SAT* Exam

SECRETS

Study Guide
Your Key to Exam Success

SAT Test Review for the
SAT Reasoning Test

Published by
Mometrix Test Preparation
SAT Exam Secrets Test Prep Team

Written and edited by the SAT Exam Secrets Test Prep Staff

Printed in the United States of America

This paper meets the requirements of ANSI/NISO Z39.48-1992 (Permanence of Paper).

Mometrix offers volume discount pricing to institutions. For more information or a price quote, please contact our sales department at sales@mometrix.com or 888-248-1219.

SAT® is a registered trademark of the College Entrance Examination Board, which was not involved in the production of, and does not endorse, this product.

Library of Congress Control Number: 2012938330

SAT Exam Secrets Test Prep Staff
        SAT Exam Secrets Study Guide : SAT Test Review for the SAT Reasoning Test / SAT
        Exam Secrets Test Prep Staff
        --2014 ed.
        p.   cm.
ISBN 13: 978-162120-281-3
ISBN 10: 1-62120-281-X

Dear Future Exam Success Story:

Congratulations on your purchase of our study guide. Our goal in writing our study guide was to cover the content on the test, as well as provide insight into typical test taking mistakes and how to overcome them.

Standardized tests are a key component of being successful, which only increases the importance of doing well in the high-pressure high-stakes environment of test day. How well you do on this test will have a significant impact on your future- and we have the research and practical advice to help you execute on test day.

The product you're reading now is designed to exploit weaknesses in the test itself, and help you avoid the most common errors test takers frequently make.

How to use this study guide

We don't want to waste your time. Our study guide is fast-paced and fluff-free. We suggest going through it a number of times, as repetition is an important part of learning new information and concepts.

First, read through the study guide completely to get a feel for the content and organization. Read the general success strategies first, and then proceed to the content sections. Each tip has been carefully selected for its effectiveness.

Second, read through the study guide again, and take notes in the margins and highlight those sections where you may have a particular weakness.

Finally, bring the manual with you on test day and study it before the exam begins.

Your success is our success

We would be delighted to hear about your success. Send us an email and tell us your story. Thanks for your business and we wish you continued success-

Sincerely,

Mometrix Test Preparation Team

TABLE OF CONTENTS

Top 20 Test Taking Tips

1. Carefully follow all the test registration procedures
2. Know the test directions, duration, topics, question types, how many questions
3. Setup a flexible study schedule at least 3-4 weeks before test day
4. Study during the time of day you are most alert, relaxed, and stress free
5. Maximize your learning style; visual learner use visual study aids, auditory learner use auditory study aids
6. Focus on your weakest knowledge base
7. Find a study partner to review with and help clarify questions
8. Practice, practice, practice
9. Get a good night's sleep; don't try to cram the night before the test
10. Eat a well balanced meal
11. Know the exact physical location of the testing site; drive the route to the site prior to test day
12. Bring a set of ear plugs; the testing center could be noisy
13. Wear comfortable, loose fitting, layered clothing to the testing center; prepare for it to be either cold or hot during the test
14. Bring at least 2 current forms of ID to the testing center
15. Arrive to the test early; be prepared to wait and be patient
16. Eliminate the obviously wrong answer choices, then guess the first remaining choice
17. Pace yourself; don't rush, but keep working and move on if you get stuck
18. Maintain a positive attitude even if the test is going poorly
19. Keep your first answer unless you are positive it is wrong
20. Check your work, don't make a careless mistake

Critical Reading Test

The critical reading portion of the SAT consists of two 25-minute sections and one 20-minute section. It tests reading comprehension, sentence completions, and paragraph-length critical reading.

Sentence Completions

Sentence completion questions have five answer choices and either one or two blanks to be filled in. Some are primarily testing your vocabulary; others are testing your ability to use logic. The best single thing you can do to improve your score on this section is to to study advanced vocabulary words.

To answer sentence completion questions, read each sentence, inserting the answer choices in the blanks. Don't stop at the first answer choice that sounds right; read them all. What seems at first like the right choice may not be after you have seen all the choices. Be sure to read the entire sentence with your answer choice to make sure it is the *best* answer.

Do this section first, because it tends to go faster than the reading comprehension questions. Questions get more difficult as you go along, so do them in order; when they get too hard, skim the rest and move on to the reading passages. You can come back if you have time.

Mastering Sentence Completions

Vocabulary Questions: Look for Roots and Other Clues
These questions test your vocabulary. Look for familiar roots, suffixes, prefixes, and other clues to help you figure out unfamiliar words. For example, you might not recognize the word "tremulous," but the root "trem-" makes you think of "tremble." Think about it: if a person who trembles is tremulous, then he might be nervous or hesitant. How does that fit in the sentence you're given?

Logic Questions: Think Through Each Step
Some questions require you to follow the logic established by words like *because, although, in spite of, therefore*, and so on. Follow the twists and turns of a sentence to make sure you're selecting the right choice. If there are two words in an answer, make sure they *both* fit.

Example:
Although the judge seemed _____ at first, by the time the trial ended, the jurors decided he was merely _____.
    a. officious ... lavish
    b. loquacious ... histrionic
    c. brusque ... taciturn
    d. ostentatious ... despotic
    e. illicit ... capricious

The word "although" may sometimes be a hint that you will be looking for opposites; however, in this case, you will notice there are no pairs of opposites in the choices. So you know you'll be looking for contrast of a different kind.

You can quickly rule out choices A and E because "lavish" and "illicit" couldn't possibly fit. Read option B in context; the word "merely" rules it out: no judge would be "merely histrionic." Choice D does not make sense because ostentatious (showy) and despotic (acting like a tyrant) don't fit the "although this, really that" logic.

Choice C is correct: "Although the judge seemed <u>brusque</u> (blunt or abrupt) at first, by the time the trial ended, the jurors decided he was merely <u>taciturn</u> (quiet; not talking much).

Multiple Blanks Are an Opportunity
Some questions have two blanks, and others have one. The two-blank questions give you more opportunities to rule out incorrect answers: *both* words must fit the blanks. If you can rule out one of the words, that answer choice must be wrong. Be very sure to check both words in an answer, instead of jumping immediately to a choice where the first word seems to fit perfectly.

You can also use this technique to spot likely pairs of correct answers. Read the sentence, and think about the relationship between the words. Are you looking for opposites (antonyms)? Synonyms, or words with different shadings of the same meaning?

Also consider whether a word is the correct part of speech. If the blank needs two adjectives, don't pick an answer that has one adjective and one noun.

Adjectives Give It Away
Adjectives and adverbs often hold the clue to determining which answer choice is correct.

Example:
Searching for ancient, hidden insights, the historian spent years searching out _____ old texts.
  a. esoteric
  b. quotidian
  c. languid
  d. epistolary
  e. derelict

Look at the adjectives "ancient" and "hidden." "Derelict" and "esoteric" could both describe old books; however, "derelict" means neglected and in bad condition, even falling apart, whereas "esoteric" means obscure and hard to understand. Therefore, A is the best answer.

Looking for Roots
Incidentally, the incorrect choices in the last example offer a good opportunity to practice looking for roots. "Quotidian" means daily, routinely; do you see the root "quo", as in "quota"? Now look at "epistolary." An epistle is a letter; similarly, "epistolary" means involving or made up of letters or correspondence.

Transitional Words
Watch out for key transitional words. These can include "however," "but," "yet," "although," "so," "because," etc. These may change the meaning of a sentence and the context of the missing word.

Example:
Frank had was famous for his largesse to the symphony, yet he was _____ with his own family.
  a. lavish
  b. parsimonious

c. exorbitant
d. apathetic
e. egalitarian

The word "yet" is your hint that the correct answer will contrast with "largesse," or open-handedness. The only such choice is "parsimonious," B, which means stingy.

Tricky Negatives
Watch out for "not", "no," "never," and similar words indicating a negative, especially in the logic-based questions. Even trickier, some sentences include negatives in both clauses: "Betty's coach said *never* to bunt on the first pitch, because then she *would have no chance* of hitting the ball out of the park."

The Trap of Familiarity
Don't choose a word just because you recognize it. On difficult questions, you may only recognize one or two of the five answer choices. SAT doesn't put "make-believe words" on the test, so don't think that recognizing a word means it must be correct. If you don't recognize four words, then focus on the one that you do recognize. Is it correct? Try your best to determine if it fits the sentence. If it does, that's great; but if it doesn't, move to the next question.

Shades of Meaning
The SAT will often have two answers that are very similar, and at least one that is wildly wrong. If you recognize that two words in a list are near-synonyms, examine them carefully. One of them is likely to be the best answer. In a two-blank question, the other word of the pair will likely determine which is correct.

Example:
Even though the book's cover was downright _____, the writing itself was sophisticated, scholarly, and even _____.
    a. odious ... archaic
    b. lurid ... bombastic
    c. garish ... erudite
    d. cryptic ... intricate
    e. insipid ... soporific

Because of the words "even though," you know you are looking for a pair of words that somehow contrast. You can rule out choices D and E because those word pairs don't offer a contrast. Choice A is clearly nonsensical.

In choices B and C, "lurid" and "garish" have similar meanings; therefore, look at the second words of each pair. Read the sentence: "...sophisticated, scholarly, and even bombastic"? "...sophisticated, scholarly, and even erudite" is a better choice. Note that B would not be an impossible choice; however, "erudite" (learned) is a better fit.

Reading Passages

The reading passages test how well you can read and understand college-level material about the humanities, social studies, natural sciences, and literary fiction. Some sections involve a single passage, and others include two related passages for you to compare and contrast. There are four categories of questions:

- Reasoning questions — making inferences based on the passage, recognizing the main idea or author's purpose, identifying tone or attitude, recognizing parallel or analogous ideas, and interpreting particular words, phrases, imagery, and literary devices.
- Vocabulary questions — what does a word mean in the context of a specific passage?
- Comprehension — understanding the ideas presented in a passage.
- Paired selections — identifying the ways two passages support, contradict, or otherwise relate to each other.

Everything you need to know to answer the questions will be contained within the passages themselves.

Unlike the other sections, the reading passages questions do not get harder as you go. Feel free to skip around the questions for a given passage, answering easier ones first, then figuring out the hard ones. However, do *not* skip between passages: you will waste time re-reading when you go back, and you're likely to confuse yourself.

Use a Strategic Approach

Read the questions first.
Before you begin to read a passage, look ahead and read the questions that refer to it, so you'll know what kinds of information you're looking for. Mark key words to look for in the passages.

Read the passage, marking key words and main ideas.
Use your knowledge of the questions (which you've already read) to mark places you'll need to refer back to. In general, it's best to put a line or bracket in the margin near the main idea of the passage as a whole, and underline a few key words you identified in the questions.

Marking just a few places—not too many—will later help you skim quickly for the section you need to answer each question.

Focus on paragraphs.
Focus upon the first sentence of each paragraph, which is usually the most important. Remember learning about "topic sentences"? (If it's not the first sentence, it's probably the last.) In most cases, the key words you're looking for will be in the topic sentence.
When you return to the questions, start by locating which paragraph will have the answer. It will save time if you can jump straight to the place you need.

Each paragraph will have its own main idea, but the main idea of a *passage* is typically spread across all or most of its paragraphs. For questions asking about the main idea of a passage as a whole, look for an idea that is repeated or addressed in different ways across multiple paragraphs.

Often, for a question asking for the main idea of the passage, the answer choices will include incorrect choices that are main ideas of individual paragraphs. That is why it is crucial to choose ideas that are supported by most of the paragraphs, not just one.

Think: Is it a fact? An assumption? An opinion? An inference?
As you read, be mindful of the difference among facts, assumptions, and inferences.

A *fact* is demonstrably true. An *inference* is an idea that a reader can conclude, or reason out, from the ideas presented; it is not directly stated. And an *assumption* is a statement that the author makes without evidence: for example, an argument based on the assumption that Ivy League colleges provide the best education, without data to support that idea.

Distinguishing fact from inference, or facts from assumptions, is important in reading comprehension questions. Words like "apparently," "seems," and "suggests," as well as the obvious terms "implied" and "inferred," indicate that you are being asked to make or identify an inference. (Remember: authors imply; readers infer.)

Opinions usually place a value judgment on a conclusion or inference. Look for words like "thought," "believed," or "should"/"should not" to help you identify opinions.

Look back at the passage.
Find the key word or idea in the question, and look back to the passage. Re-read that section. Is the author stating a fact? Making an assumption? Implying an idea without stating it directly? Arguing against someone else's inference? Comparisons and contrasts are important.

What is the author's purpose? It might be to entertain, or to persuade the reader to believe something, or to argue against someone else's opinion. Look at the words the author chooses: are they scientific? Emotional? Is the author forceful or subtle?

Vocabulary questions should be relatively easy, but you must look back at the passage. These questions involve words that can have more than one meaning, and you must select the one that author intended. It may be a metaphorical or ironic meaning, not one you would expect.

Don't try to remember everything in the passage — especially when there are two passages.
You won't be able to remember everything, so don't risk errors by trying. Especially for sections with two passages, mark the key words and ideas, then look back at the text to answer the questions.

For the answers that you think are correct, read them carefully and find the one that answers the question. (A common testing trick is to throw in a fact or quote from the passage that is irrelevant to the question being asked.) Additionally, two answers can both be seemingly correct, so be sure to read all of the answer choices and make sure that you get the one that BEST answers the question.

Two passages: Compare and contrast.
For many two-passage sections, you'll have a few questions that refer to the passages individually ("The author of Passage 1 implies that...") and several that require you to compare the two in some way. You may be asked to identify a common theme or literary device, or determine their relationship, for example:
> a. Passage 2 supports the argument made in Passage 1.
> b. Passage 2 provides an explanation for a phenomenon that Passage 1 describes as inexplicable.
> c. Passage 1 is a satirical take on the situation described objectively in Passage 2.
> d. Passage 1 rebuts the premise of Passage 2.
> e. Passages 1 and 2 provide different arguments against the same public policy.

Stick to the passage itself.
Avoid the temptation to bring your own ideas and judgment. Passages may involve controversial subjects, such as global warming, that evoke strong opinions. You must answer questions with the **writer's** opinion, ideas, and purpose — not yours. Remember: **an answer can be true but still the wrong answer**.

More Tips and Strategies

Watch out for negatives, absolutes, and "hedge" words.
Don't read so quickly that you miss important words like "not." Qualifiers such as "always," "sometimes," "except," "only," and "rarely" are often traps for the unwary. Skim to locate the section you need, then slow down and read carefully to make sure you understand it accurately.

Read all the answer choices.
You're looking for the BEST choice. There may be more than one that could be arguably correct; you need the best answer.

Eliminate the obvious.
Some answers may be obviously wrong: they contradict the passage, contain assumptions or ideas that weren't in the passage, or are irrelevant. Mark them out; remember you can write anywhere in the test booklet.

For example, when trying to answer a question such as "the passage indicates all of the following EXCEPT" quickly skim the paragraph searching for references to each choice. If the reference exists, scratch it off as a choice.

Beware of directly quoted answers.
Once you've quickly found the correct section of the passage to find the answer, focus upon the answer choices. Sometimes a choice will repeat word for word a portion of the passage near the answer. However, beware of such duplication—it may be a trap! More than likely, the correct choice will paraphrase or summarize the related portion of the passage, rather than having exactly the same wording.

When there's no key word...
Some questions will not have a key word. For example, "Which of the following would the author of this passage likely agree with?"

In these cases, look for key words in the answer choices. Then skim the passage to find where those words occur. Often the answer choices can all be found in the same paragraph, which can quickly narrow your search. If you marked key words when reading the first time, you should be able to find the place quickly and save time.

Check your answers.
For *every* question, once you've selected an answer, check it. If it's a vocabulary word, read the sentence with the answer choice instead of the original word. If it's an idea or a factual detail, compare your answer to the relevant section of the passage itself.

Truth does not equal correctness.
If your answer is based on what you know, rather than what's written on the page, it's likely to be wrong. The **correct answer** is not necessarily **true.** Be very careful not to let your own ideas, experience, and opinions lead you astray.

It bears repeating: Just because an answer is true, that doesn't make it the right answer.
A warning about similar answer choices
Watch for answers that are similarly worded. If they *really* mean the same thing and one answer is wrong, you can eliminate the other choice as well.

However, similar answers are often there to draw a fine distinction. For example, consider these two choices:
A) Alistair is upset because he believes that Sue insulted the quality of his compositions.
B) Alistair is upset because he believes Sue does not think he is a good musician.

Look back at the passage: Was Alistair worried about whether Sue disliked his songs or his playing? Or is neither of these true? (Maybe Alistair is angry because Sue was late for dinner, in which case both of these are wrong.)

Contextual clues
Look for contextual clues in the passage, especially for the vocabulary questions. You may need to identify an uncommon use of a common word. Always re-read the passage before answering vocabulary-in-context questions such as "What does the word *smart* mean in this sentence?"

Time Management

In technical passages, do not get lost on the technical terms. Note them and move on. You want a general understanding of what is going on, not a mastery of the content. If you can recognize the terms, you don't need to understand exactly what each one means.

When you encounter material in the selection that seems difficult to understand, bracket it. If no question addresses that passage, don't spend time on it. (This is another reason to read the questions first.) Don't waste time trying to understand a difficult section if it's not going to be relevant to a question.

Answer general questions before detail questions. A reader with a good understanding of the whole passage can often answer general questions without rereading a word. Get the easier questions out of the way before tackling the more time-consuming ones. Remember, questions in this section do not get harder as you go along—the easiest question may be last.

Identify each question by type. Is it a question of fact? Finding the main idea? Identifying inferences? You alone know which question types you customarily handle with ease and which give you trouble and will require more time. Save the difficult questions for last.

Skip around within the questions for a given passage, but don't move around between passages. You'll just waste time having to re-read the selections.

Mathematics Test

The math portion of the SAT consists of two 25-minute sections and one 20-minute section. The questions cover numbers and operations, algebra and functions, geometry, statistics, probability, and data analysis.

Don't be intimidated by the questions presented on the math exam. They do not require highly advanced math knowledge, but only the ability to recognize basic problem types and apply simple formulas and methods to solving them. This guide outlines the concepts you will need to know and presents some basic tips for approaching problems on the test. It is not intended to cover every concept that might be tested, but to provide an overview so you can use your study time most effectively.

Use the practice tests.
The best thing you can do to prepare for the SAT is to take several practice tests and review all your wrong answers very carefully. Work back through those problems until you understand how the answer was derived and you're confident you could answer a similar problem on your own.

Concepts covered
SAT questions fall into four categories:
- Numbers and operations
- Algebra and functions
- Geometry and measurements
- Data analysis, statistics, and probabilities

The SAT does *not* include any questions involving complex numbers, logarithms, trigonometry, calculus, geometric proofs, or computations of standard deviation. If you understand basic algebra, geometry, and statistics, you'll be able to figure all of the questions out.

This Guide includes a practice test with answer key and explanations. Examples are also available on the College Board website. If you feel uncertain on a particular concept or problem type, use these tests to practice.

How to Approach SAT Math Questions

Take an approved calculator you're familiar with. Check its batteries.
If you normally use a scientific or graphic calculator, check the SAT website to make sure it's one you'll be allowed to use. Use that calculator as you work through the practice tests.

Remember that the test provides all the information you need.
There's even a handy chart of "reference information" in the textbook with geometry formulas you might need, including the Pythagorean Theorem and special right triangles. The chart even tells you that the sum of angles in a triangle equals 180. Don't worry about cramming to memorize the formula for calculating the area of a circle. All you need to know is that A = area, C = circumference, and r = radius.

Read carefully.
Yes, it's a math test, but these questions require careful reading. Look for key words such as "is" (equals), "more than," "less than," "of" (percentage, ratio, or multiplication), and so forth. Ask yourself:

- "What do I know?"
- "What information does the problem provide?"
- "What is the question asking, exactly?"

Remember that you don't always have to solve the whole problem to answer the question.
Especially with algebra problems, answering the question may not actually require solving the entire equation or finding all the variables. This is another example of "read carefully" — be sure you understand what the question is asking for.

Look at the answers before you begin calculating.
What form do the possible answers take? If they're fractions, then work in fractions rather than decimals. Do they include negative numbers? (Negative numbers are an often-forgotten option for many problems involving exponents, roots, and absolute values.)

Take it one step at a time.
If a problem seems overwhelming at first, just look for the first step. Write down what information you know. Break it down. And remember that by just using logic and basic techniques, you can work through even the most complex multi-step problems.

Draw a picture or write down expressions as you read.
Many of the problems require more logic than raw mathematical knowledge. As you read a problem, make a sketch in the margin, draw on the figure in the test book, or write out the mathematical expression described. (For example, if you read "The area of Circle A is twice the area of Circle B," write down "A = 2B.")

Substitute numbers for variables.
Sometimes the easiest thing to do is pick a value for x, n, or another variable, and work through the problem using that number. It may be easier to worth through that way, especially for geometry problems. (Just remember that the value isn't "true," merely convenient.)

Use elimination.
As with all SAT questions, the first thing to do is eliminate obviously wrong answers. Are there choices that are clearly too big or too small? In an impossible form? Based on a common error, such as a sign or exponent error?

Check your answers.
When you solve a problem, plug the answer back in to confirm it makes sense. Make sure you haven't made careless mistakes such as skipping a step or making an arithmetic error.

Fill in all the circles, then double-check.
For the "student-produced" responses, where you have to supply the actual number instead of selecting from multiple choices, make sure to fill in all the circles. You get no credit for the number written at the top — those boxes are only there to help you mark the circles accurately. Make sure you've filled in the right spots.

Go ahead and guess on student-produced answers.

Those fill-in-the-blank responses don't count against you if you get them wrong. If you can make a good guess, go ahead.

Don't get mired down on any one question.
The first, easiest problem on the test is worth the same points as the last, hardest question. If one problem is taking a long time, move on. You can come back to it later if you have time.

Numbers and Operations

Topics to study:
- Properties of integers (positive and negative, 0, odd and even numbers)
- Number lines
- Sequences
- Word problems
- Sets
- Ratios, proportions, and percents
- Counting problems (how many combinations can you make of a given set)
- Fractions and rational numbers
- Factors, multiples, and remainders
- Prime numbers
- Square and square roots
- Logical reasoning

Even though you're allowed to use calculators, the SAT doesn't have problems with long, tedious arithmetic computations. That doesn't mean every answer will be neat and simple, but it does mean that if you're getting wrapped up in lots of arithmetic, you're probably taking the wrong approach.
Anticipate the negative.
When you solve problems, remember to consider the possibility of a negative answer. Your answer might have two possible solutions, or might be an absolute value. Remember that multiplying two negatives makes a positive, and that a negative exponent means an inversion (1 over x). All squares, therefore, are positive, but square roots can be negative. (The SAT does not include imaginary numbers.)

Review common squares.
If you don't know the squares of all integers between 1 and 12 (and therefore –1 through –12), spend a few minutes reviewing them before the test. Even though you have a calculator, knowing these squares will save you time. Also, remember that to square a fraction, you square the numerator and denominator both, producing a number that is smaller than the original.

Approaching sequences.
These problems have a series of number that are related by some pattern. Your first task will usually be to figure out the pattern, then use it to find the *n*th term, or the average of certain terms, etc. Arithmetical sequences, derived by adding or subtracting, are usually obvious. If you can't spot the pattern right off, consider multiplication and exponents. Is each number a multiple of the one before it (3, 9, 27, 81)? The square of consecutive integers (25, 36, 49, 64)?

The problem *will* have the information you need to solve it. You may be given a rule and asked to find a particular number in the sequence by applying it, or given the sequence and asked to find the rule.

Practice fraction techniques:
- Adding, subtracting, multiplying, and dividing fractions
- Finding the lowest common denominator
- Converting mixed numbers (1½) to improper (3/2) fractions, or vice versa
- Converting fractions to decimals or decimals to fractions — know the common equivalents such as 2/3 = .6666667 and ¼ = .25
- Finding and using reciprocals

Practice scientific notation.
The SAT often writes very large or very small numbers as a power of 10. For example, $3{,}700{,}000{,}000 = 3.7 \times 10^9$. Use the exponent to count places left or right of the decimal: if the exponent is 9, add zeros until you have moved the decimal 9 places to the right. The same technique works for negative exponents, except that the decimal moves left ($3.7 \times 10^{-9} = 0.0000000037$).

Remember that ratios, percents, and proportions are essentially the same.
If you are struggling with one form, you can use the form that seems most natural to you. Just make sure to convert your answer back to the form the question is asked: for example, ¾ might need to be given as 3:4 or 75%.

Draw a picture.
Especially for word problems, counting problems ("how many possible 5-character passwords can be created with 4 digits and 1 letter?"), and logical reasoning problems, draw a sketch as you read the problem. Write down what you know from the question and put statements into formulas as you go. The resulting sketch or equation will usually make it clear what you need to do.

Algebra, Functions, and Graphs

Topics to study:
- Manipulating algebraic formulas
- Functions, including graphs, translations, domain, and range
- Solving equations, including solving one equation in terms of another (two variables)
- Word problems
- Factoring
- Exponents and roots
- Absolute value
- Inequalities
- Equation systems
- Quadratic equations
- Rational equations
- Direct and inverse variation

The SAT does *not* cover complex numbers (*i*, the imaginary root of a negative number), logarithms, trigonometry, or calculus.

Review these key formulas and approaches:

Difference of two squares (factoring)
$$(a^2 - b^2) = (a + b)(a - b)$$

Common factors
$$8x - 16y = 8(x - 2y)$$

In this case, 8 is a factor of both terms, so you can extract it to factor the expression.

FOIL (first, outer, inner, last)
$$(x + 2)(x - 3)$$

To multiply two expressions like this, use FOIL:
First parts: $(x)(x) = x^2$
Outer: $(x)(-3) = -3x$
Inner: $(2)(x) = 2x$
Last: $(2)(-3) = -6$
Result: $x^2 + -3x + 2x + -6 = x^2 - x - 6$

Quadratic equations
Solve by factoring and setting equal to 0. Sample question:
"For what values of x is $x^2 + 3x - 1 = 3$?"

First, subtract 3 from both sides to produce the standard quadratic equation, then factor:
$$x^2 + 3x - 4 = 0$$
$$(x + 4)(x - 1) = 0$$
$$x = -4 \text{ and } x = 1$$
Special case: $x^2 + 2x + 1 = (x+1)^2$

Exponents
A negative exponent produces the inverse (divide 1 by the number or expression).

Any number with an exponent of 0 = 1, regardless of the number.

Fractional exponents indicate roots; $x^{\frac{1}{2}} = \sqrt{x}$

To multiply numbers with the same base, add exponents; to divide, subtract.

An exponent raised to another exponent is multiplied: $(x^2)^3 = x^6$

Inequalities
When working with inequalities, remember that multiplying or dividing both sides by a negative number reverses the direction of the inequality.

Systems of equations; answers that are expressions, not numbers
Remember that you will not always be solving for a number. Some questions may require you to solve for an expression, such as $(2x - y)$, rather than the individual values of x and y. If you have two

equations with two variables, you can use the combination to eliminate one of the variables and arrive at a solution. Find a value for one variable, then plug it in to get the other:

Example:
   $2x - 3y = -2$
   $4x + y = 24$
The second equation can be transformed to $y = 24 - 4x$.

   Now substitute and solve:
   $2x - 3(24 - 4x) = -2$
   $2x - 72 + 12x = -2$
   $14x - 72 = -2$
   $14x = 70$
   $x = 5$

Slope-Intercept formula
This standard formula, often used in graphing, takes this form: $y = mx + b$, where m is the slope of the line and b is the y-intercept (where the line crosses the y-axis).

Example:
   In the (x,y) coordinate plane, what is the slope of the line $2y = x - 4$?

   First convert to slope-intercept form by dividing both sides by 2.
   $2y/2 = (x - 4)/2$
   $y = (x/2) - 2$
   $y = \frac{1}{2}(x) - 2$
   The slope is ½.

Slope formula
The slope formula is $m = (y1 - y2) / (x1 - x2)$, where m is the slope of the line and two points on the line are given by (x1, y1) and (x2, y2).

Remember the formula as "rise over run": the y-values (rise, or vertical axis) on the top of the ratio, with the x-values (run, or horizontal axis) on the bottom.

Functions
Functions involve relating numbers in a particular *domain* (such as all nonnegative integers) to those in another group, the *range*. The range is essentially the result of applying the function.

You may be asked to find the domain and/or range of a given function; that is, what numbers is it valid for? Look at whether you can eliminate, for example, all negative numbers. Then look at what the output or result would be for any number you can plug in — that's the range. These answers will generally be broad categories, not individual numbers.

Check that your answers make sense.
Whenever you finish any problem, ask yourself, "Does this fit?" Is it reasonable? Does it answer the question that was asked?

Geometry

Topics to study:
- Geometric notation
- Points and lines
- Angles
- Triangles (especially the "special" ones: equilateral, isosceles, right triangles and the Pythagorean theorem, 30-60-90 triangles, similar triangles, the triangle inequality)
- Quadrilaterals (parallelograms, rectangles, and squares)
- Other polygons
- Circles (diameter, radius, arc, tangent, circumference, area)
- Areas and perimeters
- Solid geometry (volume, surface area)
- Geometric perception
- Coordinate geometry
- Transformations

The SAT does *not* cover formal geometric proofs, trigonometry, or radian measure.

The test booklet provides a box of "reference information" such as formulas for area and volume. Don't spend your study time memorizing formulas; instead, spend it refreshing your memory of how to *use* them.

Know how to read a figure or graph.
A line is named by two points on it, represented by letters; if the line above the letters has an arrow, those points can be anywhere on the line. If the line just ends, the letter under it is an endpoint. Angles are named so that the point where the two lines join is in the center of the expression: ∠EDF is formed of lines DE and DF.

Understand supplementary and vertical angles.
If two lines intersect, the angles opposite each other will have the same measure; the two angles on one side of a line will add to 180 degrees. When one line intersects parallel lines, the corresponding angles will have the same measure (i.e., the top left angle of one intersection will be the same as the top left angle of the other).

In the example below, knowing that the two angles on one side of a line will total 180, you can find the size of the missing angles 180 – 128 = 52 degrees. Because vertical (opposite) angles are the same and angles formed by parallel lines are the same, all four of the missing angles are 52 degrees.

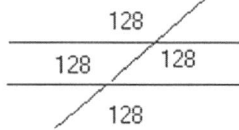

When a question asks about two similar shapes, expect a ratio problem.
Remember that similar figures (for example) are the same shape but different sizes. To find a missing value, set up ratios of corresponding sides and angles. Just be careful to set up the ratios correctly, so that values for Figure A are always on top or always on bottom of the ratio, and that you're using the matching sides or angles. (Figures may be rotated in the illustration, so be careful.)

Example:

> Take 2 triangles, where triangle ABC ~ A'B'C'. In these similar triangles, a = 3, b = 4, c = 5, and a' = 6. What is the value of b'?
>
> Use the ratio of a/a' to find b': 3/6 = 4/b'. To solve, cross-multiply the two sides: (6)(4) = 3b'; 24 = 3b', and b' =8.

Review these key formulas and approaches:

Equilateral triangles: All three sides are equal in length; all three angles = 60°.

Isosceles triangles: Two sides of equal length; angles opposite those equal sides will also be equal.

Right triangles: Any triangle with a right angle. The longest side is the hypotenuse, opposite the right angle. You will usually use the Pythagorean theorem with these: $a^2 + b^2 = c^2$, where c is the hypotenuse. Special right triangles (30-60-90 and 45-45-90) have special formulas for the lengths of their sides, given in the Reference Information chart.

Congruent triangles have the same size and shape.

Similar triangles have the same shape (angles are the same), but are different sizes (sides are different lengths).

The triangle inequality is the fact that the sum of any two sides of a triangle will be greater than the length of the third side. (If they were the same, the lines would lie on top of each other; less than, and the remaining side would have to be an arc.)

Quadrilaterals: Parallelograms, rectangles, and squares all have opposite angles and opposite sides the same size. Their angles will always total 360 degrees. The diagonal of any rectangle or square will form two identical right triangles; in a square, those will be 45-45-90 triangles. Because of that, if the side of a square is x, the length of its diagonal is $x\sqrt{2}$.

Areas and perimeters: Formulas for common figures (triangles, rectangles, circles) are given in the Reference Information. Remember that, to find the area or perimeter of an irregular polygon (i.e., not one with a formula), you can divide it into triangles and quadrilaterals, then apply their formulas.

Interior angles: For most polygons, you can find out the total number of degrees in interior angles by dividing the figure into triangles (all sharing a point at one vertex). Each triangle has angles totaling 180 degrees. Therefore, multiply the number of triangles by 180 to find the sum of angles in the polygon.

Tangents: A tangent is perpendicular to the radius of the circle at the point where it touches.

Surface area: Calculate surface area by figuring the area of each face, then adding them all together. Don't forget the back and bottom or base!

Midpoints: For a line on a coordinate plane, find the midpoint by averaging the *x* values and the *y* values.

Translation, rotation, and reflection: Translation just slides a shape on a graph (in any direction). Rotation leaves its center in place, but turns the figure. Reflection produces a mirror image across a line, which can be an axis or any other line. For example, to create a reflection across the y-axis, you would multiply the x coordinates of all the points by –1.

Note whether the drawing is to scale or not.
Figures in the SAT exam are drawn to scale unless they're marked "not to scale." If you're comparing sides of a triangle, for example, that's a useful thing to know.

Data Analysis, Statistics, and Probability

Topics to study:
Data interpretation (graphs and charts)
- Statistics
- Probability
- Geometric probability

The SAT does *not* cover standard deviations or *p*-values (significance).

Example:

Springfield Workforce

	Employed	Unemployed	**Total**
Men	12,570		**13,520**
Women			
Total	23,780		**26,800**

Based on the information given above, how many women in the Springfield workforce are unemployed?
- a. 510
- b. 950
- c. 2,070
- d. 2,700
- e. 3,020

Subtract employed men from total men, then total employed from total workforce. Then subtract the unemployed men from the unemployed total to yield the correct answer, C.

Approaching the Questions

Look carefully at the chart or table.
What kind of information is being displayed? What are the units? The scale? How precise is it?

As always, read the question carefully.
Is it asking for an interpolation or projection, rather than just reading a number off a graph?

In these questions, your starting questions are especially important. Ask yourself:
- "What do I know?"

- "What information does the problem provide?"
- "What is the question asking, exactly?"

For probability questions, ask "are they independent events?"
The results of a coin toss are not affected by the tosses that come before or after. Each toss is independent. However, if you're considered the probability of coming down either heads or tails in the same toss, those *are* dependent events — the coin cannot do both at once. The answer to this question determines how you calculate the probability (see below).

Review these key formulas and approaches:

Mean: the "average."

Median: the middle value when the items are in order. May not be anywhere close to the mean. If there are an even number of items, average the two in the middle.

Mode: the value that appears the most times.

> ➤ **Review Video: Mean, Median, and Mode**
> *Visit mometrix.com/academy and enter Code: 286207*

Using an average to find a missing value: If you know the average or mean of a group of values and either the sum or the number of values, you can find a missing value. Just plug the numbers into the formula: average = sum / [number of values].

Finding probabilities: Probability is a ratio: the target over the total possibilities. The ratio is always expressed as a number between 0 and 1, where 1 = 100% probability (aka "certainty"). If you have 12 black marbles and 7 white marbles, the odds of picking a white one at random are 7/19.

Independent events: If you have multiple independent events, you can find the probability they will all occur by multiplying the individual probabilities.

Dependent events: You can't just multiply probabilities of dependent events. You'll have to analyze each question logically; if you can untangle a series of independent events, *then* you can multiply.

Geometric probability: The same concepts apply, but instead of events such as winning a game or tossing a coin, the questions may involve areas or volumes of different figures. First calculate the areas (e.g.) of the different possibilities, then calculate the probability as usual.

Student-Produced Response

The SAT test includes 10 questions that are not multiple choice. Instead, they require you to solve the problem, then fill the exact number into a grid very similar to the one you used to enter your name and address on the form. The grid has a row of four boxes on top, with a column of numbers 0–9, a slash, and a decimal beneath each box.

To fill in the grid, write your answer in the boxes on top, then fill in the corresponding circle underneath. Use the slash to indicate fractions. It's a machine-scored test, so you don't get any credit for the number you write on top — that's strictly to help you fill in the circles correctly. If your answer doesn't fill up all four columns, that's okay. And it doesn't matter whether you left-justify or right-justify your answers. What *does* matter is that the circles be filled in correctly.

If you can't write it using the characters provided, it's not right.
No student-produced response will be a negative number or a percent. If you get a negative number, you've made a mistake. Percentages should be expressed as a ratio or decimal; for example, 50% can be written as .50.

Start on the left.
There are a few reasons to start with the first box every time. For one thing, it's faster. It will also help you be as precise as possible. If your answer is <1, though, don't use a leading 0 before the decimal. The SAT omits the 0 from column one to help you be as precise as possible. For decimals, use as many columns as you can. Don't round or truncate answers. If you calculate an answer to be .125, enter the full number, not .13.

Repeat a repeating decimal.
Repeating decimals such as .666666 are only counted correct if you fill all the available columns. Either .666 or .667 will get credit. However, .66 will be counted as wrong.

Don't use mixed numbers.
If you try to write 2½ , the computer will think you've written 21/2 and count it wrong. Instead, use the improper form of such fractions; for example, 2½ = 5/2.

Use your calculator.
You brought a calculator; use it. Work the problem twice to make sure you entered all the numbers correctly.

Check your work.
More than any other questions in the math section, student-produced responses need to be double-checked. Try working the problem backward, plugging answers back into the original equation.
It's okay to get multiple answers.
Some questions may have more than one answer. In that case, any (positive) answer will do.

There's no penalty for guessing on these.
These 10 questions do *not* subtract points if you get them wrong. Even if you're not completely sure of your answer, it's better to attempt these than to leave them blank.

In general:
Approach the problem systematically. Take time to understand what is being asked for. In many cases there is a drawing or graph that you can write on. Draw lines, jot notes, do whatever is necessary to create a visual picture and to allow you to understand what is being asked.

Final Note

The SAT math test doesn't require advanced techniques to succeed. There's no trigonometry or calculus. If you've had geometry and algebra, you should have the concepts you need to do well. Reference information is even printed in the test booklet so you don't have to worry about remembering common formulas.

What the SAT math section does require is careful thought. Many problems require several steps or multiple techniques. Draw in the test book, mark up the word problems, and take notes as you read. The techniques in this guide will help you approach problems successfully.

Finally, work practice tests. They are available in this book and on the SAT website, as well as in the other study guides listed in the Special Report. Math, more than any other section, benefits from practice. Not only will you be more familiar with the kinds of questions to expect, you'll boost your confidence that you can do well on this section.

Writing Test

The Writing test of the SAT consists of a 25-minute section of multiple-choice questions and a 25-minute essay. The multiple-choice questions ask you to identify errors in sentences, improve sentences, or improve paragraphs.

Multiple-Choice Questions

There are two kinds of questions on the SAT Writing test that require you to find grammatical or usage errors.

The first kind asks you to replace an underlined phrase with a phrase that makes the sentence correct. The first choice is always the original wording, which you should choose if there is no error.

Example:
Though he is now considered one of the 20ᵗʰ century's greatest writers, <u>critics originally accused James Joyce</u> of being obscene and incomprehensible.
    a. critics originally accused James Joyce
    b. critics were originally accusing James Joyce
    c. James Joyce was originally accused
    d. James Joyce, having originally been accused,
    e. critics accused James Joyce originally

Answer: C. The original sentence has a dangling modifier, with its introductory clause improperly modifying "critics." Possible choices to correct that error are C and D; however, D eliminates the main verb and creates a sentence fragment.

The second kind of question has four underlined words or phrases, and you must identify which, if any, is an error. The fifth choice is always "E, No error."

Example:
    Mona <u>was unprepared</u> for her visitors,
              a.
    <u>as</u> pieces of the quilt <u>was lying</u>
     b.   **c**.
    scattered <u>on every surface</u>. <u>No error</u>.
           d.   **e**.

Answer: C. The verb "was" should agree with "pieces," not "quilt."

Common Errors to Look For

Pronoun case.
If a pronoun is underlined, check it carefully. Should that "him" be "he" instead? Is "who" the subject, or is it an object ("whom")? Hint: "between you and I" is *never* correct. (Quick "whom" test: Would you replace the word with "he" or with "him"? If it would be "him," then use "whom.")

Pronoun agreement and antecedents.

Check pronouns to make sure they have correct antecedents (the noun that the pronoun is standing in for). Does the pronoun switch (person, number, or case) in the middle of a sentence without justification? Especially be on the lookout for "his" and "their" used incorrectly. "Their" is the plural possessive and should never be used to refer to a single person.

> ➢ **Review Video: <u>Pronoun Antecedent Agreement</u>**
> *Visit **mometrix.com/academy** and enter **Code: 919704***

Subject-verb agreement.

A favorite trick is to interpose a prepositional phrase between a subject and verb so you don't immediately spot the agreement problem: "All the tall people on the boat <u>was</u> cramped." The subject is "people," which is plural, requiring the verb "were."

> ➢ **Review Video: <u>Subject-Verb Agreement</u>**
> *Visit **mometrix.com/academy** and enter **Code: 479190***

Danglers (very common, and sometimes subtle).

Watch out for gerund or participial phrases that aren't properly attached to the word they modify. These are especially common in introductory phrases: "While <u>brushing my teeth</u>, the phone rang." The phone wasn't brushing your teeth! The underlined phrase is an error. (This is easy to fix, by the way: "While I was brushing my teeth, the phone rang" is correct.) Danglers can happen anywhere in a sentence ("The phone lights up when <u>touching the screen</u>"); suspect one whenever you see an underlined phrase beginning with an *–ing* word.

Comma errors.

These errors will not be ambiguous: they will involve clearly wrong usage such as a comma between a subject and verb, or a comma splice (run-on sentence). Watch for commas between two parts of a compound predicate, which can look like a compound sentence if you're reading too quickly. For example, "They were accustomed to a hard life, and could watch a man die without blinking" should not have a comma after "life."

Adjectives and adverbs.

Make sure that adverbs modify verbs ("finish quickly," not "quick"), and that adjectives agree in number. You cannot have the ____*est* anything if there are only two. (With two objects, one is big*ger*, not big*gest*.)

Pronouns vs. possessives.

There are several common usage errors that fall in this category:
- *"It's" and "its"* — If you can replace the word with "his," it should be "its"; if could can replace it with "it is," then "it's" is correct.
- <u>They're</u>/their/there — Check for errors by substitution: "They're" means "they are"; "their" is possessive; otherwise, the word should be "there."

- *Who's/whose* — Try replacing the word with "Who is"; if that doesn't make sense, you need the possessive, "whose."

Lie and lay.
If Sam is tired, he will *lie* down. If his arms are tired, he will *lay* the heavy books down.

Tips and Strategies for Finding Sentence Errors

Read the sentence straight through once.
The error may be obvious.

Take each underlined section individually.
Look at each one; ask, "is this correct?" If it involves a pronoun, a gerund or participle, or a verb, look very carefully. (See the next section for a discussion of participles.)

Quickly run through common errors.
Do the subject and verb agree? Are all pronouns correct in case and number? Is the underlined phrase a dangler? An adjective used instead of an adverb? Misplaced comma?

Watch out for intervening phrases or clauses.
A common SAT trick is to insert a prepositional phrase or restrictive clause between a subject and verb or between a noun and pronoun. Don't be fooled! In the phrase "one of the team members," for example, "one" is the subject. The verb must be singular.

Check idioms.
These are set phrases, and although some seem strange if you try to analyze them grammatically, they are part of the language. We "agree on" a contract but "agree with" a person, for example. Your ear is a good guide here.

Remember that some sentences have no error.
Don't linger on these questions. You will need the time on the questions that require you to improve sentences and paragraphs.

Improving Sentences

Like sentence error questions, these questions involve a sentence with part or all of it underlined. Your five answer choices will offer different ways to reword or rephrase the underlined portion of the sentence. The first answer choice merely repeats the original underlined text, while the other four offer different wording.

These questions will test your recognition of correct and effective expression. Choose your answer carefully, looking not only for grammar but also for parallelism, placement of modifiers, and the use of clauses. The correct answer will flow smoothly and be both clear and concise.

Example:
The band's latest release quickly shot to the top of the charts because it was catchy, <u>uptempo, and you could dance to it.</u>
  a. uptempo, and you could dance to it.
  b. uptempo, and easy to dance to.
  c. it was uptempo, and danceable.
  d. uptempo, and people could dance to it.
  e. uptempo, and it could be danced to.

Answer: B. The issue here is parallelism: only answer B puts all three predicate adjectives in parallel form.

Example:
Brought to Florida as a teenager to attend a special tennis training center, <u>his first big tournament win made Oskar the center of an international publicity storm.</u>
    a. his first big tournament win made Oskar the center of an international publicity storm.
    b. Oskar's first big tournament win swept him up in an international publicity storm.
    an international publicity storm engulfed
    c. Oskar after his first big tournament win.
    d. Oskar was swept up in an international publicity storm after his first big tournament win.
    e. Oskar's winning his first big tournament was the center of an international publicity storm.

Answer: D. In all the others, the introductory clause dangles. It must be securely attached to the word it modifies, "Oskar."

Put participles in their place.
Participles are a common source of errors in everyday writing and probably the single biggest error type you'll be asked to identify in the SAT. Here's a quick refresher:
- Participles are verbs (or phrases starting with a verb) that function as adjectives. They commonly end in *–ing* (present tense), but can also end in *–ed* or *–en* (past tense). Single-word participles ("watched," "buzzing") rarely cause problems.
- Participial phrases are often misplaced, which changes the meaning of a sentence. They must be placed right next to the word they modify. Compare these sentences:
  - *Tourists in Washington, D.C., see lots of statues walking around the National Mall.* (Are the statues walking around?)
  - *Tourists walking around the National Mall in Washington, D.C., see lots of statues.*
- If you see a phrase introduced by an *–ing* or *–ed* word, think carefully: is it in the right place? If you moved the phrase, would it make more sense?

Tips and Strategies for Improving Sentences

Read all the choices in context.
Read the sentence five times, once with each possible wording. (Choice A will always represent no change.) Don't try read the choices on their own; that will only waste your time.

Look for common errors.
As you read, check first for subject-verb agreement, pronoun agreement, and other common errors described above in the Sentence Errors section.

Match punctuation.
Make sure that your answer choice fits the original sentence in terms of opening or closing punctuation. If the underlined passage is an introductory phrase ending in a comma, your answer should probably end in a comma. (Do be aware, though, that sometimes the punctuation itself is the error. If you're consciously looking at punctuation, you'll probably spot it.)

Don't dangle.

As in questions on sentence errors, watch for participial phrases and other dangling modifiers. Any participle (discussed above) deserves a moment of your attention.

Be parallel.
Elements in a series must take the same form, whatever that is (number, tense, infinitive or participle, etc.). Phrases should begin with the same preposition. This is a very common issue in SAT questions, so look carefully.

Be clear.
Don't pick a choice because you think it sounds fancier or more "educated." If in doubt, choose the answer that is clearest and most concise.

Follow the logic.
Look for sudden changes in meaning, especially if two contradictory statements are joined by the word "and."

Improving Paragraphs

These questions generally begin with a short "draft" passage followed by several questions. Sentences in the passage are numbered. Each of the questions will specify a particular sentence or sentences, then ask you to select the best rewrite for that section.

These questions rely on sense and context. They generally require you to
- Eliminate redundancy (unnecessary repetition).
- Eliminate unnecessary wordiness.
- Improve clarity and consistency.

Tips and Strategies for Improving Paragraphs

First, read the whole essay slowly, focusing on its meaning and organization.
You must have a sense of the passage's purpose and structure in order to answer the individual questions. Expect errors, but don't try to fix them during this reading.

Read all of the choices before deciding.
Read each one in context of the paragraph. The instructions ask you to be "the best" answer, so there may be more than one that is grammatically correct. You want the answer that creates the most effective, concise paragraph.

Make sense.
Look for the answer that is most logical and consistent with the rest of the paragraph and the passage as a whole.

When in doubt, choose the simplest option.
Eliminating extra words and unnecessary fluff is one of the goals of this section. It's okay to trust your ear. If it makes sense and sounds natural, it's probably correct.

Remember that "as it is now" is a choice.
Sometimes the original passage is the best choice. Don't be afraid of that answer.

Writing an Essay

A topic will be presented to you and you must write out a discussion on it within the 25 minutes allowed. There is not a "correct" answer to the topic. You must evaluate the topic, organize your ideas, and develop them into a cohesive and coherent response.

You will be scored on how well you are able to utilize standard written English, organize and explain your thoughts, and support those thoughts with reasons and examples.

Preparing for the Essay Section

Practice, and compare your results to examples in this book and one the College Board website.
The only way to get better at writing is to write. This book has some suggestions for making your practice more effective, but you cannot expect to just read this section, write your first essay on test day, and get a score of 6. You must write some practice essays.

Read examples of high-scoring essays.
Examples are available in this book and on the College Board website. Note that first-person essays (using "I") are just fine.

Practice writing your essays by hand, in pencil.
Those are the test conditions, and you should get accustomed to fitting a substantial essay onto the lines provided. Illegible handwriting will lower your score.

Understand the SAT scoring standards.
An essay does not have to be perfect to earn a score of 6. Pay attention to mechanics, but organization, supporting detail, and clarity are the most important.
- Score of 6: An "outstanding" essay demonstrates
  - *Clear and consistent mastery.*
  - *Outstanding critical thinking, with supporting and contrasting examples that develop an idea.*
  - *Smooth, coherent organization.*
  - *Skillful use of language, such as metaphor and varied sentence structure.*
  - *A clear authorial voice.*
  - *Varied, accurate, and apt vocabulary.*
  - *Supporting detail.*
- Score of 5: An "effective" essay demonstrates
  - *Reasonably consistent mastery.*
  - *Effective development of a main idea.*
  - *Strong critical thinking, with supporting and contrasting examples.*
  - *Effective use of language, such as varied sentence structure.*

  It may lack
  - *A well-developed organizational structure.*
  - *A smooth progression of ideas.*
  - *Development of insightful conclusions from examples.*
- Score of 4: An "adequate" essay
  - *Demonstrates adequate mastery.*
  - *Develops a point of view.*

- o *Includes examples to support and contrast with the main idea.*
- o *Exhibits general focus and some progression of ideas from beginning to end.*
- o *Uses* language competently.

It may lack
- o *A well-developed organizational structure, with clear focus and point of view.*
- o *A smooth progression of ideas.*
- o *Development of insightful conclusions from examples.*
- o *Skillful use of language, with varied sentence structure, metaphors, and apt vocabulary.*

- Score of 3: An essay of "developing mastery"
  - o *Asserts a point of view.*
  - o *Attempts to support the main idea, although evidence may be limited and repetitive.*
  - o *Demonstrates some critical thinking.*

It may lack
- o A well-*developed organizational structure, with clear focus and point of view.*
- o *A smooth progression of ideas.*
- o *Robust and appropriate examples.*
- o *Development of insightful conclusions from examples.*
- o *Skillful use of language, with varied sentence structure, metaphors, and apt vocabulary.*

- Score of 2: A "seriously limited" essay
  - o Begins *to develop a point of view.*
  - o *Attempts to support the main idea, although evidence may be limited and repetitive.*
  - o *Uses limited vocabulary and unvaried,* simplistic language.

It may lack
- o *Organization and focus.*
- o *A smooth progression of ideas.*
- o *Effective examples that support and contrast with the main idea.*
- o *Development of insightful conclusions from examples.*
- o *Evidence of critical thinking.*
- o *Skillful use of language, with varied sentence structure, metaphors, and apt vocabulary.*

- Score of 1: A "fundamentally lacking" essay
  - o May *attempt to develop a point of view.*
  - o *Provides little evidence to support the main idea.*
  - o *Is vague and unfocused.*
  - o *Fails to develop ideas.*
  - o *Uses limited vocabulary and unvaried, simplistic* language.

It may lack
- o *Coherent organization and focus.*
- o *Effective examples that support and contrast with the main idea.*
- o *A smooth progression of ideas.*
- o *Evidence of critical thinking.*
- o *Development of insightful conclusions from examples.*
- o *Skillful use of language, with varied sentence structure, metaphors, and apt vocabulary.*

On Test Day

Think about the prompt.
Essays that are off-topic or do not respond to the prompt will receive a score of 0. Don't disqualify yourself before you've even started.

Brainstorm and organize.
With only 25 minutes, you may be tempted to go straight into writing the introduction. Don't. Spend a couple of minutes brainstorming ideas, then organizing them into a logical flow. Choose an opinion to express and a point of view.

Plan your examples and supporting evidence.
Jot down a few notes about how you will support and develop your ideas. Be sure to include both supporting and contrasting examples. The best essays tend to have at least three or four examples or facts to support their main ideas.

Acknowledge the other side.
The best essays recognize that there is an opposing point of view, acknowledge it with examples, then present an argument against that opposing side.

Weed the garden.
As you think about your ideas and examples, ask, "Are these relevant? Do they wander from my main point?" Those are weeds. Eliminate them.

Plan your path.
How will you progress from the first idea to the conclusion? A clear progression of ideas differentiates a 6 essay from a 4 or 5. Think about your conclusion and how your introduction will set it up. How will you step smoothly from one idea to the next along the path?

The writing.
- Pace yourself. Be aware of the time and how much writing you still need to do. If you haven't finished by the 20-minute mark, jump to the conclusion. Try to allow a few minutes for proofreading.
- Have an introduction. It doesn't have to be fancy, but you need to give readers a ramp onto your main idea.
- Next, state your idea and offer your examples. You should have a 2–3 paragraphs of supporting and contrasting examples to illustrate critical thinking and develop your main idea.
- Use varied, expressive language. Be sure to use both long, complex sentences with multiple clauses and short, declarative sentences. Employ metaphors and similes. Write with expressive verbs, rather than loading your sentences with strings of adjectives and adverbs.
- Wrap it up with a conclusion. This is where you tie everything neatly together in a final sentence or two. Bring your examples back to your main idea. If you can refer to or restate an analogy or metaphor from the introduction, even better.

Breathe. If you get stuck, just write something.
You can always erase or mark through text if you change your mind. If you're feeling stuck, writing *something* down will often break through the logjam.

Proofread.
A longer essay isn't necessarily better. If you find that you're repeating yourself, mark it out and move to the next idea. Strike out any extraneous "detours" that arise during the drafting process. Finally, be sure to save a few minutes to check your punctuation and spelling. When you're writing quickly, it's easy to omit or repeat words.

Final Note

Essay writing takes planning and practice, but the scoring is predictable. Anyone can do well on the essay by

- Developing a main idea.
- Including appropriate supporting and contrasting examples (three or four of them),
- Sticking to a clear organization and progression of ideas, and
- Using varied sentence structure and expressive vocabulary.

Review the scoring criteria described in this section, read high-scoring essays, and practice before test day, and you'll be able to create an essay you're proud to turn in.

SAT Exam Secrets in Action

Critical Reading Subtest

Sentence Completion Question

Louisa May Alcott's _____ the philosophical brilliance of her father's intellect was _____ by her impatience with his unworldliness

    a. exasperation with . . contradicted
    b. concealment of . . supplanted
    c. respect for . . augmented
    d. rebellion against . . qualified
    e. reverence for . . tempered

Let's look at a couple of different methods of solving this problem.

1. Understand What to Expect

Before you have read any of the answer choices and begin to stumble over some of the complicated vocabulary words used in the answer choices, see if you can predict what the answer might be, based on the information provided to you in the problem sentence. You aren't trying to guess the exact word that might be in the correct answer choice, but only the type of word that you should expect. Is it a positive word, negative word, etc.

Ask yourself what sort of words would likely fill the blanks provided. Consider the first blank, which comes directly before a description of the intellectual brilliance of Louisa's father. It is likely that she loved her father and thought highly of him, particularly with regards to his intelligence. Therefore, you should expect a verb with a positive meaning to fill the first blank.

The second blank comes directly before a description of her impatience with her father over his unworldliness. Her father's brilliance is a positive attribute, the unworldliness is a negative. The missing word is a verb that allows a transition

between these two, somehow reconciling the positive and negative aspects of her father's character.

Now that you have an idea of what to expect in a correct answer choice, review the choices provided. Choices C and E both have a positive word to fill the first blank, "respect" and "reverence" respectively, so either could be correct. Moving to the second word to clarify which is the correct answer, you encounter the words "augmented" and "tempered". Augmenting deals with increasing or supporting. It doesn't make sense that a positive attribute of her father's would increase her impatience, making choice C incorrect. Tempering deals with modifying or adjusting. It does make sense that her perception of a positive attribute of her father's would be modified or adjusted by a negative attribute, making choice E correct.

2. Group the Answers

Review the answer choices and try to identify the common aspects of each answer choice. Are any of the words synonyms or antonyms?

Without ever having looked at the problem, but simply reviewing the answer choices can tell you a lot of information. Classify the words in the answer choice as positive or negative words and group them together. For example, you can tell that both answer choice A and D deal with "anger", using the words "exasperation" and "rebellion". Answer choices C and E deal with "appreciation", using the words "respect" and "reverence". Answer choice B stands alone, and in many cases can be immediately eliminated from consideration.

Grouping answers makes it easy to accept or reject more than one answer at a time. By reviewing the context of the sentence, "appreciation" makes more sense than "anger" in describing a woman's perception of her father's intellectual brilliance. Therefore, answer choices A and D can both be rejected simultaneously. Because "appreciation" is a likely description of Louisa's perception of her father's brilliance, choice B can be dismissed temporarily. If on further inspection answer choice C and E do not continue to make sense, then you can easily return to choice B for consideration.

Once again, in comparing the remaining words in choice C and E, "augmented" and "tempered", the meaning of the root word "temper" as a modifying agent makes it the better answer, and choice E correct.

3. Make it Easier

As you go through and read the sentence and answer choices, don't allow a complicated wording to confuse you. If you know the meaning of a phrase and it is over complicated, be sure to mentally substitute or scratch through and write above the phrase an easier word that means the same thing.

For example, you can rewrite "Louisa May Alcott's -------- the philosophical brilliance of her father's intellect was ------- by her impatience with his unworldliness" as "Louisa May Alcott's -------- her father's intelligence was ------- by her impatience with his simplicity.

Using words that are simpler and may make it easier for you to understand the true context of the sentence will make it easier for you to identify the correct answer choice. Similarly, you can use synonyms of difficult words as a mental replacement of the words in the answer choices to make it easier for you to understand how the word fits into the sentence.

For example, if you know the meaning of the word "supplanted" in choice B, but have difficulty understanding how it fits into the sentence, mentally replace it with the word "displaced." Displaced means the same thing and may be easier for you to read and understand in the context of the sentence.

Reading Passages Question

Mark Twain was well aware of his celebrity. He was among the first authors to employ a clipping service to track press coverage of himself, and it was not unusual for him to issue his own press statements if he wanted to influence or "spin" coverage of a particular story. The celebrity Twain achieved during his last ten years still reverberates today. Nearly all of his most popular novels were published before 1890, long before his hair grayed or he began to wear his famous white suit in public. We appreciate the author but seem to remember the celebrity.

Based on the passage above, Mark Twain seemed interested in:
   a. maintaining his celebrity
   b. selling more of his books
   c. hiding his private life
   d. gaining popularity
   e. writing the perfect novel

Let's look at a couple of different methods of solving this problem.

1. Identify the key words in each answer choice. These are the nouns and verbs that are the most important words in the answer choice.
   a. maintaining, celebrity
   b. selling, books
   c. hiding, life
   d. gaining, popularity
   e. writing, novel

Now try to match up each of the key words with the passage and see where they fit. You're trying to find synonyms and/or exact replication between the key words in the answer choices and key words in the passage.
   a. maintaining – no matches; celebrity – matches in sentences 1, 3, and 5
   b. selling – no matches; books – matches with "novels" in sentence 4.
   c. hiding – no matches; life – no matches
   d. gaining – no matches; popularity – matches with "celebrity" in sentences 1, 3, and 5, because they can be synonyms
   e. writing – no matches; novel – matches in sentence 4

At this point there are only two choices that have more than one match, choices A and D, and they both have the same number of matches, and with the same word in the passage, which is the word "celebrity" in the passage. This is a good sign, because SAT will often write two answer choices that are close. Having two answer choices pointing towards the same key word is a strong indicator that those key words hold the "key" to finding the right answer.

Now let's compare choice A and D and the unmatched key words. Choice A still has "maintaining" which doesn't have a clear match, while choice D has "gaining" which doesn't have a clear match. While neither of those have clear matches in the passage, ask yourself what are the best arguments that would support any kind of connection with either of those two words.

"Maintaining" makes sense when you consider that Twain was interested in tracking his press coverage and that he was actively managing the "spin" of certain stories.

"Gaining" makes sense when you consider that Twain was actively issuing his own press releases, however one key point to remember is that he was only issuing these press releases after another story was already in existence.

Since Twain's press releases were not being released in a news vacuum, but rather as a response mechanism to ensure control over the angle of a story, his releases were more to *maintain* control over his image, rather than *gain* an image in the first place.

Furthermore, when comparing the terms "popularity" and "celebrity", there are similarities between the words, but in referring back to the passage, it is clear that "celebrity" has a stronger connection to the passage, being the exact word used three times in the passage.

Since "celebrity" has a stronger match than "popularity" and "maintaining" makes more sense than "gaining," it is clear that choice A is correct.

2. Use a process of elimination.
a. maintaining his celebrity – The passage discusses how Mark Twain was both aware of his celebrity status and would take steps to ensure that he got the proper coverage in any news story and maintained the image he desired. This is the correct answer.

b. selling more of his books – Mark Twain's novels are mentioned for their popularity and while common sense would dictate that he would be interested in selling more of his books, the passage makes no mention of him doing anything to promote sales.

c. hiding his private life – While the passage demonstrates that Mark Twain was keenly interested in how the public viewed his life, it does not indicate that he cared about hiding his private life, not even mentioning his life outside of the public eye. The passage deals with how he was seen by the public.

d. gaining popularity – At first, this sounds like a good answer choice, because Mark Twain's popularity is mentioned several times. The main difference though is that he wasn't trying to gain popularity, but simply ensuring that the popularity he had was not distorted by bad press.

e. writing the perfect novel – Though every author of fiction may strive to write the perfect novel, and Mark Twain was a famous author, the passage makes no mention of any quest of his to write a perfect novel.

Mathematics Subtest

Standard Multiple-Choice Question

Three coins are tossed up in the air. What is the probability that two of them will land heads and one will land tails?

    a. 0
    b. 1/8
    c. 1/4
    d. 3/8
    e. 1/2

Let's look at a few different methods and steps to solving this problem.

1. Reduction and Division

Quickly eliminate the probabilities that you immediately know. You know to roll all heads is a 1/8 probability, and to roll all tails is a 1/8 probability. Since there are in total 8/8 probabilities, you can subtract those two out, leaving you with 8/8 – 1/8 – 1/8 = 6/8. So after eliminating the possibilities of getting all heads or all tails, you're left with 6/8 probability. Because there are only three coins, all other combinations are going to involve one of either head or tail, and two of the other. All other combinations will either be 2 heads and 1 tail, or 2 tails and 1 head. Those remaining combinations both have the same chance of occurring, meaning that you can just cut the remaining 6/8 probability in half, leaving you with a 3/8ths chance that there will be 2 heads and 1 tail, and another 3/8ths chance that there will be 2 tails and 1 head, making choice D correct.

2. Run Through the Possibilities for that Outcome

You know that you have to have two heads and one tail for the three coins. There are only so many combinations, so quickly run through them all.
You could have:

    H, H, H
    H, H, T
    H, T, H
    T, H, H
    T, T, H
    T, H, T

    H, T, T
    T, T, T

Reviewing these choices, you can see that three of the eight have two heads and one tail, making choice D correct.

3. Fill in the Blanks with Symbology and Odds

Many probability problems can be solved by drawing blanks on a piece of scratch paper (or making mental notes) for each object used in the problem, then filling in probabilities and multiplying them out. In this case, since there are three coins being flipped, draw three blanks. In the first blank, put an "H" and over it write "1/2". This represents the case where the first coin is flipped as heads. In that case (where the first coin comes up heads), one of the other two coins must come up tails and one must come up heads to fulfill the criteria posed in the problem (2 heads and 1 tail). In the second blank, put a "1" or "1/1". This is because it doesn't matter what is flipped for the second coin, so long as the first coin is heads. In the third blank, put a "1/2". This is because the third coin must be the exact opposite of whatever is in the second blank. Half the time the third coin will be the same as the second coin, and half the time the third coin will be the opposite, hence the "1/2". Now multiply out the odds. There is a half chance that the first coin will come up "heads", then it doesn't matter for the second coin, then there is a half chance that the third coin will be the opposite of the second coin, which will give the desired result of 2 heads and 1 tail. So, that gives 1/2*1/1*1/2 = 1/4.

But, now you must calculate the probabilities that result if the first coin is flipped tails. So draw another group of three blanks. In the first blank, put a "T" and over it write "1/2". This represents the case where the first coin is flipped as tails. In that case (where the first coin comes up tails), both of the other two coins must come up heads to fulfill the criteria posed in the problem. In the second blank, put an "H" and over it write "1/2". In

the third blank, put an "H" and over it write "1/2". Now multiply out the odds. There is a half chance that the first coin will come up "tails", then there is a half chance that the second coin will be heads, and a half chance that the third coin will be heads. So, that gives 1/2*1/2*1/2 = 1/8.
Now, add those two probabilities together. If you flip heads with the first coin, there is a 1/4 chance of ultimately meeting the problem's criteria. If you flip tails with the first coin, there is a 1/8 chance of ultimately meeting the problem's criteria. So, that gives 1/4 + 1/8 = 2/8 + 1/8 = 3/8, which makes choice D correct.

Student Produced Response Question

Data Table

Length of 0.10 mm diameter aluminum wire(m)	Resistance (ohms) at 20° C
1	3.55
2	7.10
4	14.20
10	35.50

Based on the information in the Data Table, what would be the predicted resistance in ohms that a 20 m length of aluminum wire with a 0.10 mm diameter would have?

Let's look at a few different methods and steps to solving this problem.

1. Create a Proportion or Ratio
The first way you could approach this problem is by setting up a proportion or ratio. You will find that many of the problems on the SAT can be solved using this simple technique. Usually whenever you have a given pair of numbers (this number goes with that number) and you are given a third number and asked to find what number would be its match, then you have a problem that can be converted into an easy proportion or ratio.

In this case you can take any of the pairs of numbers from the Data Table. As an example, let's choose the second set of numbers (2 m and 7.10 ohms).

Form a question with the information you have at your disposal: 2 meters goes to 7.10 ohms as 20 meters (from the question) goes to which resistance?

From your ratio: 2 m / 7.10 ohms = 20 m / x "x" is used as the missing number that you will solve for.

Cross multiplication provides us with 2*x = 7.10*20 or 2x = 142.

Dividing both sides by 2 gives us 2x/2 = 142/2 or x = 71, making 71 the correct answer.

2. Use Algebra
While you might think that creating an algebra problem is the last thing that you would want to do, it actually can make the problem extremely simple.

The question is asking for the resistance of a 20 m length of wire. The resistance is a function of the length of the wire, so you know that you could probably set up an algebra problem that would have 20 multiplied by some factor "x" that would give you your answer.

So, now you have 20*x = ?

But what exactly is "x"? If 20*x would give you the resistance of a 20 meter piece of wire, than 1*x would give you the resistance of a 1 meter piece of wire. Remember though, the table already told you the resistance of a 1 meter piece of wire – it's 3.55 ohms.

So, if 1*x = 3.55 ohms, then solving for "x" gives you x = 3.55 ohms.

Plugging your solution for "x" back into your initial equation of 20*x = ?, you now have

20*3.55 ohms = 71 ohms, making 71 the correct answer.

3. Look for a Pattern

Much of the time you can get by with just looking for patterns on problems that provide you with a lot of different numbers. In this case, consider the provided table.

      1 – 3.55
      2 – 7.10
      4 – 14.20
      10 – 35.50

What patterns do you see in the above number sequences. It appears that when the number in the first column doubled from 1 to 2, the numbers in the second column doubled as well, going from 3.55 to 7.10. Further inspection shows that when the numbers in the first column doubled from 2 to 4, the numbers in the second column doubled again, going from 7.10 to 14.20. Now you've got a pattern, when the first column of numbers doubles, so does the second column.

Since the question asked about a resistance of 20, you should recognize that 20 is the double of 10. Since a length of 10 meant a resistance of 35.50 ohms, then doubling the length of 10 should double the resistance, making 71 ohms, or 71 the correct answer.

Writing Subtest

Sample Question

Improving Sentences Problem – Choose which of five ways of writing the underlined part of the sentence is correct.

While a leader, one can decide to allow the group to determine its course by a simple vote of majority, or we can choose to guide the group without allowing the opportunity for discussion.
    a. While a leader, one can decide
    b. While leaders, we can decide
    c. While a leader, we can decide
    d. While leaders, one can decide

    e. While leading, one can decide

Let's look at a couple of different methods and steps to solving this problem.

1. Agreement in Pronoun Number

All pronouns have to agree in number to their antecedent or noun that they are representing. In the underlined portion, the pronoun "one" has as its antecedent the noun "leader".

Go through and match up each of the pronouns in the answer choices with their antecedents.
    a. leader, one – correctly matches singular antecedent to singular pronoun
    b. leaders, we – correctly matches plural antecedent to plural pronoun
    c. leader, we – incorrectly matches singular antecedent to plural pronoun
    d. leaders, one – incorrectly matches plural antecedent to singular pronoun
    e. ?, one – no antecedent

Based on pronoun number agreement, you can eliminate choices C and D from consideration, because they fail the test.

2. Parallelism

Not only do the pronouns and antecedents in the underlined portion of the sentence have to be correct, but the rest of the sentence has to match as well. The remainder of the sentence has to be parallel to the underlined portion. Part of the sentence that is not underlined has the phrase "we can choose." Notice how this phrase uses the plural pronoun "we". This means that the underlined portion of the sentence has to be plural to agree with the rest of the sentence and have matching plural pronouns and nouns as well.

Quickly review the answer choices and look for whether the nouns and pronouns in the answer choices are singular or plural.
    a. leader, one – singular noun, singular pronoun

- 35 -

b. leaders, we – plural noun, plural pronoun
c. leader, we – singular noun, plural pronoun
d. leaders, one – plural noun, singular pronoun
e. ?, one – singular pronoun

Only choice B has both a plural noun and a plural pronoun, making choice B correct.

Sample Question
Identifying Sentence Errors Problem – Choose which, if any, of the four underlined sections of the sentence is incorrect. If there are no errors, choose "no error".

Each of the top picks of last year was quickly dismissed as a possibility when the newest selections arrives on the market a month ago. No error

Let's look at a few different methods and steps to solving this problem.

1. Subject-Verb Agreement
Go through and look at each subject-verb pair in the sentence.

"Was dismissed" is the first verb encountered. At first you may get distracted and not see the correct subject for this verb. You may think the subject is "picks," but note that "picks" is in the prepositional phrase "of the top picks," meaning it cannot be the subject of a verb outside of the prepositional phrase. The actual subject is "Each," and the subject and verb are in agreement. "Each was dismissed" is grammatically correct.

"Arrives" is the second verb encountered. "Selections" is its subject, and the two are not in agreement, as "selections" is plural, and "arrives" is singular. This makes choice D the correct answer choice.

2. View the Choices as Part of a Whole
Go through and look at each underlined answer choice as a part of the larger sentence. View each choice as part of a greater whole.

Some answer choices will appear correct when viewed independently (particularly if they are a single word answer choice), and can only be properly viewed as part of the entire sentence, where it can be placed into a proper context.
   a. of the top – this is part of a prepositional phrase and fits appropriately into the sentence.
   b. year was – "year" is part of another prepositional phrase, and "was" is the verb for "each" at the beginning of the sentence. Both are correctly used.
   c. quickly dismissed – quickly is an adverb describing how the picks were dismissed and is correctly used.
   d. selections arrives – when considered by itself, this subject/verb pair is already wrong, but you can also factor into the decision the last part of the sentence. The sentence is describing an event that occurred a month ago. "Arrives" is present tense and even if it were "arrive" (which would make the subject/verb be in agreement), it would still be incorrect, as it needs to be "arrived," to match with the past tense indicated by the phrase "a month ago". This is the underlined portion that is wrong and is the correct answer choice.
   e. no error – N/A

Sample Topic
What is the most important thing in your life? Discuss why?

Let's look at a few different methods and steps to solving this problem.

1. What's the goal?
Remember that on the essay portion of the SAT, there isn't a "correct" answer. The answer you choose to give to the topic provided does not have to be the first thing that comes to your mind.

For example, with this topic, your first thought might be your home or car, which are necessary for the basic functions of life, such as providing a roof over your head and a method of transportation. Yet, what would be your supporting answer as to why you would pick your car? Some possibilities might be: "it gets me where I need to go, it is brand new, it is expensive, I like it a lot, it would be difficult to replace, it's shiny."

These answer choices may fill up some space, but don't have much meaning. There are probably things in your life that have much more meaning and priority in other ways that would be better to write about.

The goal is to think of something that has meaning beyond the mere basics of shelter or transportation. You want a topic that you could potentially write pages and pages about, filling each of them with depths of passionate detail. While you probably won't have time to write pages and pages, it's good to have a topic that has plenty of room to be expanded upon.

2. Make a Short List
The best way to think of a good topic would be to create a short list of possibilities.

What are some alternative things that you have that are important? What are things that you would regret and miss for years to come? Perhaps your family, your friends, a relationship, or your faith would be better choices.

After you've made your list, look back over it and see which choice you could write the most information about. That is the one you want to choose.

3. Answer "Why"
Notice that choosing a topic and writing about it does not completely answer the topic question. There are two little words hidden at the back of the initial question, "Discuss why?"

You have to answer that all-important question. If you wrote a sentence as part of your response and one of the essay scorer

looked over your shoulder and said, "but why?" would your next sentence answer their question.

For example, suppose you wrote, "The relationship that I have with my father has a lot of meaning."

If someone asked, "But why?" would your next sentence answer it.

Your next sentence should say, "The relationship has meaning because he was there to support me when my mother died. We depended upon each other to get through that period, which was extremely difficult."

Answering the question posed is crucial to your success at writing a great essay. It doesn't do any good to write a good essay if it doesn't answer the question.

Practice Test #1

Practice Questions

Section 1

Essay

Time – 25 minutes

Consider the issue presented below:

Merit pay for teachers is the practice of giving increased pay based upon the improvement in student performance. It is a controversial idea among educators and policy makers. Those who support this idea say that, with it, school districts are able to select and retain the best teachers and to improve student performance. Others argue that merit pay systems lead to teacher competition for the best students and to test-driven teaching practices that are detrimental to the overall quality of education.

Assignment:

Should teachers receive merit pay based on student performance? Write an essay developing your point of view on this issue. Support your position with evidence from your reading, experience, and personal observations.

Time -- 25 minutes

20 Questions

For this section, solve each problem and decide which of the choices given is the best.

Question 1 is based on the following figure.

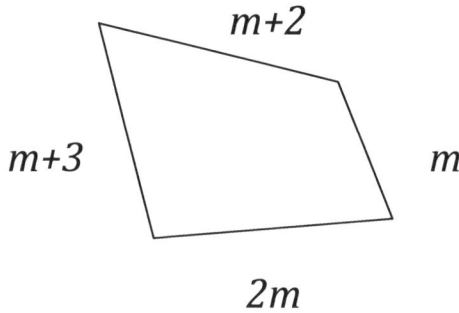

1. The figure shows an irregular quadrilateral and the lengths of its individual sides. Which of the following equations best represents the perimeter of the quadrilateral?

(A) $m^4 + 5$
(B) $2m^4 + 5$
(C) $4m + 5$
(D) $5m + 5$
(E) $4m^2 + 5$

Question 2 is based upon the following diagram.

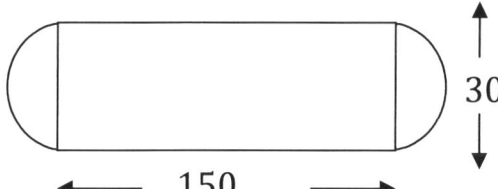

2. The diagram shows the outline of a racetrack for skaters, which consists of two long straight sections and two semi-circular turns. Given the dimensions shown, which of the following most closely measures the perimeter of the entire track?

(A) 300 yards
(B) 180 yards
(C) 360 yards
(D) 395 yards
(E) 425 yards

3. A motorcycle manufacturer offers 3 different models, each available in 6 different colors. How many different combinations of model and color are available?

(A) 9
(B) 6
(C) 12
(D) 18
(E) 24

4. If $x + y > 0$ when $x > y$, which of the following cannot be true?

(A) $x = 3$ and $y = 0$
(B) $x = 6$ and $y = -1$
(C) $x = -3$ and $y = 0$
(D) $x = -4$ and $y = -3$
(E) $x = 3$ and $y = -3$

5. Which of the following could be a graph of the function y = 1/x?

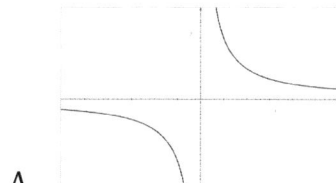

A.

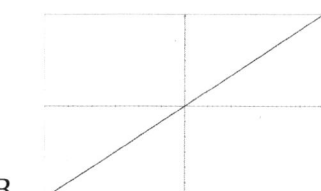

B.

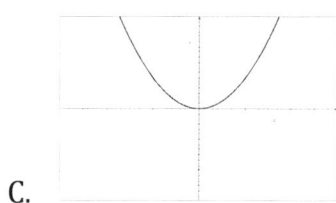

C.

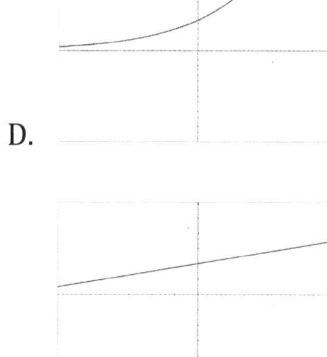

D.

E.

Question 6 is based on the following table.

Hours	1	2	3
Cost	$3.60	$7.20	$10.80

6. The table shows the cost of renting a bicycle for 1, 2 or 3 hours. Which of the following equations best represents the data, if C represents the cost and h represents the time of the rental?

(A) $C = 3.60h$
(B) $C = h + 3.60$
(C) $C = 3.60h + 10.80$
(D) $C = 10.80/h$
(E) $C = 3.60 + 7.20h$

7. Which of the following statements is true?

(A) Perpendicular lines have opposite slopes
(B) Perpendicular lines have the same slopes
(C) Perpendicular lines have reciprocal slopes
(D) Perpendicular lines have opposite reciprocal slopes
(E) Perpendicular lines have slopes that are unrelated

8. There are 64 squares on a checkerboard. Bobby puts one penny on the first square, two on the second square, four on the fourth, eight on the fifth, and continues to double the number of coins at each square until he has covered all 64 squares. How many coins must he place upon the last square?

(A) 2^{64}
(B) $2^{64} - 1$
(C) 2^{63}
(D) $2^{63} + 1$
(E) $2^{64} - 2$

9. Carrie wants to decorate her party with bundles of balloons containing three balloons each. Balloons are available in 4 different colors. There must be three different colors in each bundle. How many different kinds of bundles can she make?

(A) 18
(B) 12
(C) 4
(D) 6
(E) 10

Question 10 is based upon the following figure:

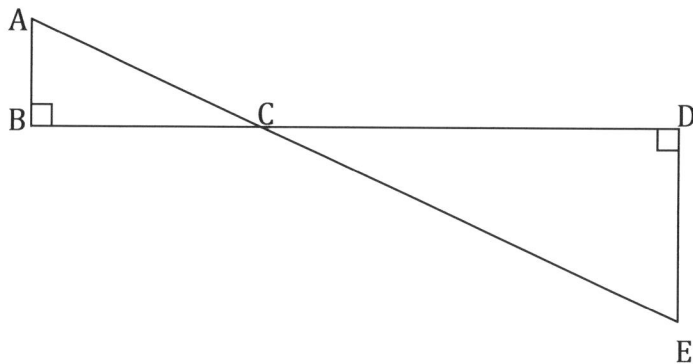

10. In the figure above, segment BC is 4 units long, segment CD is 8 units long, and segment DE is 6 units long. What is the length of segment AC?

(A) 7 units
(B) 5 units
(C) 3 units
(D) 2.5 units
(E) 4 units

11. Rafael has a business selling computers. He buys computers from the manufacturer for $450 each and sells them for $800. Each month, he must also pay fixed costs of $3000 for rent and utilities at his store. If he sells *n* computers in a month, which of the following equations can be used to calculate his profit?

(A) $P = n(800 - 450)$
(B) $P = n(800 - 450 - 3000)$
(C) $P = 3000n(800 - 450)$
(D) $P = n(800 - 450) - 3000$
(E) $P = n(800 - 450) + 3000$

12. Arrange the following numbers in order from the least to greatest 2^3, 4^2, 6^0, 9, 10^1.

    (A) 2^3, 4^2, 6^0, 9, 10^1
    (B) 6^0, 9, 10^1, 2^3, 4^2
    (C) 10^1, 2^3, 6^0, 9, 4^2
    (D) 6^0, 2^3, 9, 10^1, 4^2
    (E) 9, 6^0, 10^1, 4^2, 2^3

13. Dorothy is half her sister's age. She will be three fourths of her sister's age in 20 years. How many years old is she?

    (A) 10
    (B) 15
    (C) 20
    (D) 25
    (E) 30

Question 14 is based on the following diagram:

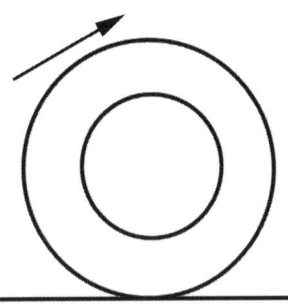

14. A tire on a car rotates at 500 RPM (revolutions per minute) when the car is traveling at 50 km/hr (kilometers per hour). What is the circumference of the tire, in meters?

    (A) $50{,}000/2\pi$

    (B) $50{,}000/60 * 2\pi$

    (C) $50{,}000/500 * 2\pi$

    (D) $50{,}000/60$

    (E) $10/6$

- 44 -

15. Which of the following expressions is equivalent to $(a + b)(a - b)$?
    (A) $a^2 - b^2$
    (B) $(a + b)^2$
    (C) $(a - b)^2$
    (D) $ab(a - b)$
    (E) $ab(a + b)$

16. Which of the following expressions represents the ratio of the area of a circle to its circumference?

    (A) πr^2
    (B) $\dfrac{\pi r^2}{2\pi}$
    (C) $\dfrac{2\pi r}{r^2}$
    (D) $2\pi r^{1/2}$
    (E) $\dfrac{r}{2}$

17. Jack and Kevin play in a basketball game. If the ratio of points scored by Jack to points scored by Kevin is 4 to 3, which of the following could NOT be the total number of points scored by the two boys?

    (A) 7
    (B) 14
    (C) 16
    (D) 28
    (E) 35

18. The average of six numbers is 4. If the average of two of those numbers is 2, what is the average of the other four numbers?

    (A) 5
    (B) 6
    (C) 7
    (D) 8
    (E) 9

19. How many 3-inch segments can a 4.5-yard line be divided into?

(A) 15
(B) 45
(C) 54
(D) 64
(E) 84

20. If −1/3x + 7 = 4, what is the value for 1/3x + 3?

(A) 3
(B) 6
(C) 9
(D) 12
(E) 15

Section 3

Time – 25 minutes

24 Questions

Questions 1-5: Each sentence below has one or more blanks. Beneath each sentence are five words or sets of words labeled A through E. Choose the word or set of words that best fits the meaning of the sentence as a whole.

1. He believed that in order to _____ the problem fully, he would need to understand all of its _____.

   (A) solve...positions
   (B) comprehend...extreme
   (C) experience...thoughts
   (D) embrace...nuances
   (E) address...intricacies

2. The author's novel was _____ but she managed to develop numerous _____ fully and enjoyably by its end.

   (A) thought-provoking...storylines
   (B) brief...characters
   (C) uninsightful...answers
   (D) surprising...plots
   (E) long-winded...chapters

3. The rumors were _____ and she welcomed the opportunity to _____ them.

   (A) true...repudiate
   (B) fabricated...correction
   (C) believable...enjoy
   (D) odious...refute
   (E) pertinent...demystify

4. I was sorry to see her in that _____, she looked so _____.

    (A) condition...despondent
    (B) situation...arbitrary
    (C) state...demure
    (D) position...pensive
    (E) mood...abstruse

5. The disarray was _____; the office had to be closed for the day so all the furniture could be placed where it belonged, papers could be re-filed and a general cleaning done.

    (A) inconsequential
    (B) contemptible
    (C) severe
    (D) intermittent
    (E) trifling

Questions 6-10 are based upon the following passage:

What Is Disturbing the Fun?

It was in this apartment, also, that there stood against the western wall, a gigantic clock of ebony. Its pendulum swung to and fro with a dull, heavy, monotonous clang; and when the minute-hand made the circuit of the face, and the hour was to be stricken, there came from the brazen lungs of the clock a sound which was clear and loud and deep and exceedingly musical, but of so peculiar a note and emphasis that, at each lapse of an hour, the musicians of the orchestra were constrained to pause, momentarily, in their performance, to harken to the sound; and thus the waltzers perforce ceased their evolutions; and there was a brief disconcert of the whole gay company; and, while the chimes of the clock yet rang, it was observed that the giddiest grew pale, and the more aged and sedate passed their hands over their brows as if in confused revery or meditation. But when the echoes had fully ceased, a light laughter at once pervaded the assembly; the musicians looked at each other and smiled as if at their own nervousness and folly, and made whispering vows, each to the other, that the next chiming of the clock should produce in them no similar emotion; and then, after the lapse of sixty minutes (which embrace three thousand and six hundred seconds of the

Time that flies), there came yet another chiming of the clock, and then were the same disconcert and tremulousness and meditation as before.

—Excerpted from "The Masque of the Red Death" by Edgar Allan Poe

6. The clock in this passage symbolizes

   (A) the brief amount of time the orchestra played.
   (B) the movement from early morning to evening.
   (C) the passage of time and nearness of death.
   (D) the fading beauty of all things.
   (E) the lack of attention the dancers paid to the music.

7. The scene that is being described is of a

   (A) concert.
   (B) formal dinner.
   (C) garden party.
   (D) boating tournament.
   (E) ball.

8. The action stops when

   (A) the host announces dinner.
   (B) the clock chimes the hour.
   (C) an uninvited guest arrives.
   (D) guests are asked to remove their masks.
   (E) members of the orchestra leave.

9. What does the reader infer will happen in the story?

   (A) The musicians will soon be playing for the king.
   (B) The police will arrive to stop the evening's pleasures.
   (C) The clock will explode at midnight.
   (D) At least one person there will die.
   (E) The host will throw out the rowdy guests.

10. Which words best describes the tone of this passage?

   (A) lighthearted and sunny
   (B) humorous and merry
   (C) mysterious and forbidding
   (D) angry and bitter
   (E) negative and sarcastic

Questions 6-17 are based upon the following passage:

In the United States, where we have more land than people, it is not at all difficult for persons in good health to make money. In this comparatively new field there are so many avenues of success open, so many vocations which are not crowded, that any person of either sex who is willing, at least for the time being, to engage in any respectable occupation that offers, may find lucrative employment.

Those who really desire to attain an independence, have only to set their minds upon it, and adopt the proper means, as they do in regard to any other object which they wish to accomplish, and the thing is easily done. But however easy it may be found to make money, I have no doubt many of my hearers will agree it is the most difficult thing in the world to keep it. The road to wealth is, as Dr. Franklin truly says, "as plain as the road to the mill." It consists simply in expending less than we earn; that seems to be a very simple problem. Mr. Micawber, one of those happy creations of the genial Dickens, puts the case in a strong light when he says that to have annual income of twenty pounds per annum, and spend twenty pounds and sixpence, is to be the most miserable of men; whereas, to have an income of only twenty pounds, and spend but nineteen pounds and sixpence is to be the happiest of mortals.

Many of my readers may say, "we understand this: this is economy, and we know economy is wealth; we know we can't eat our cake and keep it also." Yet I beg to say that perhaps more cases of failure arise from mistakes on this point than almost any other. The fact is, many people think they understand economy when they really do not.

11. Which of the following statements best expresses the main idea of the passage?

   (A) Getting a job is easier now than it ever has been before.
   (B) Earning money is much less difficult than managing it properly.
   (C) Dr. Franklin advocated getting a job in a mill.
   (D) Spending money is the greatest temptation in the world.
   (E) There is no way to predict changes in the economy.

12. What would this author's attitude likely be to a person unable to find employment?

    (A) descriptive
    (B) conciliatory
    (C) ingenuous
    (D) incredulous
    (E) exculpatory

13. According to the author, what is more difficult than making money?

    (A) getting a job
    (B) traveling to a mill
    (C) reading Dickens
    (D) understanding the economy
    (E) managing money

14. Who is the most likely audience for this passage?

    (A) economists
    (B) general readers
    (C) teachers
    (D) philanthropists
    (E) children

15. What is the best definition of *economy* as it is used in this passage?

    (A) exchange of money, goods, and services
    (B) delegation of household affairs
    (C) efficient money management
    (D) less expensive
    (E) luxurious accommodations

16. Which word best describes the author's attitude towards those who believe they

understand money?

    (A) supportive
    (B) incriminating
    (C) excessive
    (D) patronizing
    (E) incendiary

17. This passage is most likely taken from a(n) ____.

(A) self-help manual
(B) autobiography
(C) epistle
(D) novel
(E) brochure

Questions 18-24 are based upon the following passage:

We all know the drill: the consequences of urban sprawl, American's long work hours, and devotion to television and the internet are doing nothing good for American communities.

A new study by sociologists at Duke University and the University of Arizona adds more grist to this mill, noting that Americans in 2004 had smaller networks of people with whom they talk about matters important to them than they did in 1985. (*Social Isolation in America: Changes in Core Discussion Networks Over Two Decades*, American Sociological Review, June 2006.) In 1985, Americans had three confidants, in 2004, we averaged two. The number of Americans who had no one with whom to talk about important matters almost doubled in 2004 to over 25%. Increasingly, most confidants are family: in 2004, 80% of people talked only to family about important matters and about 9% people depended totally on their spouse.

This decrease in confidants is part (a result) of the same trend that's leaving fewer people knowing their neighbors or participating in social clubs or public affairs than in the past (phenomena noted in the book <u>Better Together: Restoring the American Community</u> by Robert Putnam and Lewis Feldstein). We know a lot of people, but not necessarily very well.

Left to our own devices and cultural trends then, we seem to be moving in an unpleasant direction. Communities are formed ad hoc, around specific shared individual interests. This wouldn't be bad, of course, except that those communities seem to exist only within the constraints of those shared interests, and don't develop into close and meaningful relationships. The transient and specific nature of many of our relationships today can keep us socially busy without building the lasting relationships and communities that we want.

So what do we do about it if we want to change things? Harvard University's School of Government put together 150 ways to increase what they call "social capital" (the value of our social networks). Among their suggestions are: support local merchants; audition for community theater or volunteer to usher; participate in political campaigns; start or join a carpool; eat breakfast at a local gathering spot on Saturdays; and stop and make sure the person on the side of the highway is OK.

18. According to the author, which of the following was true in 2004:

(A) The average American had three confidants and 9% of people depended totally on their spouse for discussion of important matters.
(B) The average American had two confidants, and 80% of people discussed important matters only with their spouses.
(C) The average American had two confidants, and 9% of people discussed important matters only with family members.
(D) The average American had two confidants, and 80% of people discussed important matters only with family members.
(E) The average American had three confidants, and 80% of people discussed important matters only with family members.

19. The author argues that the transient nature of many of today's relationships is problematic because:

(A) we don't share specific interests
(B) we don't know many people
(C) it prevents us building lasting relationships and communities
(D) we have too much social capital
(E) we talk to too many people about private matters

20. Which of the following are some of the causes to which the author attributes problems in American communities:

    (A) too much homework and devotion to television
    (B) devotion to television and decline of sports team membership
    (C) long work hours and too much homework
    (D) urban sprawl and decline of sports team membership
    (E) urban sprawl and long work hours

21. Which of the following is not something the author states was suggested by Harvard University as a way to increase social capital:

    (A) eat breakfast at a local gathering spot
    (B) join a bowling team
    (C) support local merchants
    (D) join a carpool
    (E) audition for community theater

22. In what year was the Duke University study cited by the author published?

    (A) 2006
    (B) 2000
    (C) 1985
    (D) 2002
    (E) 2004

23. How many ways did Harvard University's School of Government suggest to increase social capital?

    (A) 25
    (B) 80
    (C) 100
    (D) 150
    (E) 200

24. According to the author, "social capital" means which of the following:

    (A) the value of our social networks
    (B) the number of confidants with whom we share information
    (C) the value we place on friendships outside family members
    (D) the number of activities in which we engage
    (E) the difference between our relationships in 1985 and 2004

Time – 25 minutes

35 Questions

> *Questions 1-11*: A portion of each of the following sentences is underlined. Following the text there are five ways of phrasing the underlined material. Choice A is the original text; the other four choices are different. Select the choice that produces the best sentence.

1. Minerals are nutritionally significant elements <u>that assist to make your body</u> work properly.

    (A) that assist to make your body
    (B) that help your body
    (C) that making your body
    (D) that work to make your body
    (E) that hinder your body to

2. Of the two, <u>the oldest brother</u> had a much more difficult time in school.

    (A) the oldest brother
    (B) the older brother
    (C) the earliest brother
    (D) the best brother
    (E) the better brother

3. The duck waddled towards the pond, <u>her five ducklings following just behind her</u>.

    (A) her five ducklings following just behind her
    (B) and then there were five ducklings following in back of her
    (C) therefore the ducklings were following behind
    (D) and so her five ducklings were following just behind her
    (E) her five ducklings

4. <u>Fair teachers understand that he or she</u> cannot treat any student with favoritism.

   (A) Fair teachers understand that he or she
   (B) Fair teachers understand that he
   (C) Fair teachers understand that she
   (D) Fair teachers understand that they
   (E) Fair teachers understand that their

5. We will begin with painting <u>first, and then secondly</u> we will start the decoupage process.

   (A) first, and then secondly
   (B) firstly, and then secondly
   (C) first, and then second
   (D) first, then second
   (E) first, second

6. The hidden passageway in the bowels of the castle <u>remained a well kept secret</u>.

   (A) remained a well kept secret
   (B) remained a well-kept secret
   (C) remained a wellkept secret
   (D) was always going to be a secret
   (E) would always be a secret

7. <u>Another view of the test results had been planned to be provided by a different doctor.</u>

   (A) Another view of the test results had been planned to be provided by a different doctor.
   (B) She will need to get new test results from a different doctor.
   (C) A different doctor has planned to provide another view of the test results.
   (D) Several new views of the results are provided and planned with a different doctor.
   (E) A couple of views of the test results are planned to be provided by a different doctor.

8. <u>I dare not whisper</u> the deadly secret to a single soul.

   (A) I dare not whisper
   (B) I should not whisper
   (C) I cannot tell anyone
   (D) I swore not to tell
   (E) I whispered

9. <u>The scientist said we did need not trouble</u> our minds with trivial details.

(A) The scientist said we did need not trouble
(B) The scientist said we did not trouble
(C) The scientist said do not worry
(D) The scientist did not need to do
(E) The scientist said we need not trouble

10. <u>Every teacher ought set a good example</u> for his or her students.

(A) Every teacher ought set a good example
(B) Every teacher ought to set a good example
(C) Teachers are required to set a good example
(D) It is important for teachers to set good examples
(E) One teachers should set a good example

11. The Math Committee worked to make sure students <u>had options to participate in</u>

contests, book work, computer games or memory practice games.

(A) had options to participate in
(B) met the requirements for
(C) were allowed to do
(D) could choose one of the following:
(E) opted to do one of the following:

Questions 12-29: The following sentences test your ability to recognize grammar and usage errors. Each sentence contains either one error or no error at all. No sentence contains more than one error. The error, if there is one, is underlined. If the sentence contains an error, select the underlined part that must be changed to make the sentence correct. If the sentence is correct, select choice E.

12. The information that (A) <u>he was given</u> by the two doctors (B) <u>make him realize</u> how much his (C) <u>grandfather's health</u> (D) <u>had declined</u>. (E) <u>No error</u>.

13. Quincy and his son Zane, (A) <u>neither of</u> (B) <u>whom</u> enjoy sporting events, (C) <u>is going</u> to see a movie (D) <u>instead</u>. (E) <u>No error</u>.

14. The entire audience (A) <u>are</u> rapt for the (B) <u>duration</u> of the performance and applaud (C) <u>loudly</u> when the (D) <u>curtain falls</u>. (E) <u>No error</u>.

15. (A) <u>When asked about</u> her major job responsibilities, (B) <u>Jodi answered that</u> she (C) <u>responded to</u> client questions, conducted interviews, wrote reports, and (D) <u>giving presentations</u>. (E) <u>No error</u>.

16. In the time of the dinosaurs, other (A) <u>flora and fauna</u> on earth (B) <u>are</u> (C) <u>very different</u> from what we're (D) <u>used to</u> today. (E) <u>No error</u>.

17. Our (A) <u>dogs don't</u> (B) <u>behave well</u> at home with us, (C) <u>but may</u> be (D) <u>a good achiever</u> in obedience school. (E) <u>No error</u>.

18. Everyone (A) <u>in the firm</u> (B) <u>participated in</u> the gift exchange and brought (C) <u>their present</u> to the reception desk (D) <u>for distribution</u>. (E) <u>No error</u>.

19. My (A) <u>aunt was</u> very surprised when my mom (B) <u>told her</u> that (C) <u>Henry was</u> better at Spanish than (D) <u>my sister</u>. (E) <u>No error</u>.

20. (A) Between the two dresses she (B) was considering for the event, she liked the one (C) with the green piping (D) most. (E) No error.

21. (A) She acknowledged in her speech that she was (B) indebted with (C) many people, including her family, her friends, (D) her agent, and her publisher. (E) No error.

22. The paintings of local artist Dana Smith (A) are often compared to (B) Pablo Picasso, (C) although Smith denies that Picasso was a (D) significant influence for him. (E) No error.

23. (A) Of our (B) set of dinner plates, (C) less than five (D) are without chips or cracks. (E) No error.

24. Neither the gift (A) from his father (B) or the gift from his mother (C) was what (D) he expected for his birthday this year. (E) No error.

25. The employees (A) were all worried (B) about layoffs, but each (C) remained positive (D) and upbeat throughout the day. (E) No error

26. (A) Being an honor student with a (B) penchant with reading, she (C) loves to pick up a book during every spare (D) moment. (E) No error

27. At the (A) full arena, (B) filled with 15,000 concert-goers, the two friends (C) were still somehow capable (D) to find each other. (E) No error

28. While the (A) TV anchorman (B) relayed the (C) details of the storm, the family (D) fell silent. (E) No error.

29. I (A) had already read (B) the book (C) before, so I knew what (D) to expect. (E) No error

- 59 -

Questions 30-35: The following passage is an early draft of an essay. Some parts of the passage need to be rewritten. Read the passage and select the best answers for the questions that follow. Some questions are about particular sentences or parts of sentences and ask you to improve sentence structure or word choice. Other questions ask you to consider organization and development. In choosing answers, follow the requirements of standard written English.

Questions 30-35 refer to the following passage:

(1) Even before women had the right to vote, women have attempted to gain the nation's highest executive office. (2) Victoria Woodhull ran as a third party candidate in 1872. (3) Although she did not win, she became the first woman who owned an investment firm on wall street. (4) In 1884 and 1888, the lawyer Belva Lockwood also ran as a third party candidate. (5) Margaret Chase Smith (who served in both houses of Congress) was the first woman nominated by a major party, the Republicans.

B

(6) Nine other women have seeked for the presidency since the 1970s. (7) Five of them were Democrats and one was a Republican and three represented third parties. (8) I think it's about time this country had a woman as president. (9) Only two women have been nominated as vice president—Democrat Geraldine Ferraro in 1984 and Republican Sarah Palin in 2008. (10) Many people believe that soon the United States will join countries such as Britain, India, Germany, Chile, and Liberia, that have women heads of state.

30. Sentence (1): *"Even before women had the right to vote, women have attempted to gain the nation's highest executive office."*

If you rewrote sentence (1) beginning with the words <u>Women have attempted to gain the nation's highest executive office,</u> the next words should be

    (A) to vote
    (B) women had
    (C) even before
    (D) the right
    (E) had the

31. Sentence (3): *"Although she did not win, she became the first woman who owned an investment firm on wall street."*

What correction should be made to this sentence?

    (A) change <u>became</u> to <u>become</u>
    (B) capitalize <u>wall street</u>
    (C) change <u>Although</u> to <u>Though</u>
    (D) capitalize <u>investment firm</u>
    (E) place a question mark at the end of the sentence

32. Sentence (5): *"Margaret Chase Smith (who served in both houses of Congress) was the first woman nominated by a major party, the Republicans."*

What correction should be made to this sentence?

    (A) place commas before and after the parentheses
    (B) do not capitalize <u>Republicans</u>
    (C) change <u>woman</u> to <u>women</u>
    (D) change <u>nominated</u> to <u>nomminated</u>
    (E) no correction is necessary

33. Sentence (6): "*Nine other women have seeked for the presidency since the 1970s.*"

Which of the following is the best way to write the underlined portion of this sentence? If you think the original is the best way to write the sentence, choose option 1.

(A) women have seeked for
(B) woman have seeked for
(C) women have seek for
(D) women have sought
(E) woman had seeked for

34. Sentence (7): "*Five of them were Democrats and one was a Republican, and three represented third parties.*"

What correction should be made to this sentence?

(A) add a comma after Democrats and delete and
(B) change them to those
(C) change were to was
(D) capitalize third parties
(E) no correction is necessary

35. Which revision would improve the overall organization of this article?

(A) switch paragraphs A and B
(B) place the final sentence at the beginning of paragraph B
(C) delete sentence (8)
(D) place sentence 2. at the end of paragraph A
(E) begin the article with sentence (6)

Time – 25 minutes

18 Questions

Questions 1-8: Solve each problem and decide which of the choices given is the best.

1. A combination lock uses a 3-digit code. Each digit can be any one of the ten available integers 0-9. How many different combinations are possible?

    (A) 9
    (B) 1000
    (C) 30
    (D) 81
    (E) 100

2. A mother is currently three times as old as her daughter. In fifteen years the mother will be twice as old as the daughter. The mother's present age is

    (A) 30
    (B) 42
    (C) 45
    (D) 50
    (E) 52

3. The cost, in dollars, of shipping x computers to California for sale is 3000 + 100x. The amount received when selling these computers is 400x dollars. What is the least number of computers that must be shipped and sold so that the amount received is at least equal to the shipping cost?

    (A) 10
    (B) 15
    (C) 20
    (D) 25
    (E) 30

4. If a rectangle's length and width are doubled, by what percentage does its area increase?

    (A) 20
    (B) 80
    (C) 160
    (D) 240
    (E) 300

5. If $3/s = 7$ and $4/t = 12$, then $s - t =$

    (A) -1/12
    (B) -1/7
    (C) 2/12
    (D) 2/7
    (E) 2/21

6. Which of the following are complementary angles?

    (A) 71° and 19°
    (B) 18° and 18°
    (C) 90° and 90°
    (D) 90° and 45°
    (E) 15° and 30°

7. In the following figure, angle b = 120°. What is the measurement of angle a?

    (A) 40°
    (B) 60°
    (C) 90°
    (D) 100°
    (E) 180°

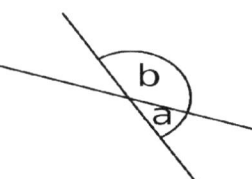

8. Which of the following figures has rotational symmetry?

(A)

(B)

(C)

(D)

(E)

Questions 9-18: Use the grids on the answer sheet page where you have answered.

9. Jesse invests $7,000 in a certificate of deposit that pays interest at the rate of 7.5% annually. How much interest (in dollars) does Jesse gain from this investment during the first year that he holds the certificate? Mark your answer in the circles on the grid on the answer sheet.

Question 10 is based upon the following figure:

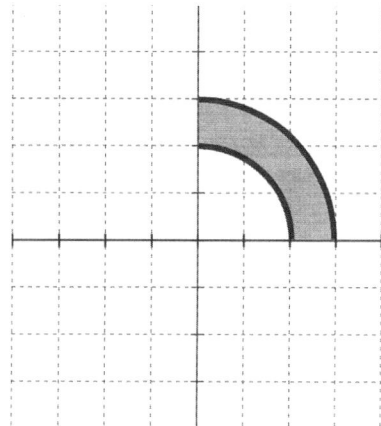

10. Figure shows two quarter circles centered on the origin of the Cartesian coordinate plane. The inner circle has a radius of two units; the outer circle has a radius of three units. What is the area of the shaded region? Mark your answer in the circles on the grid on the answer sheet.

Question 11 is based on the following table, which describes the closing prices of a number of stocks traded on the New York Stock Exchange.

Stock	Price per Share	Shares Traded
Microsoft	$31.44	48,681,000
Oracle	$28.74	24,817,000
Apple Computer	$514.85	17,125,000
Cisco Systems	$19.80	36,405,000
Garmin	$44.69	7,971,000

11. Pradip decides to invest $4500 in Cisco Systems stock and buys it at the price shown in the table. At what price should he sell it to obtain a profit of 10%? Mark your answer in the circles on the grid on the answer sheet.

12. The distance traveled by a moving object is computed from the relation $d = rt$, where r is the rate of travel(speed) and t is the time of travel. A major league pitcher throws a fastball at a speed of 125 ft/sec. The distance from the pitching rubber to home plate is 60.5 feet. How long, in seconds, does it take a fastball to travel this distance? Compute your answer to the nearest hundredth of a second and mark your answer in the circles on the grid on the answer sheet.

Question 13 is based upon the following figure:

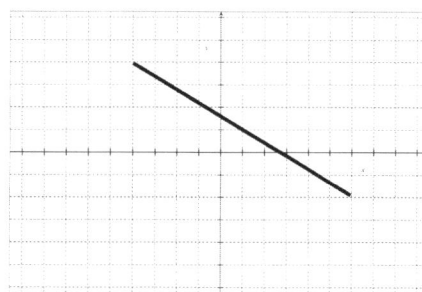

13. Determine the midpoint of the line shown in the figure. Mark your answer in the circles on the coordinate plane grid on your answer sheet.

14. The expressions $y = -3x + 6$ and $y = 2x - 4$ represent straight lines. Compute the coordinates of the point at which they intersect and mark your answer in the circles on the coordinate plane grid on your answer sheet.

15. Chan receives a bonus from his job. He pays 30% in taxes, gives 30% to charity, and uses another 25% to pay off an old debt. He has $600 remaining from his bonus. What was the total amount of Chan's bonus? Mark your answer in the circles on the grid on the answer sheet.

16. If number x is subtracted from 27, the result is -5. What is number x?

17. A wall clock has the numbers 1 through 12 written on it. If you spin the second hand, what is the probability of landing on an even number?

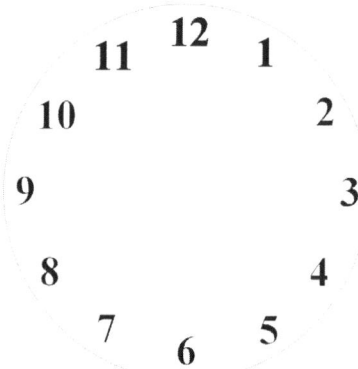

18. A rectangle is divided into two squares, each with a perimeter of 20. What is the perimeter of the rectangle?

Time -- 25 minutes

23 Questions

Questions 1-8: Each sentence below has one or more blanks, each blank indicating that something has been omitted. Beneath each sentence are five words or sets of words labeled A through E. Choose the word or set of words that, when inserted in the sentence, best fits the meaning of the sentence as a whole.

1. He told the kids not to be so _____ when he was gone. He was afraid they would _____ the babysitter.

   (A) placid...frighten
   (B) boisterous...overwhelm
   (C) obedient...enrage
   (D) truculent...appease
   (E) egotistical...endear

2. It was an _____ house with its vaulted ceilings, obviously expensive furniture and extravagant art covering the walls.

   (A) off-kilter
   (B) obstreperous
   (C) odious
   (D) obscure
   (E) ostentatious

3. They chalked their meeting up to _____; it was the kind of lucky thing that could never have happened by design.

   (A) preparation
   (B) serendipity
   (C) extravagance
   (D) peculiarity
   (E) concatenation

4. He was modest in his _____ and did not _____ a promotion to higher levels of responsibility at work.

   (A) dreams...refuse
   (B) failures...question
   (C) habits...necessitate
   (D) vision...challenge
   (E) ambition...pursue

5. History did not feel _____ to her. Seeking a more _____ major she decided to study economics.

   (A) relevant...topical
   (B) important...literary
   (C) familiar...theatrical
   (D) esoteric...sycophantic
   (E) important...trivial

6. She considered herself to be _____ and liked to predict events before they occurred.

   (A) precocious
   (B) prescient
   (C) predated
   (D) prefatory
   (E) preferential

7. "If the yeti is _____", he asked, "then who made these _____ footprints?"

   (A) genuine...invisible
   (B) dangerous...massive
   (C) imaginary...colossal
   (D) welcoming...cavernous
   (E) mysterious...unfathomable

8. Elijah noticed that the crowd had _____ and it was possible once again to walk around the museum _____.

   (A) thickened...confidently
   (B) intensified...on foot
   (C) vanished...en masse
   (D) dispersed...with ease
   (E) startled...convincingly

Questions 9-15 are based on the following passage:

For those of you not in the know in the world of invented languages, Esperanto was created in the late 1800s by a Mr. Ludwik Zamenhof of Poland. Zamenhof bemoaned the tension created by the literal inability of we humans to understand each other. In Esperanto he sought to provide a sort of neutral universal second language that privileged no one linguistically, confining us all only by our ability to be articulate, rather than by our familiarity with whatever language happens to be spoken at a given time.

While not the world-wide form of communication Zamenhof and other Esperantists have hoped for, Esperanto has grown impressively since its inception. Estimates of numbers of speakers range from 100,000 to 2 million, in 115 different countries; native speakers are estimated to number more than 1000. Many books have been translated and written in Esperanto, and two movies have been made in Esperanto – including Incubus starring William Shatner.

Reasons to Learn Esperanto:

It's Easy. A common argument for learning Esperanto is the ease of learning it: it's phonetic, grammatically regular, and a relatively small amount of words can be combined to create additional words -- so you need to know less vocabulary to sound smart than you would in other languages. In addition to being able to be learned many times more quickly than anything else, studies show that learning Esperanto increases people's ability to learn a next language.

You Can Stay in People's Houses for Free. Some of these Esperanto-speakers really put their money where their mouths are when it comes to supporting international understanding. There's a list Esperantists can put themselves on called the *Pasporta Serva*; speak Esperanto and, bang, you can stay with any of those fellow speakers for free. The list currently has around 1350 hosts in more than 85 countries.   Does any other language come with that kind of perk?

I am Esperanto. A final reason to pin a green 5-pointed star (symbol of Esperanto) to your shirt and try and learn this crazy human-made language is to support the ideals that motivated Zamenhof to create the thing in the first place. He wanted to help usher in peace among cultures by giving people a place to be on equal footing, at least linguistically. In this time of tensions and divisions between pretty much every group you can find, that seems like a goal worth sharing. So, go ahead and call yourself Esperanto – it means, in Esperanto, "one who hopes."

Some Esperanto Phrases to Use to Impress Your Friends

Hello	Saluton
Good Night	Bonan nokton
I speak Esperanto	Mi parolas Esperanton
I love you	Mi amas vin
You smell like a crocodile	Vi odoras kiel krokodilo

9. According to the author, estimates of Esperanto speakers range from:

   (A) 115 to 1000
   (B) 100,000 to 2 million
   (C) around 1350
   (D) 85 to 1350
   (E) more than 1000

10. Which of the following is <u>not</u> a reason given by the author for learning Esperanto?

   (A) Esperanto speakers can stay in some other speakers' homes for free
   (B) It is phonetic
   (C) It increases speakers' ability to learn a next language.
   (D) It is spoken by most Europeans
   (E) It is grammatically regular

11. According to the author, why did Zamenhof create Esperanto?

(A) To help people learn additional languages
(B) To assist people in staying with other speakers around the world
(C) To combine what he thought were the best elements of Spanish and English in   one language
(D) To eliminate political differences
(E) To give people a place to be on equal footing and thereby help create peace among cultures

12. According to the author, in how many countries is Esperanto spoken, and how many countries are represented on the *Pasporta Serva*?

(A) 115/ more than 1000
(B) 1350/more than 85
(C) 115/ more than 85
(D) 1350/ more than 1000
(E) 1000/ more than 1350

13. The author writes that "he sought to provide a sort of neutral universal second language that privileged no one linguistically..." Which of the following words is most synonymous with the word "privileged" as used in that sentence?

(A) benefited
(B) hindered
(C) advantage
(D) fortunate
(E) confidential

14. What are Esperanto speakers called?

(A) Esperantos
(B) Esperantis
(C) Esperantists
(D) Esperantons
(E) Esperantins

15. According to the author, what have studies shown about Esperanto?

(A) That it is spoken in 115 countries
(B) That two movies have been made in Esperanto
(C) That it has grown impressively since its inception
(D) That it increases global understanding and communication
(E) That learning it increases people's ability to learn a next language

Questions 16 - 19 are based on the following passage:

It could be argued that all American war movies take as their governing paradigm that of the Western, and that we, as viewers, don't think critically enough about this fact. The virtuous hero in the white hat, the evil villain in the black hat, the community threatened by violence; these are the obvious elements of the paradigm. In addition, the hero is highly skilled at warfare, though reluctant to use it, the community is made up of morally upstanding citizens, and there is no place for violence in the community: the hero himself must leave the community he has saved once the battle is complete. This way of seeing the world has soaked into our storytelling of battle and conflict. It's hard to find a U.S.-made war movie that, for example, presents the enemy as complex and potentially fighting a legitimate cause, or that presents the hero (usually the U.S.) as anything other than supremely morally worthy. It is important to step back and think about the assumptions and frameworks that shape the stories we're exposed to; if we're careless and unquestioning, we absorb biases and world views with which we may not agree.

16. The primary purpose of this passage is to:

(A) analyze an interesting feature of American cinema.
(B) refute the Western paradigm.
(C) suggest a way that war movies could be made better.
(D) suggest that viewers think critically about underlying assumptions in the movies we watch.
(E) explain the Western paradigm.

17. The author claims that it is hard to find a U.S. made movie that "presents the hero (usually the U.S.) as anything other than supremely morally worthy." Does the author imply that she:

(A) believes the hero should always appear to be morally worthy.
(B) believes the hero should never appear to be morally worthy.
(C) believes the hero should be more nuanced and less unconditionally good.
(D) believes the hero is an uninteresting character.
(E) believes the hero is not the U.S.

18. Which of the following is <u>not</u> an example given by the author of an element of the Western paradigm:

    (A) Hero highly skilled at warfare
    (B) Evil villain in black hat
    (C) Everyone riding horses
    (D) Community made up of upstanding citizens
    (E) Virtuous hero

19. Which of the following is part of the world view, with which we may not agree, that the author implies we might absorb from these movies if we're careless and unquestioning:

    (A) Enemies of the U.S. do not ever fight for legitimate causes.
    (B) The community is morally bankrupt.
    (C) The U.S. is complex.
    (D) The U.S. is not skilled at warfare.
    (E) The community welcomes violence.

Questions 20 - 23 are based on the following passage.

In the American Southwest of the late 1800s, the introduction of barbed wire fencing led to fierce disputes between ranchers and farmers, both eager to protect their rights and their livelihood. The farmers were the clear winners of the two groups, and the barbed wire fences stayed and proliferated. Barbed wire proved to be ideal for use in western conditions; it was cheaper and easier to use than the alternatives of wood fences, stone walls or hedges. Within a few decades all the previously open range land became fenced-in private property. This change was so dramatic to the western culture that some consider the introduction of barbed wire fencing to be the event that ended the Old West period of our history.

20. According to the author, which group supported the use of barbed wire fences?

    (A) the ranchers
    (B) the farmers
    (C) both the ranchers and the farmers
    (D) neither the ranchers nor the farmers
    (E) the American Southwest

21. According to the author, what do some believe the introduction of barbed wire ended?

    (A) the disputes between the farmers and the ranchers
    (B) the controversy over whether wood fences or stone walls were better
    (C) the Old West period of our history
    (D) the livelihood of the farmers
    (E) the existence of public property

22. Which of the following did the author <u>not</u> imply would have been found in the Old West prior to the introduction of barbed wire fencing?

    (A) no fencing in some places
    (B) wood fences
    (C) hedges
    (D) brick walls
    (E) stone walls

23. According to the author, when did the introduction of barbed wire fencing occur?

    (A) the late 16th century
    (B) the late 17th century
    (C) the late 18th century
    (D) the late 19th century
    (E) the late 20th century

Time – 20 minutes

16 Questions

For this section, solve each problem and decide which of the choices given is the best.

1. Which of the following letters has a vertical line of symmetry?

    (A) E
    (B) V
    (C) K
    (D) B
    (E) L

2. Angle AEC is a straight line. Angle BEC is 45°. What is the measure for angle AEB?

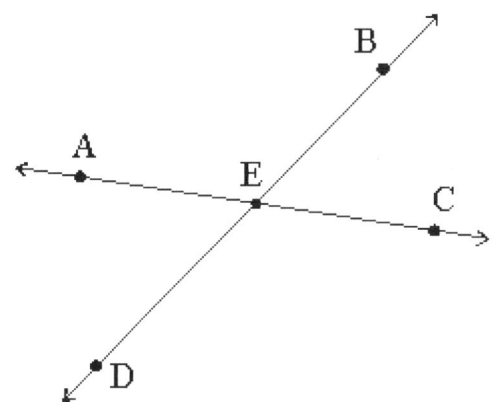

    (A) Angle AEB is 90°
    (B) Angle AEB is 115°
    (C) Angle AEB is 135°
    (D) Angle AEB is 180°
    (E) Angle AEB is 360°

Use the figure below to answer questions 3, 4 and 5.

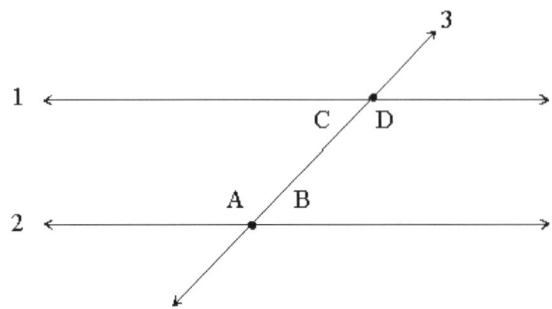

3. Which of the following statements is true about the figure above?

   (A) Lines 1 and 2 are parallel.
   (B) Lines 1 and 3 are parallel.
   (C) Lines 1 and 2 intersect.
   (D) Line 1 bisects line 3.
   (E) Line 2 corresponds with Angle B.

4. In the figure above, which of the following is a pair of alternate interior angles?

   (A) Angle C and Angle D
   (B) Angle A and Angle B
   (C) Angle A and Angle C
   (D) Angle B and Angle D
   (E) Angle A and Angle D

5. In the figure above, which of the following is an obtuse angle?

   (A) Line 1
   (B) Line 2
   (C) Line 3
   (D) Angle A
   (E) Angle B

6. All of the children are girls. Some of the girls like soccer. Some of the girls like cheerleading. Based on this data, which statement has to be correct?

   (A) All girls like to play soccer.
   (B) Some of the girls are 3 years old.
   (C) Some of the girls like both soccer and cheerleading.
   (D) Some of the children like soccer.
   (E) Some of the girls do not like soccer or cheerleading.

- 78 -

7. If the average of 7 and x is equal to the average of 9, 4, and x, what is the value of x?

   (A) 4
   (B) 5
   (C) 6
   (D) 7
   (E) 8

8. If $2^4 = 4^x$, then x =

   (A) 2
   (B) 4
   (C) 6
   (D) 8
   (E) 16

9. If 2x + 3y = 13 and 4x – y = 5, then 3x + 2y =

   (A) 2
   (B) 3
   (C) 6
   (D) 12
   (E) 24

10. How many integers are solutions of the inequality |x| < 4?

   (A) An infinite number
   (B) 0
   (C) 3
   (D) 6
   (E) 7

11. For what real number x is it true that 3(2x – 10) = x?

   (A) -6
   (B) -5
   (C) 5
   (D) 6
   (E) 30

12. A two-digit number is chosen at random. What is the probability that the chosen number is a multiple of 7?

(A) 1/10
(B) 1/9
(C) 11/90
(D) 12/90
(E) 13/90

13. If the measures of the three angles in a triangle are 2 : 6 : 10, what is the measure of the smallest angle?

(A) 20 degrees
(B) 40 degrees
(C) 60 degrees
(D) 80 degrees
(E) 100 degrees

14. Henry is three times as old as Truman. Two years ago, Henry was five times as old as Truman. How old is Henry now?

(A) 4
(B) 8
(C) 12
(D) 16
(E) 20

15. The bowl of change on your dresser totals $2.17. Which combination of coins could NOT be in the bowl?

(A) 8 quarters, 1 dime, 1 nickel, and 2 pennies
(B) 192 pennies and 1 quarter
(C) 25 nickels, 11 dimes, and 2 pennies
(D) 6 quarters, 6 dimes, 1 nickel, and 2 pennies
(E) Any of these is possible

16. Which number could fill in the blank in this sequence? 1, 6, 16, __, 51

(A) 31
(B) 26
(C) 41
(D) 21
(E) 46

Time – 20 minutes

19 Questions

> *Questions 1-6*: Each sentence below has one or more blanks, each blank indicating that something has been omitted. Beneath each sentence are five words or sets of words labeled A through E. Choose the word or set of words that, when inserted in the sentence, best fits the meaning of the sentence as a whole.

1. The trip was very _____ and they vowed to each other that they would not take another for the _____ future.

    (A) enjoyable...near
    (B) unpleasant...so-called
    (C) fruitful...distant
    (D) dignified...immediate
    (E) taxing...foreseeable

2. The investigative reporter was extremely _____ and was able to _____ facts about the scandal that had not previously come to light.

    (A) inscrutable... indict
    (B) circumspect... insinuate
    (C) astute... ascertain
    (D) pragmatic... renounce
    (E) pedantic... vindicate

3. Once known for her nonstop conversation, Lucy had become more _____ of late.

    (A) reticent
    (B) vituperative
    (C) bombastic
    (D) redundant
    (E) duplicitous

4. The two brothers were equally _____ and thus inevitably had a _____ relationship.

    (A) belligerent... byzantine
    (B) insolent... pernicious
    (C) cantankerous... rancorous
    (D) jocular... dogmatic
    (E) meticulous... fastidious

5. The high school sponsored a presentation on the _____ effects of smoking.

    (A) banal
    (B) benign
    (C) scintillating
    (D) quiescent
    (E) deleterious

6. Emma found the professor's class so _____ that she always drank a big cup of coffee before it.

    (A) austere
    (B) soporific
    (C) copious
    (D) tumultuous
    (E) dilatory

Questions 7-18 are based on the following two passages:

Passage 1

Black History Month is unnecessary. In a place and time in which we overwhelmingly elected an African American president, we can and should move to a post-racial approach to education. As *Detroit Free Press* columnist Rochelle Riley wrote in a February 1 column calling for an end to Black History Month, "I propose that, for the first time in American history, this country has reached a point where we can stop celebrating separately, stop learning separately, stop being American separately."

In addition to being unnecessary, the idea that African American history should be focused on in a given month suggests that it belongs in that month alone. It is important to instead incorporate African American history into what is taught every day as American history. It needs to be recreated as

- 82 -

part of mainstream thought and not as an optional, often irrelevant, side note. We should focus efforts on pushing schools to diversify and broaden their curricula.

There are a number of other reasons to abolish it: first, it has become a shallow commercial ritual that does not even succeed in its (limited and misguided) goal of focusing for one month on a sophisticated, intelligent appraisal of the contributions and experiences of African Americans throughout history. Second, there is a paternalistic flavor to the mandated bestowing of a month in which to study African American history that is overcome if we instead assert the need for a comprehensive curriculum. Third, the idea of Black History Month suggests that the knowledge imparted in that month is for African Americans only, rather than for all people.

Passage 2

Black History Month is still an important observance. Despite the important achievement of the election of our first African American president, the need for knowledge and education about African American history is still unmet to a substantial degree. Black History Month is a powerful tool in working towards meeting that need. There is no reason to give up that tool now, and it can easily coexist with an effort to develop a more comprehensive and inclusive yearly curriculum.

Having a month set aside for the study of African American history doesn't limit its study and celebration to that month; it merely focuses complete attention on it for that month. There is absolutely no contradiction between having a set-aside month and having it be present in the curriculum the rest of the year.

Equally important is that the debate *itself* about the usefulness of Black History Month can, and should, remind parents that they can't necessarily count on schools to teach African American history as thoroughly as many parents would want.

Although Black History Month has, to an extent, become a shallow ritual, it doesn't have to be. Good teachers and good materials could make the February curriculum deeply informative, thought-provoking, and inspiring. The range of material that can be covered is rich, varied, and full of limitless possibilities.

Finally, it is worthwhile to remind ourselves and our children of the key events that happened during the month of February. In 1926, Woodson organized the first Black History Week to honor the birthdays of essential civil rights activists Abraham Lincoln and Frederick Douglass. W. E. B. DuBois was born on February 23, 1868. The 15th Amendment, which granted African Americans the right to vote, was passed on February 3, 1870. The first black U.S. senator, Hiram R. Revels, took his oath of office on February 25, 1870. The National Association for the Advancement of Colored People (NAACP) was founded on February 12, 1909. Malcolm X was shot on February 21, 1965.

7. The author's primary purpose in Passage 1 is to:
   (A) argue that Black History Month should not be so commercial.
   (B) argue that Black History Month should be abolished.
   (C) argue that Black History Month should be maintained.
   (D) suggest that African American history should be taught in two months rather than just one.
   (E) argue that African American history is not part of mainstream curriculum.

8. It can be inferred that the term "post-racial" in the second sentence of Passage 1 refers to an approach that:

(A) treats race as the most important factor in determining an individual's experience.
(B) treats race as one factor, but not the most important, in determining an individual's experience.
(C) considers race after considering all other elements of a person's identity.
(D) prohibits discussion of race.
(E) is not based on or organized around concepts of race.

9. Which of the following statements is true?

(A) The author of Passage 1 thinks that it is important for students to learn about the achievements and experience of African Americans, while the author of Passage 2 does not think this is important.
(B) The author of Passage 2 thinks that it is important for students to learn about the achievements and experience of African Americans, while the author of Passage 1 does not think this is important.
(C) Neither author thinks that it is important for students to learn about the achievements and experience of African Americans.
(D) Both authors think that it is important for students to learn about the achievements and experience of African Americans.
(E) It is unclear from the passages whether either author thinks that it is important for students to learn about the achievements and experience of African Americans.

10. The author of Passage 1 argues that celebrating Black History Month suggests that the study of African American history can and should be limited to one month of the year. What is the author of Passage 2's response?

(A) Black History Month is still an important observance.
(B) Black History Month is a powerful tool in meeting the need for education about African American history.
(C) Having a month set aside for the study of African American history does not limit its study and celebration to that month.
(D) Black History Month does not have to be a shallow ritual.
(E) Black History Month can make parents realize they can't rely on schools to teach African American history.

11. Why does the author of Passage 2 believe that the debate itself about Black History Month can be useful?

(A) The people on opposing sides can come to an intelligent resolution about whether to keep it.
(B) African American history is discussed in the media when the debate is ongoing.
(C) The debate is a reminder to parents that they can't count on schools to teach their children about African American history.
(D) Black History Month doesn't have to be a shallow ritual.
(E) Black History Month can remind us of the many important events that happened in February.

12. Which of the following does the author of Passage 1 not give as a reason for abolishing Black History Month?

(A) It has become a shallow ritual.
(B) There is a paternalistic feel to being granted one month of focus.
(C) It suggests that the month's education is only for African Americans.
(D) No one learns anything during the month.
(E) It suggests that African American history need not be incorporated into the curriculum for the rest of the year.

13. Who is Hiram R. Revels?

(A) An influential high school teacher
(B) A Detroit Free Press columnist
(C) The founder of the NAACP
(D) The first black U.S. senator
(E) The creator of Black History Month

14. Which of the following does neither author claim occurred in February?
(A) W.E.B. DuBois's birthday
(B) Abraham Lincoln's birthday
(C) The signing of the Emancipation Proclamation
(D) The founding of the NAACP
(E) Frederick Douglass's birthday

15. What does the author of Passage 2 say about the range of material that can be taught during Black History Month?
(A) It is rich and varied.
(B) It is important.
(C) It is an unmet need.
(D) It is comprehensive.
(E) It is surprising.

16. Which event happened first?
    (A) The passing of the 15th Amendment
    (B) The birth of W.E.B. DuBois
    (C) The establishment of Black History Month
    (D) The founding of the NAACP
    (E) The murder of Malcolm X

17. What did the Fifteenth Amendment do?
    (A) Prohibit racial discrimination
    (B) Create Black History Month
    (C) Emancipate the slaves
    (D) Create the NAACP
    (E) Give African Americans the right to vote

18. Which individuals are described in either Passage 1 or Passage 2 as "essential civil rights activists?"
    (A) Abraham Lincoln and Malcolm X
    (B) Abraham Lincoln and W.E.B. DuBois
    (C) Malcolm X and W.E.B. DuBois
    (D) Abraham Lincoln and Frederick Douglass
    (E) Malcolm X and Frederick Douglass

Questions 19-20 are based on the following passage:

On April 30, 1803, the United States bought the Louisiana Territory from the French. Astounded and excited by the offer of a sale and all that it would mean, it took less than a month to hear the offer and determine to buy it for $15 million. Right away the United States had more than twice the amount of land as before, giving the country more of a chance to become powerful. They had to move in military and governmental power in this region, but even as this was happening they had very little knowledge about the area. They did not even really know where the land boundaries were, nor did they have any how many people lived there. They needed to explore.

19. Based on the facts in the passage, what prediction could you make about the time immediately following the Louisiana Purchase?
    (A) Explorers were already on the way to the region.
    (B) The government wanted to become powerful.
    (C) People in government would make sure explorers went to the region.
    (D) Explorers would want to be paid for their work.
    (E) Government workers would become explorers.

20. Why did the United States decide to buy the Louisiana Territory?
    (A) They needed to expand the military.
    (B) They wanted to find out the land boundaries.
    (C) They wanted to know how many people lived there.
    (D) They were astounded.
    (E) They wanted to be more powerful.

Time – 10 minutes

14 Questions

Questions 1 – 14: A portion of each of the following sentences is underlined. Following the text there are five ways of phrasing the underlined material. Choice A is the original text; the other four choices are different. Select the choice that, in your judgment, produces the best sentence.

1. <u>Forgetting to feed the dog was a honest mistake.</u>

    (A) Forgetting to feed the dog was a honest mistake.
    (B) She honestly forgot to feed the dog.
    (C) The dog went hungry.
    (D) Forgetting to feed the dog was an honest mistake.
    (E) Forgetting to feed her dog was an honest mistake.

2. On his first day at the news station, the new anchorman had to determine <u>where his desk was at</u>.

    (A) where his desk was at
    (B) the location of the desk
    (C) which desk would belong to him
    (D) what to put on his new desk
    (E) where his desk was

3. <u>The gentleness of the summer sky while the buttercups shined like the stars.</u>

    (A) The gentleness of the summer sky while the buttercups shined like the stars.
    (B) There was the gentleness of the summer sky while the buttercups shined like the stars.
    (C) The gentle summer sky even as the buttercups shined as though they were stars.
    (D) The summer sky gentleness while the buttercups shined like the stars.
    (E) The gentleness of the summer sky at the same time that the buttercups shined like the stars.

4. <u>He got up bright and early and he spent</u> a whole hour taking a shower.

    (A) He got up bright and early and he spent
    (B) He got up as early as he could and he took
    (C) He arose before the dawn; and he spent
    (D) He got up bright, and early, and he spent
    (E) He got up bright and early, and he spent

5. <u>The principal added an additional break time</u> into the teachers' busy schedules.

    (A) The principal added an additional break time
    (B) The principal decided that he needed to add another break time
    (C) The principal added another break time
    (D) The principal added a third break time
    (E) The principal gave the teachers another break time

6. <u>The cow cumbersome crossed the wide, grassy field.</u>

    (A) The cow cumbersome crossed the wide, grassy field.
    (B) The cow cumbersome crossed the wide grassy field.
    (C) The cow cumbersomely crossed the wide, grassy field.
    (D) The cow did his best to cross the wide, grassy field.
    (E) The cow went across the field.

7. The girl was so popular in her own school <u>that the other students treated her like a God</u>.

    (A) that the other students treated her like a God.
    (B) that the other students treated her like a god.
    (C) and so all the other students wanted her to be a god.
    (D) that she thought she was a god.
    (E) that she felt like a god.

8. <u>Cecile White is from Sylacauga, Alabama, the teacher of the year.</u>

    (A) Cecile White is from Sylacauga, Alabama, the teacher of the year.
    (B) Cecile White is the teacher of the year and was from Sylacauga, Alabama.
    (C) Cecile White, who is from Sylacauga, Alabama, is the teacher of the year.
    (D) Cecile White was the teacher of the year in Sylacauga, Alabama.
    (E) Although Cecile White is from Sylacauga, Alabama, she is the teacher of the year.

9. <u>The family, as a whole, are united</u> against the sale of the land.

    (A) The family, as a whole, are united
    (B) The family, as a whole, is united
    (C) As a whole, the family are united
    (D) The family are united as a whole
    (E) The family are unified as a whole

10. Anyone on the girls' Junior Varsity Team <u>was invited to put their name</u> on the list to try

out for the Varsity Team.

    (A) was invited to put their name
    (B) was invited to put her name
    (C) is invited to put their name
    (D) puts their name by invitation
    (E) can put their name

11. All last summer, despite the sweltering heat and humidity, <u>I wear a suit, tie and closed</u>

<u>shoes for work.</u>

    (A) I wear a suit, tie and closed shoes for work.
    (B) I nevertheless wear a suit, tie, and closed shoes for work.
    (C) I wear a suit, a tie, and closed shoes for work.
    (D) I work in a suit, tie, and closed shoes.
    (E) I wore a suit, tie and closed shoes for work.

12. People who like jazz don't usually turn into <u>someone who likes country music</u>.

    (A) someone who likes country music
    (B) someone who also likes country music
    (C) people who like country music
    (D) people who likes country music
    (E) someone who likes country

13. We all are unique and <u>each of us has our own way</u> of solving problems.

    (A) each of us has our own way
    (B) each of us have our own way
    (C) has our own way
    (D) each have our own way
    (E) each with our own way

14. <u>Drinking my second cup of coffee</u>, my mind finally cleared.

    (A) Drinking my second cup of coffee,
    (B) Drinking my second cup of coffee to wake up,
    (C) Through my second cup of coffee,
    (D) As I drank my second cup of coffee,
    (E) Drinking two cups of coffee,

Answer Key

1. D: The perimeter (P) of the quadrilateral is simply the sum of its sides, or

$P = m + (m + 2) + (m + 3) + 2m$

Combine like terms by adding the variables (m terms) together and then adding the constants resulting in: $P = 5m + 5$

In this application, it appears that some of the variables do not have a number in front of them; however, the absence of a coefficient indicates multiplication by 1 hence $m = 1m$.

2. D: First add the two straight 150 yard portions. Also, note that the distance around the two semi-circle turns combine to form the circumference of a circle. The radius (r) of that circle is half of the dimension shown as the width of the track, or 15 yards. Now, taking the formula for the circumference of a circle, $2\pi r$ and adding it to the length of the two straight portions of the track, we have Length = $(2\pi * 15) + (2*150) = 394.25$ Answer D is the closest approximation to this calculated answer.

3. D: Since each of the 3 models is available in each of the 6 different colors, there are 6 x 3 = 18 different combinations available.

If we label models A, B, and C and colors as 1 through 6, then the combinations can be broken down as follows:

Models	Colors						
Model A	A1	A2	A3	A4	A5	A6	
Model B	B1	B2	B3	B4	B5	B6	
Model C	C1	C2	C3	C4	C5	C6	=18 Total Combinations

This method is more time consuming; however, it provides a visual representation as to why the total combinations is based on the product.

4. E: First, test each expression to see which satisfies the condition $x > y$. This condition is met for all the answer choices except C and D, so these need not be considered further. Next, test the remaining choices to see which satisfy the inequality $x + y > 0$. It can be seen that this inequality holds for choices A and B, but not for choice E, since: $x + y = 3 + (-3) = 3 - 3 = 0$. In this case the sum $x + y$ is not greater than 0.

5. A: This is a typical plot of an inverse variation, in which the product of the dependent and independent variables, x and y, is always equal to the same value. In this case the product is always equal to 1, so the plot occupies the first and third quadrants of the coordinate plane. As x increases and approaches infinity, y decreases and approaches zero, maintaining the constant product. In contrast, answer B is a linear plot corresponding to an equation of the form $y = x$. C is a quadratic plot corresponding to $y = x^2$. D is an exponential plot corresponding to $y = 2^x$. E is another linear plot corresponding to $y = \dfrac{x}{4} + 1$.

6. A: This equation represents a linear relationship that has a slope of 3.60 and passes through the origin. The table indicates that for each hour of rental, the cost increases by $3.60. This corresponds to the slope of the equation. Of course, if the bicycle is not rented at all (0 hours) there will be no charge ($0). If plotted on the Cartesian plane, the line would have a y intercept of 0. Relationship A is the only one that satisfies these criteria.

7. D: The slopes of perpendicular lines are reciprocals of opposite sign. For example, in the figure below, line A has a slope of -1/2, while line B has a slope of 2.

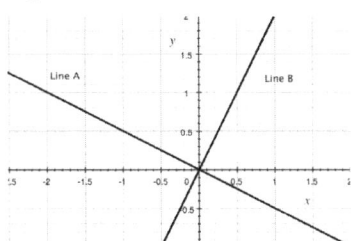

8. C: To see this, consider the following table, which shows the numbers of coins added to the first few squares, and the equivalent powers of 2:

Square	1	2	3	4
Coins	1	2	4	8
Power of 2	2^0	2^1	2^2	2^3

The table shows that in this series, the number of coins on each square represents consecutive powers of 2, since the number doubles with each consecutive square. However, the series of powers begins with 0 for the first square, so that for the 64th square, the number of coins will be 2^{63}.

9. C: Since there are four different colors, one color must be excluded from each balloon bundle. Therefore, there is one color set for each excluded color, or four in all.

This problem can also be solved mathematically as follows. An arrangement such as this, in which the order of the individual components is not important, is called a combination. The number of combinations of n objects taken k at a time is given by $C = \dfrac{n!}{(n-k)!k!}$. The ! notation indicates a *factorial* product, where $n! = 1 \times 2 \times 3 \times ... \times (n-1) \times n$. In this case, $n = 4$ colors, and $k = 3$ balloons per bundle. Substituting into the equation above, and simplifying:

$$C = \frac{4!}{(4-3)! \times 3!} = \frac{1 \times 2 \times 3 \times 4}{(1)(1 \times 2 \times 3)} = 4$$

10. B: The two right triangles are similar because they share a pair of vertical angles. Vertical angles are always congruent (angle ACB and angle DCE). Obviously both right angles (angle B and angle D) are congruent. Thus, angles A and E are congruent because of the triangular sum theorem.

With similar triangles, corresponding sides will be proportional. Segment BC is ½ the length of segment CD, therefore AC will be ½ the length of CE. The length of CE can be computed from the Pythagorean theorem, since it is the hypotenuse of a right triangle for which the lengths of the other two sides are known: $CE = \sqrt{6^2 + 8^2} = \sqrt{100} = 10$.

The length of segment AC will be ½ of this value, or 5 units.

11. D: Rafael's profit on each computer is given by the difference between the price he pays and the price he charges his customer, or $800-$450. If he sells *n* computers in a month, his total profit will be *n* times this difference, or $n(800-450)$. However, it is necessary to subtract his fixed costs of $3000 from this to compute his final profit per month.

12. D: When a number is raised to a power, it is multiplied by itself as many times as the power indicates. For example, $2^3 = 2 \times 2 \times 2 = 8$. A number raised to the power of 0 is always equal to 1, so 6^0 is the smallest number shown. Similarly, for the other numbers: $9 = 9^1 = 9$; $10^1 = 10$; $4^2 = 4 \times 4 = 16$.

13. A: Let *D* represent Dorothy's age, and *S* her sister's. Since she is half her sister's age today, we have $D = \dfrac{S}{2}$, or *S* = 2*D*. In twenty years, her age will be *D* + 20 years, and her sister's age will be *S* + 20 years. At that time, Dorothy will be ¾ of her sister's age; therefore, $D + 20 = \dfrac{3 \times (S + 20)}{4}$. Substituting 2*D* for *S* in this equation gives

$$D + 20 = \frac{3(2D + 20)}{4}$$

$$D + 20 = \frac{6D + 60}{4} \qquad \text{Use Distributive property and reduce.}$$

$$D + 20 = \frac{3}{2}D + 15$$

$$D + 20 = \frac{3D}{2} + 15$$

Gathering like terms:

$20 - 15 = \dfrac{3D}{2} - D$ which is equivalent to $5 = \dfrac{D}{2}$.

Therefore, *D* = 10 years old. Dorothy is ten years old today, and her sister is twenty years old. In twenty years, Dorothy will be 30 years old, and her sister will be 40.

14. E: It is not necessary to use the circle formula to solve the problem. Rather, note that 50 km/hr corresponds to 50,000 meters per hour. We are given the car's revolutions per minute and the answer must be represented as meters; therefore, the speed must be

converted to meters per minute. This corresponds to a speed of 50,000/60 meters per minute, as there are 60 minutes in an hour. In any given minute the car travels (50,000/60 meters/min), the tires rotate 500 times around, hence 500 times its circumference. This corresponds to $\dfrac{50,000}{60 \times 500} = \dfrac{10}{6}$ meters per revolution, which is the circumference of the tire.

15. A: Compute the product using the FOIL method, in which the *F*irst term, then the *O*uter terms, the *I*nner terms, and finally the *L*ast terms are figured in sequence of multiplication. As a result, $(a+b)(a-b) = a^2 + ba - ab - b^2$. Since ab is equal to ba, the middle terms cancel each other which leaves $a^2 - b^2$.

16. E: The area of the circle is πr² while the circumference is 2πr. Taking the ratio of these two expressions and reducing gives: $Ratio = \dfrac{\pi r^2}{2\pi r} = \dfrac{r}{2}$

17. C: Every possible combination of scores is a multiple of 7, since the two terms of the ratio have a sum of seven.

18. A: A set of six numbers with an average of 4 must have a collective sum of 24. The two numbers that average 2 will add up to 4, so the remaining numbers must add up to 20. The average of these four numbers can be calculated: 20/4 = 5.

19. C: There are 12 inches in a foot and 3 feet in a yard. Four and a half yards is equal to 162 inches. To determine the number of 3-inche segments, divide 162 by 3.

20. B: Subtracting 7 from both sides of the equation yields $-\dfrac{1}{3x} = -3$, which leads to $-9x = -1$, or $x = \dfrac{1}{9}$. Now we substitute this value into $\dfrac{1}{3x} + 3$, giving us $\dfrac{1}{3\left(\frac{1}{9}\right)} + 3$. This simplifies to $\dfrac{1}{1/3} + 3$, or $3 + 3$, which is 6.

1. E: Answer (a) is incorrect because it is not logically correct to speak of a problem's "positions." Answer (b) is incorrect because "all of its extreme" is not grammatically correct. Answer (c) is incorrect because it is not logically correct to speak of a problem's "thoughts." Answer (d) is grammatically correct, but because it is less common to "embrace" a problem than to "address" a problem, answer (e) is the better answer.

2. B: Answers (a), (d) and (e) are incorrect because the conjunction "but" in the sentence suggests that the second half happened despite the first half; in this answer, it doesn't logically make sense to say that numerous storylines were developed despite the thought-provoking nature of the book, that numerous plots were developed despite the surprising nature of the book, or that numerous chapters were developed despite the long-winded nature of the book. Answer (c) is incorrect because the second word, "answers," does not make sense in the context of the sentence. Answer (b) correctly links the two halves of the sentence: despite the brevity of the book, the author was able to develop numerous characters.

3. D: Answer (a) is incorrect because one would not repudiate true rumors. Answer (b) is incorrect; the phrase "to correction them" is not grammatically correct. Answer (c) is grammatically correct but does not make as much logical sense as answer (d). Answer (e) is incorrect; one does not demystify rumors.

4. A: Answers (b) and (e) are incorrect because one does not "look" arbitrary or abstruse. Answers (c) and (d) are grammatically correct, but answer (a) is the better answer because it explains why the speaker was sorry to see the object of the sentence: because she was despondent.

5. C: Answers (a) and (e) are incorrect because they suggest the disarray was minor; the opposite of the meaning suggested by the rest of the sentence. Answers (b) and (d) are

incorrect because they offer information about the disarray that is not relevant to the rest of the sentence.

6. C: The clock is ebony, symbolizing death, and it is placed against the western wall of the room. The sun sets in the west, another symbol of death. Words such as *dull, heavy,* and *monotonous* also provide a clue. The momentary pause of the orchestra members at the end of each hour prefigures the final pause that all the dancers and orchestra members will make. Poe writes that "the giddiest grew pale," an allusion to the pallor of death. Other words suggesting the finality of death are *nervousness, disconcert, tremulousness,* and *meditation.*

7. E: The passage refers to musicians, but choice A is not accurate because the passage also mentions waltzers who had to stop dancing when the musicians of the orchestra stopped playing, making E correct. There is no indication of food in the descriptions given of the apartment where the clock is located. A garden party would be held outdoors while this is clearly an interior scene. This need for an outdoor setting is true as well of a boating party. Thus the first four options are all incorrect, leaving only choice E.

8. B: Because of the sound of the chiming clock, the musicians stop, which means the dancers stop as well. Choice A is not accurate. The passage makes no mention of food or a meal or even of the host. Although an uninvited guest makes an appearance in the story, that scene is not included here, so choice C is incorrect. The passage does not indicate that the dancers are masked nor that they are asked to remove their masks. This means option D is not correct. The members of the orchestra do not leave during the passage, making choice E the wrong one.

9. D: The passage refers specifically to "the Time that flies," a reminder of the brevity of life. The pause of both orchestra and dancers when the clock strikes is simply a prelude to the final pause. There is not enough information in the passage to indicate that a king even exists, nor is there mention of the skill of the orchestra. Thus choice A can be eliminated. There is no indication of the need for police, making option B incorrect. The clock seems to

be in good working order, and thus the third choice is incorrect. Choice E suggests rowdy guests, which the passage does not support.

10. C: *mysterious* and *forbidding*. The passage does not answer the mystery of why the orchestra and dancers regularly halt at the sound of the chimes. Many of the words—such as *ebony, disconcert, pale, confused,* and *tremulousness*—in the passage refer to puzzles or gloominess. The other choices are extremes that cannot be supported. Choices A and B are too light for the passage, whereas choices D and E are too negative. The passage hints at negative events to come, but these are not expressed in the passage itself.

11. B: The author asserts both that earning money is increasingly easy and that managing money is difficult.

12. D: The author seems to believe that there are plenty of lucrative jobs for everyone.

13. E: The author insists that many people who have no trouble earning money waste it through lavish spending.

14. B: This passage is clearly intended for a non-expert adult readership.

15. C: Here, the author is speaking of money management on a personal or household level.

16. D: The author suggests that many people who believe they understand economy in fact do not.

17. A: It seems clear that the author is about to describe the correct means of personal economy.

18. D: This information is all given in the second paragraph.

19. C: In the fourth paragraph, the author states that the transient nature of relationships based solely on shared interests is keeping us "socially busy without building the lasting relationships and communities that we want."

20. E: The author lists urban sprawl, long work hours, and devotion to television and the internet as causes of problems for American communities.

21. B: This is the only one of the answer choices that is not listed in the fourth paragraph as suggestions put forth by the Harvard University study.

22. A: The citation of the study, given in parentheses following its first mention in the article, indicates that the study was published in June of 2006. The statistics used for the study were taken in 2004.

23. D: The author states in the fourth paragraph that Harvard University School of Government put forth 150 suggestions for increasing social capital.

24. A: The author puts this definition in parentheses immediately following his first use of the phrase "social capital."

Section 4

1. B: Answer choice B is precise and clear. Answer choice A keeps the meaning, but is awkward and wordy. Answer choice C uses the wrong verb tense. Answer choice D would put the word *work* into the sentence twice. It is not completely incorrect, but it is not the best choice. Answer choice E changes the original meaning of the sentence.

2. B: When comparing two people or things, the correct comparative word would be *older* rather than *oldest*. If there were more than two, you would use the comparative word

oldest. The other choices change the intended original meaning of the sentence. The same is true for the comparative words *better* and *best* or *less* and *least.*

3. A: The sentence is precise and clear in its original form. This type of sentence is an absolute construction, including a noun and a modifier. Absolute constructions squeeze two sentences into one. In this case the modifier is a participle phrase.

4. D: The plural subject *teachers* agrees with the pronoun *they.* Pronouns have to agree with gender, number and person. If the subject had been singular, such as *teacher,* then the pronoun would have needed to also be singular. In that case the correct sentence might have been: A fair teacher understands that he or she cannot treat any student with favoritism.

5. C: When putting things or people in order, the words must agree in the series. You can use *first, second, third,* and so forth, or you may use *firstly, secondly, thirdly,* and so forth. In this sentence, answer choice C is the best choice because the two words *first* and *second* agree in the series, and in this case it sounds better. *Firstly* and *secondly* sound awkward. Also, it is correct to use *and then* in the sentence rather than answer choice D which uses only the word *then.*

6. B: *Well* and *kept* put together forms a compound adjective. In this case the compound adjective was written with an adverb and a past participle. When the two together come before and modify a noun, such as *secret,* they must be hyphenated as such: *well-kept secret.*

7. C: The style in the original sentence is awkward because it has a double passive voice. Change the first passive verbs into an active verb and the sentence will simply sound better. Even though answer choice B sounds good and is grammatically correct, you cannot choose it because of the pronoun *she.* The original sentence does not specify gender.

8. A: The sentence is clear and precise in its original form.

9. E: The word *need* is being used as an auxillary verb in this sentence. It does not go together with *did* or any form of *do* unless it is being used as a main verb. The following is an example of *need* being used as a main verb together with *do*: *We do need to trouble our minds.*

10. B: The word *ought* is an auxiliary verb that should go together with the word *to* in formal writing. It is sometimes used in speech without the word *to* (especially in particular regions), but is not considered correct in written English. There are some cases where *ought* can be correctly used without *to* in questions, such as: *Ought the teacher set a good example?*

11. A: The sentence is clear and precise in its original form.

12. B: The verb tense is incorrect. It should be "made" rather than "make."

13. C: The verb "is" is singular, and does not agree with the plural subject "Quincy and his son Zane." The verb should be "are" instead.

14. A: A collective noun, "the audience" is singular, and takes singular verbs. Therefore, "are" is incorrect, and should be "is."

15. D: The verb "giving" is in the wrong form. It should be "gave."

16. B: In the time of the dinosaurs refers to the past. Therefore, the present "are" is incorrect. It should be "were."

17. D: "Dogs" is plural. The sentence should read "good achievers" rather than "a good achiever."

18. C: Everyone is a singular pronoun so the "their" later in the sentence is an incorrect replacement.

19. E: There are no errors in this sentence.

20. D: When two things are being compared, the correct word to use is "more," not "most."

21. B: The expression "indebted to" is an idiom; "indebted with" is not correct.

22. B: The sentence as it stands incorrectly compares the paintings of Dana Smith to Pablo Picasso, rather than to the *paintings of* Pablo Picasso.

23. C: When items can be counted, the word "fewer" should be used rather than the word "less."

24. B: The sentence should read "nor the gift" instead of "or the gift" since it begins with "neither."

25. E: There is no error in the sentence.

26. B: Penchant with reading is an incorrect idiom. If you say it out loud, you will find that it does not sound right. It should be penchant *for* reading.

27. D: To be read correctly, it should say *of finding*. The word *capable* is the key here. If the sentence had said *able to find*, it would have been correct. But the adjective *capable* is generally followed by *of*.

28. E: There is no error in this sentence.

29. C: Since the sentence uses the word *already*, the use of the word *before* is redundant. Either the word *already* or the word *before* should be taken out, and *already* was not a choice of something that could or should be changed.

30. C: The question tests students on sentence reconstruction, placing the independent clause, rather than the dependent clause, first. The first words of the dependent clause,

even before, must, therefore, come first. Option A is not correct; the sentence cannot be written beginning with these words. Option B, likewise, is incorrect; beginning with these words will not create a correct sentence. Answer D is wrong; *the right* is not the correct way to begin the dependent clause. Answer E is also not correct; the dependent clause must begin with *even*.

31. B: *Wall Street* is the name of a particular street and requires capitalization. Choice A is wrong; making such a change would create an error in verb tense. Option C is incorrect; the words *although* and *though* are nearly interchangeable; choosing *although* is not an error. Choice D is incorrect as well; *investment firm* is a common noun, not the name of a particular investment firm. No capitalization is required. Choice E is wrong; the sentence is declaratory, rather than interrogatory, and does not need a question mark.

32. E: This question tests students' knowledge of the use of parentheses, which set off unnecessary information without using commas. The sentence is correct as written. Using commas with the parentheses would be redundant and incorrect, making choice A wrong. Answer B is also wrong; *Republicans* is the name of a particular political party and requires capitalization. Choice C, likewise, is incorrect; the sentence requires a singular noun to refer *Margaret Chase Smith*. Answer D is wrong; the word is correctly spelled as it is written in the text.

33. D: The question tests knowledge of irregular verb forms. The sentence requires the past participle of *seek*, which is *sought*. Option A is incorrect; *seeked* is not the past participle of *seek*. Answer B is also wrong. Making the subject singular causes a problem in subject-verb agreement, as well as making the plural numeral *nine* disagree. Option C is incorrect; the problem is not the tense of the verb. Choice E is also incorrect; it compounds the problem with subject-verb disagreement and muddies things by using the wrong auxiliary verb.

34. A: This is a case of a run-on sentence that can be corrected by placing commas between the short independent clauses. Choice B is not correct; there is nothing wrong with the pronoun *them*. Option C is incorrect; making such a change would lead to an error in

subject-verb agreement. Choice D is also incorrect; *third parties* is a common noun, rather than the name of a specific third party. As such, the term requires no capital letters. Option E is wrong; there is a clear error to be addressed in the sentence.

35. C: Sentence (8) intrudes on the paragraph with a personal opinion that destroys the unity and coherence of the piece. Answer A is incorrect; switching the order of the paragraphs does nothing but ruin the chronological organization of the piece. Answer B is incorrect as well; moving the sentence destroys the unity and coherence of the piece. Choice D is incorrect; moving the sentence destroys the unity and coherence of the article. Choice E is also wrong; beginning with that sentence makes no sense because there is nothing for *other* to refer to.

Section 5

1. B: In this probability problem, there are three independent events (the codes for each digit), each with ten possible outcomes (the numerals 0-9). Since the events are independent, the total possible outcomes equals the product of the possible outcomes for each of the three events, that is $P = P_1 \times P_2 \times P_3 = 10 \times 10 \times 10 = 1000$
This makes sense when you also relate the problem to a sequence, beginning with the combinations 0-0-0, 0-0-1, 0-0-2......In ascending order, the last 3 digit combination would be 9-9-9. Although it may seem that there would be 999 possible combinations, you must include the initial combination, 0-0-0.

2. C: Let d be the current age of the daughter. Then the current age of the mother can be expressed as 3*d*. So the age of the daughter in fifteen years will be *d* + 15, and the age of the mother will be 3*d* + 15. Because the mother will be twice as old as the daughter at that time, we can write the equation 3*d* + 15 = 2(*d* + 15). Use the distributive property on the right side: 3*d* + 15 = 2*d* + 30. Now subtract 2*d* from both sides and subtract 15 from both sides to get *d* = 15. This is the current age of the daughter, which means the mother is currently 45.

3. A: Setting the cost of shipping equal to the amount received gives us the equation $3,000 + 100x = 400x$. Subtract 100x from both sides to get $3,000 = 300x$, then divide both sides by 300 to see that $x = 10$.

4. E: Let x stand for the length and let y stand for the width of the rectangle. Then the area is expressed as the product xy. But if the length and width are doubled to 2x and 2y respectively, the area becomes $(2x)(2y) = 4xy$, which is 4 times as large as the original rectangle. "Four times as large" is equivalent to a 300 percent increase.

5. E: Multiply both sides of the first equation by s to get 3 = 7s, then divide both sides by 7 to find that $= \frac{3}{7}$. Multiply both sides of the second equation by t to get 4 = 12t, then divide both sides by 12 to find that $= \frac{1}{3}$. To find the difference, we must convert to a common denominator. In this case, the common denominator is 21. Multiplying by appropriate fractional equivalents of 1, we find that $\frac{3}{7}\left(\frac{3}{3}\right) = \frac{9}{21}$ and $\frac{1}{3}\left(\frac{7}{7}\right) = \frac{7}{21}$. Therefore $-t = \frac{9}{21} - \frac{7}{21} = \frac{2}{21}$.

6. A: Complementary angles are two angles that equal 90° when added together.

7. B: These are supplementary angles. That means that the two angles will add up to a total of 180°, which is the angle of a straight line. To solve, subtract as follows:
b = 180° - 120°
b = 60

8. D: Rotational symmetry is defined as a figure that looks exactly the same after being rotated any amount. Answer choice D is the only example given that would stay the same if rotated.

9. The correct answer is $525. During the first year that he holds the certificate, Jesse's income will be equal to 7.5% of the principal he has invested, $7,000. Refer to the formula: I = Prt where I is interest, P is principal, r is rate (expressed as a decimal) and t is time (in years). Therefore I = $7,000 · .075 · 1, which is $525.

10. The correct answer is 3.93 square units. Note that the shaded area represents one-fourth of the difference between the areas of the inner and outer circles. The formula for computing the area of a circle is: $Area = \pi r^2$. Since the radius (r) of the outer circle is 3, we have $A_{out} = \pi \times 3^2$, or 9л. The radius of the inner circle is $A_{in} = \pi \times 2^2$, or 4 л. Therefore, the area of the shaded portion must be determined as followed:

$$Area = \frac{1}{4}(9\pi - 4\pi) \quad \text{Factor out п}$$

$$Area = \frac{1}{4}\pi(9 - 4) = \frac{5\pi}{4} = 3.93$$

11. The correct answer is $21.78. To make a profit of 10%, Pradip must sell the stock at a price that is 10% higher than what he paid for it. That is, he must sell it at 110% of the purchase price. Since he buys the stock at $19.80 per share, he must sell it at a price (P) as follows:

$$P = \frac{110 \times \$19.80}{100} = \$21.78.$$

12. The correct answer is 0.48 seconds. Modify the relationship given in the question to solve for the time. Since $d = rt$, then time (t) equals $t = \frac{d}{r} = \frac{60.5\,ft}{125\,ft/sec} = 0.484\,sec$. Rounding to the nearest hundredth of a second gives the answer 0.48 seconds.

13. The correct answer is (1,1). The line in the graph extends from a point at the upper left (IVth quadrant) with x,y coordinates (-4,4) to a point at the lower right (IInd quadrant) with coordinates (6,-2). To determine the midpoint, add the x and y coordinates for each point separately and divide by 2. Thus, for x: $x_{mid} = \frac{x_1 + x_2}{2} = \frac{(-4)+6}{2} = \frac{2}{2} = 1$

Similarly, for y

$$y_{mid} = \frac{y_1 + y_2}{2} = \frac{4+(-2)}{2} = \frac{2}{2} = 1$$

14. The correct answer is (2,0). To determine this, first set the two expressions to be equal and solve for the variable x. This is known as the substitution method which gives:

$-3x + 6 = 2x - 4$.

Gathering like terms on each side of the equation and isolating the variable gives $10 = 5x$. Finally, divide each side by 5 so that we have $x = 2$.

Now, substitute this value of x into either of the original equations to determine the y coordinate: $y = -3x + 6 = -6 + 6 = 0$.

15. The correct answer is $4000. Besides the $600 he has remaining, Chan has paid out a total of 85% (30% + 30% +25%) of his bonus for the expenses described in the question. Therefore, the $600 represents the remaining 15%. To determine his total bonus, solve $\frac{100}{15} \times 600 = 4000$ dollars.

16. $27 - x = -5$

$x = 32$

17. Out of the twelve numbers, half are even. That means there is a 50% chance that the spinner will land on an even number.

18. The perimeter of a square is four times the length of any one of its sides. If a square's perimeter is 20, the length of any side is 5. The perimeter of this rectangle is six times the length of a side, which is 30.

Section 6

1. B: Answers (A) and (C) are incorrect because placid and obedient children are easy to care for, and would not logically be expected to frighten or enrage caretakers. Similarly, answers (D) and (E) are incorrect because truculent and egotistical children might be difficult to care for and would not logically be expected to appease or endear themselves to caretakers. Answer (E) is furthermore grammatically incorrect.

2. E: All the adjectives describing the house and the things in the house suggest a showy and grandiose home; ostentatious is the only answer choice that fits this meaning.

3. B: The word sought is one that describes something lucky that does not happen through design. Answer (b), serendipity, fits this meaning. Answer (A) is incorrect as it means the opposite of the word sought. Answers (C), (D) and (E) do not relate to the rest of the sentence.

4. E: Answers (A) and (D) are incorrect because their second words suggest he didn't *deny* a promotion when offered him, while the word that best fits the meaning of the sentence will be one that indicates that he didn't *seek* a promotion. Answers (C) and (E) offer words that fit this meaning, but answer (E) is better because ambition fits more logically into the sentence than does habits. Answer (B) is wrong because it is not logically correct to say he was modest in his failures.

5. A: Answers (B), (C) and (D) are incorrect as they all provide words that do not make logical sense describing an economic major ("literary," "theatrical," and "sycophantic"). Answer (E) is incorrect as it does not make logical sense that one avoiding a major because it felt unimportant would seek a more trivial one.

6. B: prescient, which means able to anticipate the course of events. Answer (A) means early in development and is incorrect. Answer (C) means preceding in time and is incorrect. Answer (D) means related to a preface or located in front and is incorrect. Answer (E) means showing preference and is incorrect.

7. C: Answer (A) is incorrect because there is no context in the sentence for someone to discuss invisible footprints; additionally if the footprints were, despite invisibility, known of then it would be possible that the yeti had made them and the question wouldn't make sense. Answers (B), (D) and (E) are incorrect because there is no conflict between the words dangerous and massive, nor welcoming and cavernous, nor mysterious and

- 110 -

unfathomable, and the sentence requires such conflict to make sense. Answer (C) is correct because the sentence appropriately poses the conflict of what could make such colossal footprints if the yeti does not exist.

8. D: The words sought are something a crowd does that then allows for an individual to walk in a certain way. Answers (A) and (B) are incorrect because a crowd thickening or intensifying does not lead to an individual being able to walk more confidently or on foot. Answer (C) is wrong because if the crowd has vanished, an individual is unable to walk en masse. Answer (E) is incorrect because neither word logically fits the sentence: a crowd does not startle and there is no context in the sentence to speak of the individual walking convincingly.

9. B: This is stated in the second paragraph.

10. D: This is the only answer choice that is not given as a reason for learning Esperanto. The other choices are all listed in the fourth and fifth paragraphs.

11. E: Answers (A) and (B) are incorrect because, although they're benefits the author claims come from learning Esperanto, the author does not state that these are the reasons the language was initially developed. Answers (C) and (D) are incorrect as they were never brought up in the text at all.

12. C: This information is given in the second and fourth paragraphs, respectively.

13. A: In the sentence quoted, the author uses "privileged" to mean benefited or favored. Answers (B) and (C) are not meanings of the word privileged in any situation. Answers (D) and (E) are both meanings of the word privileged but are not appropriate in this context.

14. C: This word is used to refer to speakers of Esperanto in the second and fourth paragraphs.

15. E: The only answer option about which the author claimed a study had shown something is that Esperanto increased one's ability to learn a next language.

16. D: The point of the passage is to suggest that viewers should think more critically about assumptions and frameworks (such as the Western paradigm) that underlie the stories in movies they watch.

17. C: The author recommends that viewers think more critically about frameworks that underlie stories in movies; she argues that, if not, viewers may absorb biases with which they do not agree. An example the author gives of that bias is that it is hard to find a movie in which the hero is not supremely morally worthy. The author's identification of this as a bias implies that she thinks it is not the right choice. Her comment about the difficulty of finding a portrayal of an enemy that allows the enemy to be complex suggests that the author believes that more nuance and less absolutes would be an improvement in the U.S. storytelling of war.

18. C: The author said nothing about horseback riding.

19. A: The author suggests that these movies rarely show enemies of the U.S. to be complex or fighting for a legitimate cause.

20. B: This can be inferred from the second sentence which states that the farmers won the dispute and the barbed wire fences remained. The farmers supported the use of barbed wire fences because it discouraged livestock owned by the ranchers from consuming or trampling their crops. Ranchers were opposed to it because of the potential harm that the barbs could cause to their livestock.

21. C: This is stated in the fifth and final sentence of the passage.

22. D: The other fencing options were all listed as alternatives to barbed wire in the third sentence, and the fourth sentence talks about previously open range land becoming fenced-in.

23. D: The 19th century lasted from 1801-1900. The time period specified for the introduction of barbed wire is "the late 1800s."

Section 7

1. B: If you draw a vertical line down the center of the letter V, the two sides will be symmetrical.

2. C: A straight line is 180°. Subtract to solve: 180° - 45° = 135°

3. A: Lines 1 and 2 are parallel. If the parallel lines continued on into infinity, they would never cross. To *intersect* means that the lines cross. *Bisect* means that a line cuts another line or figure in two equal halves. To *correspond* means to match.

4. E: The degree measurement for alternate interior angles is exactly the same. In the figure, there are two pairs of alternate interior angles: B and C; A and D.

5. D: An obtuse angle is one that is more than 90° (a right angle) and less than 180°. Answer choices A, B and C are not angles. Answer choice E, angle B, is an acute angle since it is small than a 90° angle.

6. D: If all of the children are girls, and some of the girls like soccer, then some of the children must like soccer. None of the other statements can be deduced from the information given.

7. B: The average of 7 and x is 7 + x divided by 2. The average of 9, 4, and x is 9 + 4 + x divided by 3. $(7+x)/2 = (9+4+x)/3$. Simplify the problem and eliminate the denominators by multiplying the first side by 3 and the second side by 2. For the first equation, $(21 + 3x)/6$. For the second equation, $(18 + 8 + 2x)/6$. Since the denominators are the same, they can be eliminated, leaving $21 + 3x = 26 + 2x$. Solving for x gets $x = 26\text{-}21$. $x = 5$.

8. A: $2^4 = 2 \times 2 \times 2 \times 2 = 16$. Therefore, $4^x = 16$; $x = 2$.

9. D: Solving for y in the second equation gives $y = 4x\text{-}5$. If we plug this into the first equation we get $2x + 3(4x\text{-}5) = 13$. Solving for this equation gives us $14x = 28$, or $x = 2$. Then, plug the value of x into either equation to solve for y. $y = 3$. Therefore, $3x + 2y = 12$.

10. E: There are 7 integers whose absolute value is less than 4: -3, -2, -1, 0, 1, 2, 3.

11. D: To solve $3(2x - 10) = x$, first multiply the left side out. $6x - 30 = x$. Therefore, $5x = 30$, and $x = 6$.

12. E: There are 90 two-digit numbers (all integers from, and including, 10 to, and including, 99). Of those, there are 13 multiples of 7: 14, 21, 28, 35, 42, 49, 56, 63, 70, 77, 84, 91, 98.

13. A: The sum of the measures of the three angles of any triangle is 180. The equation of the angles of this triangle can be written as $2x + 6x + 10x = 180$, or $18x = 180$. Therefore, x = 10. Therefore, the measure of the smallest angle is 20.

14. C: If t equals Truman's age now, and 3t equals Henry's age now, t-2 equals Truman's age two years ago and 3t-2 equals Henry's age two years ago. Since Henry was 5 times as old as Truman two years ago, we can solve for $3t\text{-}2 = 5(t\text{-}2)$. Solving this gives us $3t\text{-}2 = 5t\text{-}10$ or $2t = 8$. Therefore, t = 4. Since Henry is three times as old as Truman, Henry is 12.

15. C: This combination of coins totals $2.37.

16. A: The sequence increases by multiples of 5: to get from 1 to 6, add 5. To get from 6 to 16, add 10. To get from 16 to 31, add 15. To get from 31 to 51, add 20.

Section 8

1. E: The part of the sentence provided indicates that the trip was such as to make the takers of it vow not to take another for some part of the future. Thus the first word should indicate that the trip was not a pleasant one; for this reason, answers (A), (C) and (D) are incorrect. Answer (B) is incorrect because the second word, so-called, does not logically complete the sentence.

2. C: The sentence indicates the reporter did something with information that others hadn't. An investigative reporter discovers (ascertains) facts, and her ability to do so where others hadn't shows she is astute.

3. A: The blank in this sentence needs to describe someone who would *not* be known for nonstop conversation. Reticent, which means reserved or quiet, is the best choice.

4. C: The word that describes the brothers has to inevitably lead to the word that describes their relationship. The words in choices (A) and (D) do not have that connection. The words in choice (E) have a close connection, but it is awkward to describe a relationship as fastidious. The words in choice (B) are somewhat connected, but not as closely as in the best choice, (C). Cantankerous, or bad tempered, people would likely have a rancorous, or bitter, relationship.

5. E: A high school would only present information about the negative effects of smoking. Choice (E) is therefore the only word that fits.

6. B: The word needed here is one that describes an effect that must be counteracted by coffee. Soporific, which means sleep inducing, is the best choice.

7. B: The entire passage makes the argument that Black History Month should be abolished, offering various reasons why this is the best course of action.

8. E: The context of the sentence suggests that post-racial refers to an approach in which race is not a useful or positive organizing principle.

9. D: Clearly both authors think it is important for students to learn about the achievements and experience of African Americans; their debate is whether observing Black History Month is the best way to achieve this goal.

10. C: The author of Passage 2 points out that just because there is a month focused on African American history, this doesn't mean that African American history must be ignored for the rest of the year.

11. C: The author points out in paragraph 3 of Passage 2 that the debate about how to meet the need to teach children about African American history can remind parents that this need is not yet fully met.

12. D: The author of Passage 1 never suggests that people do not learn about African American history during Black History Month.

13. D: The final paragraph of Passage 2 notes that Hiram R. Revels was the first black U.S. senator.

14. C: Neither author claims that the Emancipation Proclamation was signed in February.

15. A: In paragraph 4, the author of Passage 2 states that the material available is rich and varied.

16. B: Passage 2 states that W.E.B. DuBois was born in 1868; his birth was therefore the first of the identified events.

17. E: The Fifteenth Amendment gave African Americans the right to vote.

18. D: The last paragraph of Passage 2 states that Abraham Lincoln and Frederick Douglass were essential civil rights activists.

19. C: People in government knew that the purchase would make the country more powerful, but the last sentence specifically states that they needed to explore. Answer choice C is the best prediction of what would occur next. Answer choices A, D and E infer too much, since you cannot assume any of these based on this passage given. Answer choice B is simply a statement that does not predict anything for the future.

20. E: While all of the answer choices are in the passage, only answer choice E answers the question as it is written. The desire to become more powerful is listed in the passage as one of the reasons that the United States decided to buy the land.

Section 9

1. D: The only problem with the sentence is the use of the adjective *a* rather than *an*. You cannot assume gender (such as *she* or *her*).

2. E: The use of the word *at* at the end of the sentence is unnecessary. It is a dangling preposition. Remove the word *at* to make it clear and precise.

3. B: The original sentence has dependent clauses with words that LOOK like verbs but do not ACT like verbs. The entire sentence is a fragment. Answer choice B is the only one that adds a subject and verb to change the fragment into a complete sentence.

4. E: The original is a run-on sentence. There should be a comma to separate the two thoughts. The use of a semicolon only works if you remove the word *and*, as follows: He got up bright and early; he spent a whole hour taking a shower.

5. C: The two words *added* and *additional* are redundant. Grammatically, it is not wrong, but the two words are similar enough that they seem like the same word. It is awkward. Taking out the *additional* makes the sentence more precise without changing any of the meaning.

6. C: The word *cumbersome* is an adjective, but the placement in the sentence calls for an adverb. Add *ly* to the word to make modify the verb. If it had been used as an adjective, it would have come before the noun as follows: *the cumbersome cow*.

7. B: The word *god* should not be capitalized because it is not being used as a name. When the word is non-specific and not used as a name, it should be written with the lowercase *g*.

8. C: There are two facts in the sentence that need to be connected without ending up with a run-on sentence. The original is already a run-on sentence. Answer choice C is the only choice that is not confusing or awkward. It states the two facts and connects them in such a way that the sentence makes sense. Answer choice D actually changes the meaning of the sentence since it states that she is the teacher of the year IN Sylacauga, Alabama. The original sentence never says that. It only says that she is FROM Sylacauga. We have no idea where she lives now. Answer choice E uses the word *although*, which implies that she got the award in spite of being from that city.

9. B: The word "family" is singular. The verb thus needs to be the singular "is," rather than the plural "are."

10. B: The word "anyone" is singular, so the phrasing "their name" is incorrect.

11. E: "All last summer" indicates a time in the past, so the present tense form of "to wear" is incorrect.

12. C: The word "people" is plural, and is incorrectly matched with the singular word "someone."

13. A: Sentence is correct.

14. D: As written, the sentence suggests that "my mind" drank coffee. Choice (D) clarifies that *I* drank the coffee.

Practice Test #2

Practice Questions

Section 1

Essay

Time – 25 minutes

Consider the issue presented below:

The city council has raised the issue of setting a curfew for children under the age of 17 to keep young drivers off the road after a certain time at night. They know it is legal, but still plan to discuss it at the next meeting, including whether the idea is worthwhile, whether the curfew would be all the time or only on school nights, and whether or not the age of 17 is too high. The subject will be open for ideas.

Assignment:

Should there be a curfew for children under the age of 17? Write an essay developing your point of view on this issue. Support your position with evidence from your reading, experience, and personal observations.

Section 2

Time - 25 minutes

20 Questions

For this section, solve each problem and decide which of the choices given is the best.

1. On Frank's bus ride to work, all available seats are filled and 6 passengers are standing in the aisles. If 10 passengers get off the bus and 8 others get on, how many passengers are standing in the aisles, assuming that all available seats continue to be filled?

    (A) 2
    (B) 4
    (C) 6
    (D) 8
    (E) 10

2. The number 2 + 0.4 is how many times the number 1 – 0.2?

    (A) $1\frac{1}{3}$
    (B) 2
    (C) $2\frac{2}{5}$
    (D) $2\frac{1}{2}$
    (E) 3

3. If a movie reached the 90-minute mark 12 minutes ago, what minute mark had it reached m minutes ago?

    (A) $m – 102$
    (B) $m – 78$
    (C) $102 – m$
    (D) $78 – m$
    (E) $90 – m$

4. A bull's-eye with a 4-inch diameter covers 20 percent of a circular target. What is the area, in square inches, of the target?

    (A) 0.8π
    (B) 32π
    (C) 10π
    (D) 20π
    (E) 80π

5. The volume in a water drum is halved every 2 days of a drought. If the volume of water in the drum was initially 10^6 gallons, what was the volume after 10 days?

    (A) $(\frac{1}{2})^{10}(10^6)$
    (B) $(\frac{1}{2})^{5}(10^6)$
    (C) $2^5(10^6)$
    (D) $2^{10}(10^6)$
    (E) $(10^6)^5$

6.

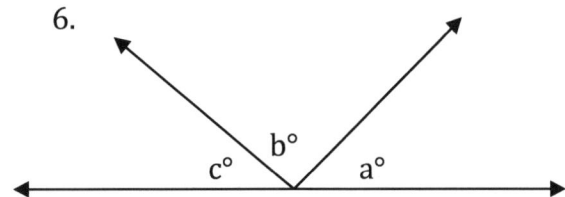

In the figure above, if $\dfrac{b}{a+b+c} = \dfrac{3}{5}$, then $b = ?$

    (A) 60
    (B) 72
    (C) 108
    (D) 120
    (E) 180

7. $3y - 2x = 9$

$2x + y = -5$

In the system of equations above, what is the value of y?

(A) −3
(B) −$\frac{1}{7}$
(C) −1
(D) 1
(E) 3

8.

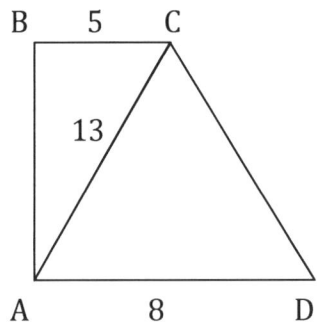

In the figure above, what is the area of triangular region ACD?

(A) 13
(B) 30
(C) 48
(D) 60
(E) 96

9. What is the maximum number of $6\frac{3}{4}$-inch strips that can be cut from a spool of ribbon that is 10 yards long?

(A) 1
(B) 17
(C) 18
(D) 53
(E) 54

10. A pilot traveled the first 1,500 miles of a 3,000-mile journey with an average speed of 400 miles per hour. At what speed must the pilot travel the remaining 1,500 miles to record an average speed of 500 miles per hour for the entire flight?

(A) $261\frac{2}{3}$ MPH
(B) 600 MPH
(C) $666\frac{2}{3}$ MPH
(D) 800 MPH
(E) 5,625 MPH

11. If the radius of circle O is one-quarter the diameter of circle P, what is the ratio of the circumference of circle O to the circumference of circle P?

(A) $\frac{1}{4}$
(B) $\frac{1}{2}$
(C) 1
(D) 2
(E) 4

12. If $x^2 + 3x - 18 = 0$ and $x < 0$, which of the following must equal 0?

I. $x^2 - 36$

II. $x^2 - 2x - 3$

III. $x^2 + 5x - 6$

(A) I only
(B) II only
(C) III only
(D) I and III only
(E) I, II, and III.

- 124 -

13. The length of the edge of cube A is three-quarters the length of the edge of cube B. What is the ratio of the volume of cube B to the volume of cube A?

(A) $\frac{1}{64}$

(B) $\frac{1}{4}$

(C) $\frac{27}{64}$

(D) $\frac{3}{4}$

(E) $\frac{64}{27}$

14. If x > 2500, then the value of $\frac{x}{1-2x}$ is closest to

(A) -1

(B) $-\frac{50}{99}$

(C) $-\frac{1}{2}$

(D) $\frac{50}{99}$

(E) $\frac{1}{2}$

15. If the area of a rectangular game board is 336 square inches and its perimeter is 76 inches, what is the length of each of the shorter sides?

(A) 10 inches
(B) 14 inches
(C) 19 inches
(D) 24 inches
(E) 65 inches

16. In a spelling bee, Anish's placement is both the 11th highest and the 25th lowest among all the spellers who participated. How many spellers participated in the spelling bee?

(A) 33
(B) 34
(C) 35
(D) 36
(E) 37

17. If c is to be chosen at random from the set $\{1, 2, 3, 4\}$ and d is to be chosen at random from the set $\{1, 2, 3, 4\}$, what is the probability cd will be odd?

(A) $\frac{1}{4}$

(B) $\frac{1}{3}$

(C) $\frac{3}{4}$

(D) 4

(E) 12

18. The length (l) of a rectangle is three times its width. What is the length of the diagonal in terms of the length (l)?

(A) $\frac{\sqrt{10}}{3}l$

(B) $\frac{10}{3}l$

(C) $\frac{10}{9}l$

(D) $\sqrt{10}\, l$

(E) $10l$

19. Two even integers and one odd integer are multiplied together. Which of the following could be their product?

(A) 3.75

(B) 9

(C) 16.2

(D) 24

(E) 69

20. If $520 \div x = 40n$, then which of the following is equal to nx?

(A) 13

(B) 40nx

(C) 26

(D) 40

(E) 13x

Section 3

Time – 25 minutes

24 Questions

Questions 1-5: Each sentence below has one or more blanks. Beneath each sentence are five words or sets of words labeled A through E. Choose the word or set of words that best fits the meaning of the sentence as a whole.

1. When the new principal realized the _____ of the school's resources, she _____ her efforts at fundraising.

    (A) ignominy... embellished
    (B) dearth... alleviated
    (C) copiousness... ameliorated
    (D) paucity... redoubled
    (E) parity... supplanted

2. He was unashamedly _____ in his _____ support of the incumbent, and in his critique of her opponent.

    (A) bombastic... magnanimous
    (B) pejorative...eminent
    (C) lugubrious... obsequious
    (D) partisan... laudatory
    (E) lavish... derogatory

3. She thought the proposed menu was unnecessarily _____ and the cost _____.

    (A) opulent... magnanimous
    (B) lavish... exorbitant
    (C) lugubrious... substantiated
    (D) multifarious... inscrutable
    (E) convoluted... abstruse

4. When they moved to a new apartment with much less storage room in the kitchen, they had to get rid of the _____ pots and pans.

    (A) jaded
    (B) tangential
    (C) eclectic
    (D) Incongruous
    (E) superfluous

5. His friends never knew what to expect from Eric; his behavior was so _____.

    (A) erratic
    (B) dubious
    (C) apathetic
    (D) specious
    (E) palliative

Questions 6-10 are based upon the following passage:

Who Was This Man?

"You have a visitor, you see," said Monsieur Defarge.

"What did you say?"

"Here is a visitor."

The shoemaker looked up as before, but without removing a hand from his work.

"Come!" said Defarge. "Here is monsieur, who knows a well-made shoe when he sees one. Show him that shoe you are working at. Take it, monsieur."

Mr. Lorry took it in his hand.

"Tell monsieur what kind of shoe it is, and the maker's name."

There was a longer pause than usual, before the shoemaker replied: "I forget what it was you asked me. What did you say?"

"I said, couldn't you describe the kind of shoe, for monsieur's information?"

"It is a lady's shoe. It is a young lady's walking-shoe. It is in the present mode. I never saw the mode. I have had a pattern in my hand."

He glanced at the shoe with some little passing touch of pride.

"And the maker's name?" said Defarge.

Now that he had no work to hold, he laid the knuckles of the right hand in the hollow of the left, and then the knuckles of the left hand in the hollow of the right, and then passed a hand across his bearded chin, and so on in regular changes, without a moment's intermission. The task of recalling him from the vagrancy into which he always sank when he had spoken, was like recalling some very weak person from a swoon, or endeavouring, in the hope of some disclosure, to stay the spirit of a fast-dying man.

"Did you ask me for my name?"

"Assuredly I did."

"One Hundred and Five, North Tower."

"Is that all?"

"One Hundred and Five, North Tower."

With a weary sound that was not a sigh, nor a groan, he bent to work again, until the silence was again broken.

"You are not a shoemaker by trade?" said Mr. Lorry, looking steadfastly at him.

His haggard eyes turned to Defarge as if he would have transferred the question to him: but as no help came from that quarter, they turned back on the questioner when they had sought the ground.

"I am not a shoemaker by trade? No, I was not a shoemaker by trade. I-I learnt it here. I taught myself. I asked leave to ... "

He lapsed away, even for minutes, ringing those measured changes on his hands the whole time. His eyes came slowly back, at last, to the face from which they had wandered; when they rested on it, he started, and resumed, in the manner of a sleeper that moment awake, reverting to a subject of last night.

"I asked leave to teach myself, and I got it with much difficulty after a long while, and I have made shoes ever since."

—Excerpted from *A Tale of Two Cities* by Charles Dickens

6. Monsieur Defarge and Mr. Lorry are visiting

    (A) an art gallery in Paris.
    (B) a man who has been ill.
    (C) a member of the British government.
    (D) a doctor making hospital calls.
    (E) a fashion designer.

7. Based on the name he gives, the reader can infer that the man

    (A) has spent time in a prison tower.
    (B) has been traveling throughout Europe.
    (C) has been homeless a long time.
    (D) first left home as a young man.
    (E) has never been married.

8. Which of the following is NOT a sign of the man's mental condition?

   (A) his inability to complete a thought
   (B) his identifying himself by a location instead of a name
   (C) the repetitive motion of his hands
   (D) his cheerful laughter
   (E) the choppy sentences he speaks

9. The man has asked to learn the trade of

   (A) woodcarving.
   (B) glassblowing.
   (C) blacksmithing.
   (D) dressmaking.
   (E) shoemaking.

10. What can the reader infer about the identity of Monsieur Defarge?

   (A) He is the unkind jailer at the prison.
   (B) He is a friend keeping the man safe.
   (C) He is the man's loving son or grandson.
   (D) He is a cruel doctor in a hospital.
   (E) He is a banker interested only in the man's money.

Questions 11-14 are based on the following passages:

Passage 1:

Fairy tales, fictional stories that involve magical occurrences and imaginary creatures like trolls, elves, giants, and talking animals, are found in similar forms throughout the world. This occurs when a story with an origin in a particular location spreads geographically to, over time, far-flung lands. All variations of the same story must logically come from a single source. As language, ideas, and goods travel from place to place through the movement of peoples, stories that catch human imagination travel as well through human retelling.

Passage 2:

Fairy tales capture basic, fundamental human desires and fears. They represent the most essential form of fictionalized human experience: the bad characters are pure evil, the good characters are pure good, the romance of royalty (and of commoners becoming royalty) is celebrated, etc. Given the nature of the fairy tale genre, it is not surprising that many different cultures come up with similar versions of the same essential story.

11. On what point would the authors of both passages agree?

   (A) Fairy tales share a common origin.
   (B) The same fairy tale may develop independently in a number of different cultures.
   (C) There are often common elements in fairy tales from different cultures.
   (D) Fairy tales capture basic human fears.
   (E) The romance of royalty is celebrated.

12. What does the "nature of the fairy tale genre" refer to in Passage 2?

   (A) The representation of basic human experience
   (B) Good characters being pure good and bad characters being pure evil
   (C) Different cultures coming up with similar versions of the same story
   (D) Commoners becoming royalty
   (E) Giants and talking animals being present

13. Which of the following is not an example of something the author of Passage 1 claims travels from place to place through human movement?

(A) Fairy tales
(B) Language
(C) Ideas
(D) Goods
(E) Foods

14. Which of the following is not an example of something that the author of Passage 1 states might be found in a fairy tale?

(A) Trolls
(B) Witches
(C) Talking animals
(D) Giants
(E) Elves

Questions 15-20 are based on the following passage:

Peanut allergy is the most prevalent food allergy in the United States, affecting around one and a half million people, and it is potentially on the rise in children in the United States. While thought to be the most common cause of food-related death, deaths from food allergies are very rare. The allergy typically begins at a very young age and remains present for life for most people. Approximately one-fifth to one-quarter of children with a peanut allergy, however, outgrow it. Treatment involves careful avoidance of peanuts or any food that may contain peanut pieces or oils. For some sufferers, exposure to even the smallest amount of peanut product can trigger a serious reaction.

Symptoms of peanut allergy can include skin reactions, itching around the mouth, digestive problems, shortness of breath, and runny or stuffy nose. The most severe peanut allergies can result in anaphylaxis, which requires immediate treatment with epinephrine. Up to one-third of people with peanut allergies have severe reactions. Without treatment, anaphylactic shock can result in death due to obstruction of the airway, or heart failure. Signs of anaphylaxis include constriction of airways and difficulty breathing, shock, a rapid pulse, and dizziness or lightheadedness.
As of yet, there is no treatment to prevent or cure allergic reactions to peanuts. In May of 2008, however, Duke University Medical Center food allergy experts announced that they expect to offer a treatment for peanut allergies within five years.

Scientists do not know for sure why peanut proteins induce allergic reactions, nor do they know why some people develop peanut allergies while others do not. There is a strong genetic component to allergies: if one of a child's parents has an allergy, the child has an almost 50% chance of developing an allergy. If both parents have an allergy, the odds increase to about 70%.

Someone suffering from a peanut allergy needs to be cautious about the foods he or she eats and the products he or she puts on his or her skin. Common foods that should be checked for peanut content are ground nuts, cereals, granola, grain breads, energy bars, and salad dressings. Store prepared cookies, pastries, and frozen desserts like ice cream can also contain peanuts. Additionally, many cuisines use peanuts in cooking – watch for peanut content in African, Chinese, Indonesian, Mexican, Thai, and Vietnamese dishes.

Parents of children with peanut allergies should notify key people (child care providers, school personnel, etc.) that their child has a peanut allergy, explain peanut allergy symptoms to them, make sure that the child's epinephrine auto injector is always available, write an action plan of care for their child when he or she has an allergic reaction to peanuts, have their child wear a medical alert bracelet or necklace, and discourage their child from sharing foods.

15. According to the passage, approximately what percentage of people with peanut allergies have severe reactions?

(A) Up to 11%
(B) Up to 22%
(C) Up to 33%
(D) Up to 44%
(E) Up to 55%

16. By what date do Duke University allergy experts expect to offer a treatment for peanut allergies?

(A) 2008
(B) 2009
(C) 2010
(D) 2012
(E) 2013

17. Which of the following is not a type of cuisine the passage suggests often contains peanuts?

(A) African
(B) Italian
(C) Vietnamese
(D) Mexican
(E) Thai

18. Which allergy does the article state is thought to be the most common cause of food-related death?

(A) Peanut
(B) Tree nut
(C) Bee sting
(D) Poison oak
(E) Shellfish

19. It can be inferred from the passage that children with peanut allergies should be discouraged from sharing food because:

(A) Peanut allergies can be contagious.
(B) People suffering from peanut allergies are more susceptible to bad hygiene.
(C) Many foods contain peanut content and it is important to be very careful when you don't know what you're eating.
(D) Scientists don't know why some people develop peanut allergies.
(E) There is no treatment yet to prevent peanut allergies.

20. Which of the following does the passage not state is a sign of anaphylaxis?

(A) constriction of airways
(B) shock
(C) a rapid pulse
(D) dizziness
(E) running or stuffy nose

Questions 21-24 refer to the following passage:

"His pride," said Miss Lucas, "does not offend *me* so much as pride often does, because there is an excuse for it. One cannot wonder that so very fine a young man, with family, fortune, everything in his favour, should think highly of himself. If I may so express it, he has a *right* to be proud."

"That is very true," replied Elizabeth, "and I could easily forgive *his* pride, if he had not mortified *mine*."

- 135 -

"Pride," observed Mary, who piqued herself upon the solidity of her reflections, "is a very common failing I believe. By all that I have ever read, I am convinced that it is very common indeed, that human nature is particularly prone to it, and that there are very few of us who do not cherish a feeling of self-complacency on the score of some quality or other, real or imaginary. Vanity and pride are different things, though the words are often used synonymously. A person may be proud without being vain. Pride relates more to our opinion of ourselves, vanity to what we would have others think of us."

21. Why doesn't the gentleman's pride offend Miss Lucas?
    (A) She admires his vanity.
    (B) He offended Elizabeth.
    (C) It is human nature to be proud.
    (D) He is poor and homeless.
    (E) He is handsome and rich.

22. What are Elizabeth's feelings towards the gentleman?
    (A) She is offended by him.
    (B) She enjoys his company.
    (C) She is proud of him.
    (D) She wants to get to know him better.
    (E) She is glad he is rich.

23. Which sentence best states the theme of this passage?
    (A) Pride and vanity are offensive.
    (B) Fame and fortune can make a person proud.
    (C) Every person is proud in one way or another.
    (D) Pride can bring you fortune.
    (E) If you have a fortune, you deserve to be proud.

24. According to the passage, what is the difference between pride and vanity?
    (A) Pride relates to a person's abilities; vanity relates to a person's looks.
    (B) Men are proud; women are vain.
    (C) Pride and vanity are synonymous.
    (D) Pride is what you think of yourself; vanity is what you want others to think of you.
    (E) Pride is part of human nature; vanity is not.

Section 4

Time – 25 minutes

35 Questions

Questions 1-11: A portion of each of the following sentences is underlined. Following the text there are five ways of phrasing the underlined material. Choice A is the original text; the other four choices are different. Select the choice that produces the best sentence.

1. Good politicians motivate us with speeches <u>and also improving</u> our communities with their actions.

    (A) and also improving
    (B) and improve
    (C) and improving
    (D) also improving
    (E) improving

2. A fast reader can get through a story in a couple of hours <u>if they're not distracted by other things</u>.

    (A) if they're not distracted by other things.
    (B) if they're not distracted.
    (C) if not distracted by other things.
    (D) so long as they are not distracted.
    (E) while distracted by other things.

3. Once considered a long shot for the presidency, <u>Barack Obama's campaign was effective at energizing voters</u>.

    (A) Barack Obama's campaign was effective at energizing voters.
    (B) Barack Obama and his campaign was effective at energizing voters.
    (C) Barack Obama's campaign effectively at energizing voters.
    (D) the campaign effectively energized Barack Obama and voters.
    (E) Barack Obama ran a campaign that was effective at energizing voters.

- 137 -

4. My grandmother came to live with us in 2002 <u>and she was 70 then</u>.

    (A) and she was 70 then.
    (B) when she was 70.
    (C) and she was 70.
    (D) upon being 70.
    (E) after becoming 70.

5. For Sara and her friends, meeting once a month for book club <u>seemed satisfying their commitment</u> to stay in touch.

    (A) seemed satisfying their commitment
    (B) satisfying their commitment
    (C) seemed to satisfy their commitment
    (D) seemed to satisfying their commitment
    (E) seemingly satisfying their commitment

6. The City Recognition Plaque went <u>to whomever in the non-profit community</u> the City Council felt had contributed most to the city's improvement the preceding year.

    (A) to whomever in the non-profit community
    (B) to who in the non-profit community
    (C) to whom in the non-profit community
    (D) to whomever in the community of non-profits
    (E) to whoever in the non-profit community

7. My aunt, along with a number of other relatives from my home town, <u>are going to stay at my house</u> for the weekend.

    (A) are going to stay at my house
    (B) are staying at my house
    (C) are all going to stay at my house
    (D) is going to stay at my house
    (E) will all stay at my house

8. <u>Before auditioning an actress for the lead role, she must have</u> a strong singing background.

    (A) Before auditioning an actress for the lead role, she must have
    (B) We won't audition an actress without
    (C) Before auditioning an actress she should have
    (D) We won't audition an actress unless she has
    (E) To consider an actress, she must have

9. Her little brother Eli is <u>one of the first graders who are going</u> on the field trip.

    (A) one of the first graders who are going
    (B) one of the first graders who is going
    (C) one first graders who are going
    (D) a first graders who are going
    (E) of the first graders who are going

10. The participants in the early morning exercise class <u>worked energetic for completing</u> the program.

    (A) worked energetic for completing
    (B) work energetic to completing
    (C) worked energetic to completing
    (D) worked energetically to complete
    (E) worked energetically for completing

11. David's home remodel allowed him to have a living room for entertaining <u>as well as relax in</u>.

    (A) as well as relax in
    (B) as well as relaxing in
    (C) and to relax in
    (D) and to relax
    (E) and also relax in

Questions 12-29: The following sentences test your ability to recognize grammar and usage errors. Each sentence contains either one error or no error at all. No sentence contains more than one error. The error, if there is one, is underlined. If the sentence contains an error, select the underlined part that must be changed to make the sentence correct. If the sentence is correct, select choice E.

12. The (A) <u>entire staff</u> is (B) <u>invited</u> to (C) <u>Barbara Schneiders</u> retirement reception on Wednesday, Oct. 8 at 2:00 p.m. (D) <u>in the community room</u>. (E) <u>NO ERROR</u>

13. If the (A) <u>substance are</u> too sticky, (B) <u>add more starch</u> in (C) <u>small amounts</u> until it becomes (D) <u>smooth and rubbery</u>. (E) <u>NO ERROR</u>

14. The young father (A) <u>lied</u> the baby (B) <u>down</u> in (C) <u>her</u> (D) <u>brand new</u> baby bed. (E) <u>NO ERROR</u>

15. (A) <u>My</u> grandparents (B) <u>gave</u> gifts to (C) <u>my brother</u> and (D) <u>myself</u>. (E) <u>NO ERROR</u>

16. The mathematicians (A) <u>experimented</u> with an (B) <u>all together</u> different (C) <u>method of</u> (D) <u>solving</u> the problem. (E) <u>NO ERROR</u>

17. The (A) <u>foundation</u> (B) <u>of the huge building</u> (C) <u>was cracked</u> pretty (D) <u>bad</u>. (E) <u>NO ERROR</u>

18. As she (A) <u>pulled into</u> the parking lot, she was surprised (B) <u>to discover</u> that (C) <u>several</u> parking places (D) <u>had been</u> blocked off due to construction. (E) <u>NO ERROR</u>

19. The company philosophy (A) <u>is to</u> strive to (B) <u>use resources wisely</u>, (C) <u>treat each employee</u> with respect, (D) <u>and an excellent product</u>. (E) <u>NO ERROR</u>

20. The boy (A) <u>could</u> take (B) <u>either</u> the goldfish (C) <u>given as a prize</u> to the winners (D) <u>or</u> choose the gift certificate instead. (E) <u>NO ERROR</u>

21. Mrs. Parker, (A) <u>teacher of a 3rd grade class</u>, said, (B) <u>"Let's all try</u> to (C) <u>remember to use</u> the (D) <u>recycling bin"</u>. (E) <u>NO ERROR</u>

22. The (A) <u>class</u> of (B) <u>8th</u> graders (C) <u>are not</u> happy (D) <u>about the field trip</u> cancellation. (E) <u>NO ERROR</u>

23. <u>If</u> wolves <u>are generally</u> pack <u>animals</u>, sometimes <u>one wolf ends up</u> alone. <u>NO ERROR</u>

24. (A) <u>Of all</u> the science (B) <u>projects</u> in (C) <u>the whole school</u>, Ben's was (D) <u>worse</u>. (E) <u>NO ERROR</u>

25. (A)<u>The teenager</u> ran as fast (B) <u>as he</u> could (C) <u>to catch</u> his dog (D) <u>wearing only his socks</u>. (E) <u>NO ERROR</u>

26. The children (A) <u>unfortunately</u> (B) <u>decided to</u> (C) <u>clean up</u> (D) <u>his own</u> mess. (E) <u>NO ERROR</u>

27. Many (A) <u>first-time</u> parents (B) <u>are surprised by</u> how much work (C) <u>it takes</u> to raise (D) <u>babies'</u>. (E) <u>NO ERROR</u>

28. (A) <u>"I'll be glad</u> when this is (B) <u>over"</u> said Nathan (C) <u>as</u> he (D) <u>stared</u> out the window. (E) <u>NO ERROR</u>

29. Talia (A) <u>twirled danced and leaped</u> (B)<u>on the sidewalk</u> on (C) <u>her way</u> (D) <u>to school</u>. (E) <u>NO ERROR</u>

Questions 30-35: The following passage is an early draft of an essay. Some parts of the passage need to be rewritten. Read the passage and select the best answers for the questions that follow. Some questions are about particular sentences or parts of sentences and ask you to improve sentence structure or word choice. Other questions ask you to consider organization and development. In choosing answers, follow the requirements of standard written English.

Questions 30-35 refer to the following passage:

Picking the Perfect Pet

A

(1) Today's choices for pets go beyond the question of whether to get a cat or a dog? (2) Gerbils, rabbits, and amphibians is all popular options. (3) Before heading to an animal shelter, it is important to know what pet makes sense for your home or classroom. (4) An obvious question to answer if you rent is if pets are permitted. (5) Some apartment complex places weight and size limits on pets or charge fees. (6) If pets are permitted, more issues need to be considered.

B

(7) If allergies effect someone in your home, be sure to select a pet that will not aggravate the condition. (8) Some dog breeds, such as schnauzer and poodle, are acceptable pets for those sensitive to fur and dander.

C

(9) Irregardless of the pet you choose, think about other costs such as veterinary care and vaccinations, food costs, licensing, and equipment. (10) Does the pet need a special kind of home? (11) Who will be responsible for feeding and cleaning up after the animal? (12) Taking time to do a little research can save you a lot of heartache and expense later.

30. Sentence (1) *"Today's choices for pets go beyond the question of whether to get a cat or a dog?"*

What correction should be made to this sentence?

    (A) change the question mark to a period
    (B) change <u>Today's</u> to <u>Todays</u>
    (C) change <u>question</u> to <u>questions</u>
    (D) change <u>whether</u> to <u>weather</u>
    (E) no correction is necessary

31. Sentence (2): *"Gerbils, rabbits, and amphibians is all popular options."*

What correction should be made to this sentence?

    (A) remove the comma after <u>Gerbils</u>
    (B) change <u>amphibians</u> to <u>amfibians</u>
    (C) change <u>is</u> to <u>are</u>
    (D) change <u>Gerbils</u> to <u>Hamsters</u>
    (E) no correction is necessary

32. Sentence (5): *"<u>Some apartment complex places weight</u> and size limits on pets or charge fees."*

Which of the following is the best way to write the underlined portion of this sentence? If you think the original is the best way to write the sentence, choose option 1.

    (A) Some apartment complex places weight
    (B) Some apartment complex places wait
    (C) Some apartment complexes places weight
    (D) Some apartment complexes place weight
    (E) Some apartment complex place wait

33. Sentence (6): *"If pets are permitted, more issues need to be considered."*

If you rewrote sentence (6) beginning with <u>More issues need to be considered,</u> the next words should be

(A) permitted pets
(B) if permitted
(C) are permitted
(D) pets are
(E) if pets

34. Sentence (7): *"<u>If allergies effect someone</u> in your home, be sure to select a pet that will not aggravate the condition."*

Which of the following is the best way to write the underlined portion of this sentence? If you think the original is the best way to write the sentence, choose option 1.

(A) If allergies effect someone
(B) If allergies affect someone
(C) If allergies affects someone
(D) If allergies effects someone
(E) If allergies affect anyone

35. Sentence (9): *"Irregardless of the pet you choose, think about other costs such as veterinary care and vaccinations, food costs, licensing and equipment."*

What correction should be made to this sentence?

(A) change <u>Irregardless</u> to <u>Regardless</u>
(B) change <u>licensing</u> to <u>lisencing</u>
(C) change the period to a question mark
(D) remove the extra commas
(E) no correction is needed

Time – 25 minutes

18 Questions

Questions 1-8: Solve each problem and decide which of the choices given is the best.

1. You are taking care of three kittens for a week. Each kitten eats 1 1/2 cans of food twice a day. The owner has left you 60 cans of food. Do you have enough food, or how many more cans do you need?

    (A) 1 can
    (B) 2 cans
    (C) 3 cans
    (D) 4 cans
    (E) There is enough food.

2. Carina consigns her children's outgrown clothing at a local consignment shop that awards her 40% of the total sales price. If she uses $28 to purchase new items and goes home with $64 in cash, what was the total sales price of her children's clothing?

    (A) $92
    (B) $153.33
    (C) $36.80
    (D) $55.20
    (E) $230

3. Each week, Zach visits his local ice cream shop and orders one of the four flavors randomly. After how many weeks can he ensure having tasted all four flavors?

    (A) 4
    (B) 5
    (C) 8
    (D) 16
    (E) Cannot be determined

4. Two angles of a triangle measure 90 degrees and 45 degrees. How many degrees is the third angle?

    (A) 45 degrees
    (B) 90 degrees
    (C) 30 degrees
    (D) 60 degrees
    (E) 180 degrees

5. If $3x = y$ and $y = 4z$, then which of the following statements is NOT true?

    (A) $3x = 4z$
    (B) y is larger than z
    (C) y is smaller than z
    (D) z is smaller than x
    (E) z is smaller than y

6. If each side of a slice of pizza is 5.5 inches long, what is the area of the whole pizza, rounded to the nearest whole number?

    (A) 55 square inches
    (B) 75 square inches
    (C) 95 square inches
    (D) 105 square inches
    (E) 115 square inches

7. Matt invests $500 in a certificate of deposit earning 3% per year. How many years will it take for his CD to earn at least $45 in simple interest?

    (A) One year
    (B) Two years
    (C) Three years
    (D) Four years
    (E) Five years

8. If Renessa earned 4 As, 2 Bs, and 1 C on her report card, what is her GPA on a scale where A is worth 4, B is worth 3, C is worth 2, D is worth 1, and F is worth 0?

    (A) 3.38
    (B) 3.43
    (C) 3.57
    (D) 3.62
    (E) 3.71

Questions 9-18: Use the grids on the answer sheet page where you have answered.

9. If 3a + 5b = 98 and a = 11, what is the value of a + b?

10. How many identical cubes, each with edges of 3 inches, can fit in a box measuring 15 inches by 9 inches by 6 inches?

11. A rectangle with a length of 5x and a width of x has an area of 245. What is the length of the longest side of the rectangle?

12. If it took Lex from 10:00a.m. to 11:45a.m. to walk 14 blocks, what was his average speed in blocks per hour?

13. The average of 4, 7, 9 and x is 9. What is the value of x?

14. A jar contains pennies and nickels. The ratio of nickels to pennies is 6:2. What percent of the coins are pennies?

15. What is the sum of the largest prime factor of 42 and the smallest prime factor of 42?

16. The flower shop puts all flowers in bouquets of 12. If the shop has 137 flowers, how many are left over when there aren't enough to make a full bouquet?

17. Larry gave 1/4 of his Halloween candy to his little sister Eva and 1/5 to his mom. What percentage of his Halloween candy did Larry have left?

18. If 24 people tried to climb a mountain and 6 people completed the climb, what percentage of people didn't climb the mountain?

Section 6

Time -- 25 minutes

23 Questions

Questions 1-8: Each sentence below has one or more blanks, each blank indicating that something has been omitted. Beneath each sentence are five words or sets of words labeled A through E. Choose the word or set of words that, when inserted in the sentence, best fits the meaning of the sentence as a whole.

1. The _____ that he used for death was so vague that people hearing it for the first time found it _____.

   (A) enigma... pragmatic
   (B) conjecture... astute
   (C) erudition... circumspect
   (D) euphemism... incoherent
   (E) potentate... pedantic

2. Her _____ was seen by so many people and was so embarrassing to her that she became very _____ for the rest of the summer.

   (A) veracity... sanctimonious
   (B) chicanery... vituperative
   (C) gaffe... reclusive
   (D) altruism... laudatory
   (E) effrontery... magnanimous

3. The realtor was _____ with calls about the new listing from the first day it was available.

   (A) supplanted
   (B) inundated
   (C) disparaged
   (D) castigated
   (E) cajoled

4. The teacher _____ her students when they gave the wrong answer.

    (A) commended
    (B) applauded
    (C) belittled
    (D) praised

5. Many rainforest species have _____ due to deforestation.

    (A) perished
    (B) persisted
    (C) survived
    (D) immigrated

6. Because of his easygoing _____, many people wanted to _____ James.

    (A) personality .. destroy
    (B) rudeness .. join
    (C) demeanor .. befriend
    (D) dominance .. ignore

7. Overcome with _____, the students built a monument to _____ their teacher after his death.

    (A) melancholy .. memorialize
    (B) sadness .. criticize
    (C) blissfulness .. commemorate
    (D) gratitude .. politicize

8. Her son's misbehavior _____ her, but she managed to calm down before she spoke to him.

    (A) exhilarated
    (B) depressed
    (C) embroiled
    (D) infuriated

Questions 9-17 are based on the following passage:

Daylight Saving Time (DST) is the practice of changing clocks so that afternoons have more daylight and mornings have less. Clocks are adjusted forward one hour in the spring and one hour backward in the fall. The main purpose of the change is to make better use of daylight.

DST began with the goal of conservation. Benjamin Franklin suggested it as a method of saving on candles. It was used during both World Wars to save energy for military needs. Although DST's potential to save energy was a primary reason behind its implementation, research into its effects on energy conservation are contradictory and unclear.

Beneficiaries of DST include all activities that can benefit from more sunlight after working hours, such as shopping and sports. A 1984 issue of *Fortune* magazine estimated that a seven-week extension of DST would yield an additional $30 million for 7-Eleven stores. Public safety may be increased by the use of DST: some research suggests that traffic fatalities may be reduced when there is additional afternoon sunlight.

On the other hand, DST complicates timekeeping and some computer systems. Tools with built-in time-keeping functions such as medical devices can be affected negatively. Agricultural and evening entertainment interests have historically opposed DST.

DST can affect health, both positively and negatively. It provides more afternoon sunlight in which to get exercise. It also impacts sunlight exposure; this is good for getting vitamin D, but bad in that it can increase skin cancer risk. DST may also disrupt sleep.

Today, daylight saving time has been adopted by more than one billion people in about 70 countries. DST is generally not observed in countries near the equator because sunrise times do not vary much there. Asia and Africa do not generally observe it. Some countries, such as Brazil, observe it only in some regions.

DST can lead to peculiar situations. One of these occurred in November, 2007 when a woman in North Carolina gave birth to one twin at 1:32 a.m. and, 34 minutes later, to the second twin. Because of DST and the time change at 2:00 a.m., the second twin was officially born at 1:06, 26 minutes earlier than her brother.

9. According to the passage, what is the main purpose of DST?

    (A) To increase public safety
    (B) To benefit retail businesses
    (C) To make better use of daylight
    (D) To promote good health
    (E) To save on candles

10. Which of the following is not mentioned in the passage as a negative effect of DST?

(A) Energy conservation
(B) Complications with time keeping
(C) Complications with computer systems
(D) Increased skin cancer risk
(E) Sleep disruption

11. The article states that DST involves:

(A) Adjusting clocks forward one hour in the spring and the fall.
(B) Adjusting clocks backward one hour in the spring and the fall.
(C) Adjusting clocks forward in the fall and backward in the spring.
(D) Adjusting clocks forward in the spring and backward in the fall.
(E) None of the above.

12. Which interests have historically opposed DST, according to the passage?

(A) retail businesses and sports
(B) evening entertainment and agriculture
(C) 7-Eleven and health
(D) medical devices and computing
(E) public safety and energy

13. According to the article, increased sunlight exposure:

(A) is only good for health.
(B) is only bad for health.
(C) has no effect on health.
(D) can be both good and bad for health.
(E) has not been studied sufficiently to determine its effect on health.

14. In what region does the article state DST is observed only in some regions?

(A) The equator
(B) Asia
(C) Africa
(D) The United States
(E) Brazil

15. What is an example given in the passage of a peculiar situation that DST has caused?

    (A) sleep disruption
    (B) driving confusion
    (C) twin birth order complications
    (D) countries with DST only in certain regions
    (E) energy conservation confusion

16. According to the passage, a 1984 magazine article estimated that a seven-week extension of DST would provide 7-Eleven stores with an extra $30 million. Approximately how much extra money is that per week of the extension?

    (A) 42,000
    (B) 420,000
    (C) 4,200,000
    (D) 42,000,000
    (E) 420,000,000

17. For what purpose did Benjamin Franklin first suggest DST?

    (A) to save money for military needs
    (B) to save candles
    (C) to reduce traffic fatalities
    (D) to promote reading
    (E) to assist agricultural interests

Questions 18-23 refer to the following passage:

Tips for Eating Calcium Rich Foods

- Include milk as a beverage at meals. Choose fat-free or low-fat milk.
- If you usually drink whole milk, switch gradually to fat-free milk to lower saturated fat and calories. Try reduced fat (2%), then low-fat (1%), and finally fat-free (skim).
- If you drink cappuccinos or lattes—ask for them with fat-free (skim) milk.
- Add fat-free or low-fat milk instead of water to oatmeal and hot cereals
- Use fat-free or low-fat milk when making condensed cream soups (such as cream of tomato).
- Have fat-free or low-fat yogurt as a snack.
- Make a dip for fruits or vegetables from yogurt.
- Make fruit-yogurt smoothies in the blender.
- For dessert, make chocolate or butterscotch pudding with fat-free or low-fat milk.
- Top cut-up fruit with flavored yogurt for a quick dessert.
- Top casseroles, soups, stews, or vegetables with shredded low-fat cheese.
- Top a baked potato with fat-free or low-fat yogurt.

For those who choose not to consume milk products

- If you avoid milk because of lactose intolerance, the most reliable way to get the health benefits of milk is to choose lactose-free alternatives within the milk group, such as cheese, yogurt, or lactose-free milk, or to consume the enzyme lactase before consuming milk products.
- Calcium choices for those who do not consume milk products include:
    o Calcium fortified juices, cereals, breads, soy beverages, or rice beverages
    o Canned fish (sardines, salmon with bones) soybeans and other soy products, some other dried beans, and some leafy greens.

- 153 -

18. According to the passage, how can you lower saturated fat and calories in your diet?

   (A) Add fat-free milk to oatmeal instead of water.
   (B) Switch to fat-free milk.
   (C) Drink calcium-fortified juice.
   (D) Make yogurt dip.
   (E) Choose lactose-free alternatives.

19. What device does the author use to organize the passage?

   (A) headings
   (B) captions
   (C) diagrams
   (D) labels
   (E) bold print

20. How much fat does reduced fat milk contain?
   (A) 0 percent
   (B) 1 percent
   (C) 2 percent
   (D) 3 percent
   (E) 100 percent

21. Which of the following is true about calcium rich foods?

   I. Canned salmon with bones contains calcium.

   II. Cheese is a lactose-free food.

   III. Condensed soup made with water is a calcium rich food.

   (A) I only
   (B) I and II only
   (C) II and III only
   (D) III only
   (E) I, II, and III

22. What information should the author include to help clarify information in the passage?

   (A) The fat content of yogurt.
   (B) How much calcium is in fortified juice.
   (C) Which leafy greens contain calcium.
   (D) The definition of lactose intolerance.
   (E) Where you can buy rice beverages.

23. The style of this passage is most like that found in a(n)
    (A) tourist guidebook.
    (B) teen magazine.
    (C) encyclopedia.
    (D) friendly letter.
    (E) health textbook.

Time – 20 minutes

16 Questions

For this section, solve each problem and decide which of the choices given is the best.

1. If $a - 16 = 8b + 6$, what does $a + 3$ equal?

    (A) b + 3
    (B) 8b + 9
    (C) 8b + 22
    (D) 8b + 25
    (E) 25

2. In the figure below, angles b and d are equal. What is the degree measure of angle d?

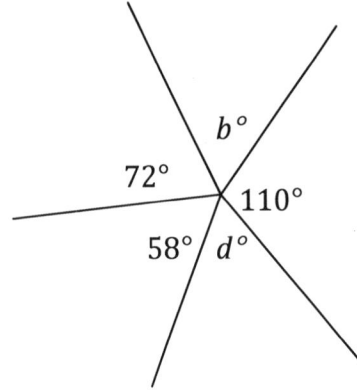

    (A) 240°
    (B) 120°
    (C) 80°
    (D) 60°
    (E) 30°

3. Janice weighs x pounds. Elaina weighs 23 pounds more than Janice. June weighs 14 pounds more than Janice. In terms of x, what is the sum of their weights minus 25 pounds?

    (A) 3x + 37
    (B) 3x + 12
    (C) x + 12
    (D) 3x - 25
    (E) x = 4

4. A bag contains 14 blue, 6 red, 12 green and 8 purple buttons. 25 buttons are removed from the bag randomly. How many of the removed buttons were red if the chance of drawing a red button from the bag is now $1/3$?

    (A) 0
    (B) 1
    (C) 3
    (D) 5
    (E) 6

5. Solve the following equation: $(y + 1)(y + 2)(y + 3)$

    (A) $y^2 + 3y + 2$
    (B) $3y^2 + 6y + 3$
    (C) $2y^2 + 11y$
    (D) $y^3 + 6y^2 + 11y + 6$
    (E) $8y^3 + 6y + 8$

6. What is the area of the parallelogram in the figure below?

    (A) 10 square feet
    (B) 12 square feet
    (C) 16 square feet
    (D) 24 square feet
    (E) 36 square feet

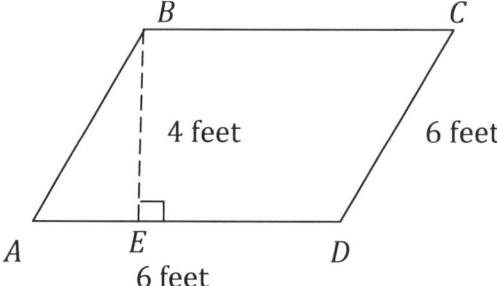

7. In the figure below, AD = 5 and AB = 12, what is the length of AC (not shown)?

(A) 10
(B) 13
(C) 17
(D) 60
(E) 169

8. A regular toilet uses 3.2 gallons of water per flush. A low flow toilet uses 1.6 gallons of water per flush. What is the difference between the number of gallons used by the regular toilet and the low flow toilet after 375 flushes?

(A) 100 gallons
(B) 525 gallons
(C) 600 gallons
(D) 1,200 gallons
(E) 1,800 gallons

9. Five dice are rolled together one time. What is the probability of rolling five 6s?

(A) $\frac{1}{6}$
(B) $\frac{1}{30}$
(C) $\frac{5}{6}$
(D) $\frac{1}{1,000}$
(E) $\frac{1}{7,776}$

10. Simplify the following equation: $4(6 - 3)^2 - (-2)$

(A) 34
(B) 38
(C) 42
(D) 48
(E) 62

11. In the figure below, find the value of *x*:

(A) 30
(B) 60
(C) 100
(D) 120
(E) 180

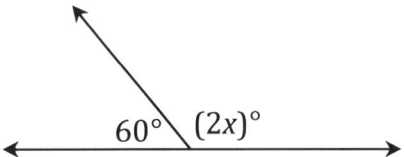

12. Solve for *n* in the following equation: $4n - p = 3r$

(A) 3r/4 - p
(B) p + 3r
(C) p - 3r
(D) 3r/4 + p
(E) 3r/4 + p/4

13. A square and an equilateral triangle have the same perimeter. If one side of the triangle measures 4 inches, how long is one side of the square?

(A) 10
(B) 8
(C) 6
(D) 4
(E) 3

14. Which of the following fractions, when entered into the triangle, makes the statement true?

$$^3/_8 < \Delta < {}^{13}/_{24}$$

(A) 7/8
(B) 5/8
(C) 5/12
(D) 1/3
(E) 1/4

15. Find the value of x in the figure below:

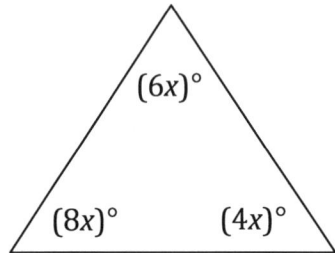

(A) 10
(B) 16
(C) 18
(D) 60
(E) 180

16. What is a good estimate of the circumference of the circle in the figure below?

(A) 6
(B) 12
(C) 24
(D) 36
(E) 48

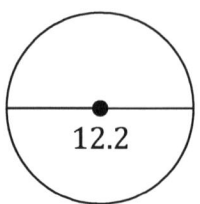

12.2

Time – 20 minutes

19 Questions

Questions 1-6: Each sentence below has one or more blanks, each blank indicating that something has been omitted. Beneath each sentence are five words or sets of words labeled A through E. Choose the word or set of words that, when inserted in the sentence, best fits the meaning of the sentence as a whole.

1. The obstacles he faced seemed _____, but through hard work and _____ he was successful in his efforts.

   (A) insuppressible .. retention
   (B) mountainous .. indolence
   (C) insurmountable .. diligence
   (D) licentious .. persistence

2. Her goal is to _____ the globe in a hot air balloon.

   (A) circumscribe
   (B) circumnavigate
   (C) circulate
   (D) circumambulate

3. Paul made a bad decision to hike in _____ weather conditions.

   (A) onerous
   (B) affable
   (C) malleable
   (D) adverse

4. The teacher's lecture was so predictable, so _____, that the students fell asleep soon after it started.

    (A) flippant
    (B) banal
    (C) inconceivable
    (D) morbid

5. The mysterious, _____ music floated through the trees and charmed the listeners.

    (A) ethereal
    (B) viable
    (C) polished
    (D) nourishing

6. Rhonda's behavior only _____ an already bad situation.

    (A) safeguarded
    (B) pursued
    (C) manifested
    (D) exacerbated

Questions 7-11 are based on the following passage:

    Harriet Tubman was a runaway slave from Maryland who became known as the "Moses of her people." Over the course of 10 years, and at great personal risk, she led hundreds of slaves to freedom along the Underground Railroad, a secret network of safe houses where runaway slaves could stay on their journey north to freedom. She later became a leader in the abolitionist movement, and during the Civil War she was a spy for the federal forces in South Carolina as well as a nurse.

    Harriet Tubman's name at birth was Araminta Ross. She was one of 11 children of Harriet and Benjamin Ross born into slavery in Dorchester County, Maryland. As a child, Ross was "hired out" by her master as a nursemaid for a small baby. Ross had to stay awake all night so that the baby wouldn't cry and wake the mother. If Ross fell asleep, the baby's mother whipped her. From a very young age, Ross was determined to gain her freedom.

    As a slave, Araminta Ross was scarred for life when she refused to help in the punishment of another young slave. A young man had gone to the store without permission, and when he returned, the overseer wanted to whip him. He asked Ross to help but she refused. When the young man started to run away, the overseer picked up a heavy iron weight and threw it at him. He missed the young man and hit Ross instead. The weight nearly crushed her skull and left a deep scar. She was unconscious for days, and suffered from seizures for the rest of her life.

- 162 -

In 1844, Ross married a free black named John Tubman and took his last name. She also changed her first name, taking her mother's name, Harriet. In 1849, worried that she and the other slaves on the plantation were going to be sold, Tubman decided to run away. Her husband refused to go with her, so she set out with her two brothers, and followed the North Star in the sky to guide her north to freedom. Her brothers became frightened and turned back, but she continued on and reached Philadelphia. There she found work as a household servant and saved her money so she could return to help others escape.

7. This passage is mainly about
   (A) slaves in the Civil War.
   (B) how slaves escaped along the Underground Railroad.
   (C) Harriet Tubman's role as an abolitionist leader.
   (D) Harriet Tubman's life as a slave.
   (E) how Harriet Tubman became a nurse.

8. The author of the passage describes Harriet Tubman's life as a slave to show
   (A) why she wanted to escape slavery.
   (B) why she was a spy during the Civil War.
   (C) why she suffered from seizures.
   (D) how she loved babies.
   (E) why she left her husband.

9. Harriet Tubman's seizures were caused by
   (A) a whipping.
   (B) a severe head injury.
   (C) loss of sleep.
   (D) a birth defect.
   (E) her escape to freedom.

10. How is this passage structured?
    (A) cause and effect
    (B) problem and solution
    (C) chronological order
    (D) compare and contrast
    (E) proposition and support

11. How did Araminta Ross come to be known as Harriet Tubman?
    (A) She took her husband's last name and changed her first name to her mother's name.
    (B) She was named after the plantation owner's wife.
    (C) She changed her name because she was wanted as an Underground Railroad runner.
    (D) She changed her name to remain anonymous as a Civil War spy.
    (E) The overseer began calling her Harriet Tubman.

Questions 12-16 are based on the following passage:

> There will come soft rains and the smell of the ground,
>
> And swallows circling with their shimmering sound;
>
> And frogs in the pools singing at night,
>
> And wild plum trees in tremulous white;
>
> Robins will wear their feathery fire
>
> Whistling their whims on a low fence-wire;
>
> And not one will know of the war, not one
>
> Will care at last when it is done.
>
> Not one would mind, neither bird nor tree
>
> If mankind perished utterly;
>
> And Spring herself, when she woke at dawn,
>
> Would scarcely know that we were gone.

12. How many stanzas does this poem have?
    (A) 2
    (B) 4
    (C) 6
    (D) 10
    (E) 12

13. Which line uses personification?
    (A) Line 2
    (B) Line 4
    (C) Line 7
    (D) Line 10
    (E) Line 11

14. The "we" used in line 12 refers to
    (A) all of mankind.
    (B) the victors of the war.
    (C) Americans.
    (D) the poet and the reader.
    (E) the animals.

15. This poem is an example of a(n)
    (A) sonnet.
    (B) rhymed verse.
    (C) free verse.
    (D) lyric.
    (E) epic.

16. Which of these statements offers the best summary of the poem?
    (A) Nature does not care about the affairs of mankind.
    (B) It is the government's responsibility to fight a war.
    (C) War has a devastating impact on nature.
    (D) Wars should not be fought in the spring.
    (E) Robins will sing about the war.

Questions 17-20 refer to the following passage:

Grapes are one of the oldest cultivated fruits. Hieroglyphics show that Egyptians were involved in grape and wine production. Also, the early Romans were known to have developed many grape varieties.

Grapes have been grown in California for more than 200 years. The tradition of viticulture (growing grapes) began in 1769 when Spanish friars established missions throughout California.

In California, the boom in grapes planted for eating arose in the early 1800s. William Wolfskill, founder of California's citrus industry, planted the first table grape vineyard in 1839 near Los Angeles.

By the 1850s, the United States had officially acquired California from Mexico and 80,000 gold prospectors had moved to the region, a few of them realizing that there was money in grapes as well as in gold.

Today, California wine, table grapes and raisins are all important agricultural commodities, with approximately 700,000 acres planted in vineyards.

About 85% of California's table grape production is in the southern San Joaquin Valley region with the Coachella Valley region accounting for most of the remaining production.

17. This passage is mainly about
    (A) how Egyptians grew wine grapes.
    (B) how to make raisins from grapes.
    (C) William Wolfskill's life as a farmer.
    (D) the history of growing grapes in California.
    (E) how grapes were involved in the Gold Rush.

18. The best title for this passage is
    (A) Early Wine Production.
    (B) California Table Grapes.
    (C) Egyptian Hieroglyphics.
    (D) The California Missions.
    (E) Viticulture in California.

19. Most of California's table grapes are grown in
    (A) the San Joaquin Valley region.
    (B) the Coachella Valley region.
    (C) Los Angeles.
    (D) the California missions.
    (E) Rome.

20. William Wolfskill is credited with
    (A) deciphering hieroglyphics about grape and wine production.
    (B) helping the United States acquire California.
    (C) planting the first table grape vineyard in California.
    (D) farming 700,000 acres of vineyards.
    (E) growing citrus in the San Joaquin Valley.

Time – 10 minutes

14 Questions

Questions 1 – 14: A portion of each of the following sentences is underlined. Following the text there are five ways of phrasing the underlined material. Choice A is the original text; the other four choices are different. Select the choice that, in your judgment, produces the best sentence.

1. Because kids often want a snack after spending time in a grocery store, <u>they are displayed near the checkout lines</u> at child height.

    (A) they are displayed near the checkout lines
    (B) they are near the checkout lines
    (C) snacks are displayed near the checkout lines
    (D) snacks are displaying near the checkout lines
    (E) they can be found near the checkout lines

2. Having eaten at the three nearby restaurants, <u>they definitely aren't as good</u> as those in our old neighborhood.

    (A) they definitely aren't as good
    (B) they definitely weren't as good
    (C) I am convinced that they are not as good
    (D) they are not as good to me
    (E) they are definitely not as good, I am convinced

3. Ian's best friend said Ian really appreciated <u>us coming to his</u> surprise party.

    (A) us coming to his
    (B) that we come to his
    (C) us since we came to his
    (D) us having come to his
    (E) our coming to his

4. If he stops to consider the ramifications of this decision, <u>it is probable that he will rethink his original decision a while longer</u>.

    (A) it is probable that he will rethink his original decision.
    (B) he will rethink his original decision over again.
    (C) he probably will rethink his original decision.
    (D) he will most likely rethink his original decision for a bit.
    (E) he probably will rethink his decision a while longer.

5. "When you get <u>older," she said "you will no doubt</u> understand what I mean."

    (A) older," she said "you will no doubt
    (B) older" she said "you will no doubt
    (C) older," she said, "you will no doubt
    (D) older," she said "you will not
    (E) older", she said, "you will no doubt

6. <u>Dr. Anderson strolled past the nurses, examining a bottle of pills.</u>

    (A) Dr. Anderson strolled past the nurses, examining a bottle of pills.
    (B) Dr. Anderson strolled past the nurses examining a bottle of pills.
    (C) Dr. Anderson strolled past, the nurses examining a bottle of pills.
    (D) Examining a bottle of pills Dr. Anderson strolled past the nurses.
    (E) Examining a bottle of pills, Dr. Anderson strolled past the nurses.

7. Karl and Henry <u>raced to the reservoir, climbed the ladder, and then they dove into</u> the cool water.

    (A) raced to the reservoir, climbed the ladder, and then they dove into
    (B) first raced to the reservoir, climbed the ladder, and then they dove into
    (C) raced to the reservoir, they climbed the ladder, and then they dove into
    (D) raced to the reservoir; climbed the ladder; and then they dove into
    (E) raced to the reservoir, climbed the ladder, and dove into

8. Did either <u>Tracy or Vanessa realize that her decision would be</u> so momentous?

    (A) Tracy or Vanessa realize that her decision would be
    (B) Tracy or Vanessa realize that each of their decision was
    (C) Tracy or Vanessa realize that her or her decision would be
    (D) Tracy or Vanessa realize that their decision would be
    (E) Tracy or Vanessa realize that their decision was

9. Despite their lucky escape, <u>Jason and his brother could not hardly enjoy themselves</u>.

    (A) Jason and his brother could not hardly enjoy themselves.
    (B) Jason and his brother could not enjoy themselves.
    (C) Jason and Jason's brother could not hardly enjoy themselves.
    (D) Jason and his brother could not enjoy them.
    (E) Jason and his brother could hardly enjoy them.

10. Stew recipes call <u>for rosemary, parsley, thyme, and these sort of herbs.</u>

    (A) for rosemary, parsley, thyme, and these sort of herbs.
    (B) for: rosemary; parsley; thyme; and these sort of herbs.
    (C) for rosemary, parsley, thyme, and these sorts of herbs.
    (D) for rosemary, parsley, thyme, and this sorts of herbs.
    (E) for rosemary, parsley, thyme, and these sorts of herb.

11. Mr. King, <u>an individual of considerable influence, created a personal fortune and gave back</u> to the community.

    (A) an individual of considerable influence, created a personal fortune and gave back
    (B) an individual of considerable influence, he created a personal fortune and gave back
    (C) an individual of considerable influence created a personal fortune and gave back
    (D) an individual of considerable influence, created a personal fortune and gave it back
    (E) an individual of considerable influence, created a personal fortune and then he gave it back

12. <u>She is the person whose opinion matters the most.</u>

    (A) She is the person whose opinion matters the most.
    (B) She is the person to whom opinion matters the most.
    (C) She is the person who matters the most, in my opinion.
    (D) She is the person for whom opinion matters the most.
    (E) She is the person which has her opinion matter the most.

13. Historians have discovered that fighting was a popular sport for ancient cultures, <u>as that of modern civilizations</u>.

    (A) as that of modern civilizations
    (B) like that for modern civilizations
    (C) exactly like modern civilizations do
    (D) as modern people do
    (E) as it still is for modern civilizations

14. Born John Joseph Lydon in North London in 1956, <u>Johnny Rotten's first number 1 song,</u> <u>*God Save the Queen* was released during the week of Queen Elizabeth II's Silver Jubilee</u> <u>when the musician was 21</u>.

    (A) Johnny Rotten's first number 1 song, *God Save the Queen* was released during the week of Queen Elizabeth II's Silver Jubilee when the musician was 21

    (B) Johnny Rotten's first number 1 song, *God Save the Queen*, released during the week of Queen Elizabeth II's Silver Jubilee when the musician was 21

    (C) Johnny Rotten's *God Save the Queen*, his first number 1 song was released during the week of Queen Elizabeth II's Silver Jubilee when the musician was 21

    (D) Johnny Rotten released his first number 1 song, *God Save the Queen*, during the week of Queen Elizabeth II's Silver Jubilee when the musician was 21

    (E) during the week of Queen Elizabeth II's Silver Jubilee, Johnny Rotten released his first number 1 song, *God Save the Queen* when the musician was 21

Answer Key

Section 2

1. B: After the 10 passengers get off the bus, presumably no one will be standing in the aisles and there will be 4 vacant seats. After the 8 new passengers board, 4 of them will fill the vacant seats and the other 4 will be left to stand in the aisles. It is also possible to calculate the answer by assigning any number to the number of seats on the bus. For instance, if there are 20 seats on the bus, then at the start of the problem there are 26 passengers. After 10 get off, there are 16 passengers, and after 8 get on, there are then 24 passengers. The first 20 passengers would fill the available seats, and the other 4 would stand in the aisles.

2. E: First perform the operations:

$2 + 0.4 = 2.4$

$1 - 0.2 = 0.8$

Next, solve the equation: $2.4 = x(0.8)$

$x = 3$

    A. Incorrect: Subtracts 2 and 0.4 instead of adding and adds 1 and 0.2 instead of subtracting.

    B. Incorrect: Adds 1 and 0.2 instead of subtracting. Or, subtracts 2 and 0.4 instead of adding.

    C. Incorrect: Adds 2 + 0.4 but doesn't subtract 0.2 from 1.

    D. Incorrect: Subtracts 0.2 from 1 but doesn't add 0.4 to 2.

    E. Correct

3. C: The movie is now at the 90 + 12 = 102-minute mark. Therefore, m minutes ago, it had reached the 102 – m mark.

      A. Incorrect: Reverses constant and variable.

      B. Incorrect: Subtracts 12 from 90 instead of adding and reverses   constant and variable.

      C. Correct

      D. Incorrect: Subtracts 12 from 90 instead of adding.

      E. Incorrect: Ignores 12 minutes ago element.

4. D: First calculate the area of the bull's-eye:

$A = \pi r^2 = \pi(4/2)^2 = \pi 2^2 = 4\pi$

Then, let x = the area of the target.

20 percent of $x = 4\pi$

$0.2x = 4\pi$

$x = 20\pi$

      A. Incorrect: Multiplies by 20 percent instead of dividing.

      B. Incorrect: Uses diameter for radius and multiplies by 2.

      C. Incorrect: Doesn't square the radius.

      D. Correct

      E. Incorrect: Uses diameter as radius.

5. B: If the volume halves every 2 days, it halves 5 times after 10 days. This halving action can be expressed as $(\frac{1}{2})(\frac{1}{2})(\frac{1}{2})(\frac{1}{2})(\frac{1}{2})$ or $(\frac{1}{2})^5$. Therefore, if the initial volume is (10^6), then the volume will be $(\frac{1}{2})^5(10^6)$ after 10 days.

      A. Incorrect: Doesn't take "every 2 days" into consideration.

      B. Correct

      C. Incorrect: Doubles instead of halving.

      D. Incorrect: Doubles instead of halving and doesn't take "every 2 days"   into consideration.

E. Incorrect: Raises initial volume to a power equal to the number of times the volume halves.

6. C: The angles a, b, and c form a straight line, so $a + b + c = 180$. Substituting 180 for $a + b + c$ in the proportion, we have:

$$\frac{b}{180} = \frac{3}{5}$$

By cross-multiplying, we can solve for b: $5b = 3(180)$ or $b = 108$.

    A. Incorrect: 180/3

    B. Incorrect: $180 - b$

    C. Correct

    D. Incorrect: $180 - (180/3)$

    E. Incorrect: $a + b + c$

7. D: First, solve the second equation for y: $y = -2x - 5$. Next, substitute that expression for y in the first equation:

$3(-2x - 5) - 2x = 9$

$-6x - 15 - 2x = 9$

$-8x = 24$

$x = -3$

Finally, substitute -3 for x in either equation in order to solve for y:

$2(-3) + y = -5$

$-6 + y = -5$

$y = 1$

    A. Incorrect: Solves for x.

    B. Incorrect: Switches x and y variables in equation #2.

    C. Incorrect: Wrong sign.

    D. Correct

    E. Incorrect: Solves for x; wrong sign.

8. C: Using the Pythagorean Theorem, we first find AB.

$AB^2 + BC^2 = AC^2$

$AB^2 + 5^2 = 13^2$

$AB^2 + 25 = 169$

$AB^2 = 144$

$AB = 12$

Next, we draw a perpendicular bisector from C to AD, forming segment CE, which is the height of triangle ACD and is equal to segment AB. Thus, the height of the triangle is 12.

We know the base of triangle ACD, AD, equals 8. So, we use the area formula.

$A = \frac{1}{2}bh = \frac{1}{2}(8)(12) = 48$

    A. Incorrect: Length of hypotenuse

    B. Incorrect: Area of ABC

    C. Correct

    D. Incorrect: Area of ABC, not halved

    E. Incorrect: Doesn't halve.

9. D: First, convert 10 yards to inches: 1 yard = 36 inches, so 10 yards = 360 inches.

Next, convert the mixed fraction $6\frac{3}{4}$ to a decimal: 6.75.

Finally, divide: 360/6.75 = 53.3333...

So, the maximum number of strips that can be cut is 53.

    A. Incorrect: Doesn't convert yards to inches.

    B. Incorrect: Converts yards to feet.

    C. Incorrect: Converts yards to feet and rounds up.

    D. Correct

    E. Incorrect: Rounds up.

10. C: Use the Distance Formula: distance = rate × time AND time = distance/rate.

1. First half of trip: 1,500 = 400 × time, so time = $\frac{15}{4}$.

2. Second half of trip: $1,500 = \text{rate} \times \text{distance/rate} = \text{rate} \times \frac{1500}{r}$.

3. Total trip: $3,000 = 500 \times \text{time}$, so total time = 6.

The total time of the trip is the sum of the times for the first 1,500 miles and the second 1,500 miles. So, $\frac{15}{4} + \frac{1500}{r} = 6$. Solving for r, we multiply both sides of the equation by $4r$ and get:

$15r + 6,000 = 24r$

$6,000 = 9r$

$r = 666\frac{2}{3}$.

    A. Incorrect: Uses time of 4/15 instead of 15/4.

    B. Incorrect: Solves $500 = (400 + r)/2$.

    C. Correct

    D. Incorrect: $3,000 \times 4/15$

    E. Incorrect: $1,500 \times 15/4$

11. B: The radius of circle O is one-fourth the diameter of circle P. The diameter is twice the radius, or $d = 2r$. So $r_o = \frac{1}{4}(2r_p) = \frac{1}{2}r_p$.

The circumference of circle P $= 2\pi\, r_p$.

The circumference of circle O $= 2\pi\, r_o = 2\pi\left(\frac{1}{2}r_p\right) = \pi\, r_p$.

The ratio of circle O's circumference to circle P's is $(\pi r_p)/(2\pi r_p) = \frac{1}{2}$.

    A. Incorrect: Doesn't convert diameter to radius.

    B. Correct

    C. Incorrect: Assumes diameter = 4r.

    D. Incorrect: Finds ratio of circle P's circumference to circle O's.

    E. Incorrect: Doesn't convert diameter to radius; Finds ratio of circle P's circumference to circle O's.

12. D: If $x^2 + 3x - 18 = 0$, then $(x + 6)(x - 3) = 0$. So $x = -6$ or 3. We are told $x < 0$, so x must equal -6.

I. $(-6)^2 - 36 = 0$ True

II. $(-6)^2 - 2(-6) - 3 \neq 0$ False

III. $(-6)^2 + 5(-6) - 6 = 0$ True

    A. Incorrect: III is also true.

    B. Incorrect: II is false.

    C. Incorrect: I is also true

    D. Correct

    E. Incorrect: II is not true.

13. E: Using the formula for volume $V = e^3$, where e represents the length of an edge of a cube, let the volume of cube B equal e^3 and so the volume of cube A is $\left(\frac{3}{4}e\right)^3 = \frac{27}{64}e^3$.

The ratio of the volume of cube B to the volume of cube A is $e^3 / \frac{27}{64}e^3 = \frac{64}{27}$.

    A. Incorrect: Uses e as the length of an edge of cube A and uses (1/4)e as the length of an edge of cube B.

    B. Incorrect: Assumes the ratio of the lengths of the edges is 1/4 and that the ratio of the volumes is the same as the ratio of the edges.

    C. Incorrect: Finds the ratio of cube A's to cube B's volume.

    D. Incorrect: Assumes that the ratio of the volumes is the same as the ratio of the lengths of the edges.

    E. Correct

14. C: For all large values of x, the value of $\frac{x}{1-2x}$ will be very close to the value of $\frac{x}{-2x} = -\frac{1}{2}$.

    A. Incorrect: Solves 1/(1 −2)

    B. Incorrect: Less than −1/2, so not closest

    C. Correct

    D. Incorrect: Wrong sign; greater than 1/2, so not closest

E. Incorrect: Wrong sign

15. B: Using the formula for the perimeter of a rectangle, we know that P = 2l + 2w. Substituting the value given, we get 76 = 2l + 2w or 38 = l + w. We can now solve for l: 38 – w = l.

Using the formula for the area of a rectangle, we know that A = lw. Substituting the value given, we get 336 = lw.

If we substitute the 38 – w we found in the first step for l, we get (38–w)w = 336. Thus:

$38w - w^2 = 336$

$0 = w^2 - 38w + 336$

$0 = (w - 14)(w - 24)$

$w = 14$ or 24

The shorter of these two possibilities is 14.

    A. Incorrect: 24 – 14

    B. Correct

    C. Incorrect: 76/4

    D. Incorrect: length of the longer sides

    E. Incorrect: (336 – 76)/4

16. C: If Anish was the 11th highest speller, 10 participants placed higher. If Anish was the 25th lowest speller, 24 participants placed lower. Therefore, the total number of participants was 10 + 24 + 1 (Anish) = 35

    A. Incorrect: 10 + 24 – 1

    B. Incorrect: 10 + 24

    C. Correct

    D. Incorrect: 11 + 25

    E. Incorrect: 11 + 25 + 1

17. A: There are 4 members of the first set and 4 members of the second set, so there are 4(4) = 16 possible products for cd. cd is odd only when both c and d are odd. There are 2 odd numbers in the first set and two in the second set, so 2(2) = 4 products are odd and the probability cd is odd is 4/16 or 1/4.

    A. Correct

    B. Incorrect: 4/12

    C. Incorrect: Probability that cd is even

    D. Incorrect: Number of possible odd products

    E. Incorrect: Number of possible even products

18. A: We are given $l = 3w$, so $w = \frac{1}{3}l$. The diagonal is the hypotenuse of the triangle with sides l and w, so we use the Pythagorean Theorem.

$$l^2 + w^2 = d^2 \qquad l^2 + \left(\tfrac{1}{3}l\right)^2 = d^2 \qquad l^2 + \tfrac{1}{9}l^2 = d^2 \qquad \tfrac{10}{9}l^2 = d^2$$

$$d = \sqrt{\tfrac{10}{9}}\, l = \tfrac{\sqrt{10}}{3}\, l$$

    A. Correct

    B. Incorrect: Doesn't take square root of numerator.

    C. Incorrect: Doesn't take square root.

    D. Incorrect: Confuses l and w.

    E. Incorrect: Confuses l and w; doesn't take square root.

19. D: Integers include all positive and negative whole numbers and the number zero. The product of three integers must be an integer, so you can eliminate any answer choice that is not a whole number: choices (A) and (C). The product of two even integers is even. The product of even and odd integers is even. The only even choice is 24.

20. A: If $520 \div x = 40n$, then

$(40n)(x) = 520$

$nx = 13$

1. D: The principal referred to in the sentence realized something about resources that changed her fundraising approach. This realization could logically either be that resources were low and she needed to increase her fundraising, or that resources were great and she could decrease her fundraising. The only choice that fits either scenario is (D).

2. D: Rule out answers that don't work at all. It doesn't make sense here to refer to support as derogatory. Similarly, it is awkward phrasing to refer to being pejorative or lugubrious in giving support. Bombastic is more plausible, but by far the better answer is (D).

3. B: The subject of the sentence thinks the menu is too something. Neither lugubrious nor multifarious make sense in terms of describing something a menu is too much of, ruling out choices (C) and (D). Neither magnanimous nor abstruse make sense in terms of describing a cost, ruling out choices (A) and (E).

4. E: The blank in this sentence should be a word that describes items one would get rid of if one had to (here, because of space concerns). Superfluous is the best fit because it indicates that the items being gotten rid of are extra and perhaps unnecessary for that reason.

5. A: The blank in this sentence needs to describe the behavior of someone who regularly does unexpected things. Erratic is the best fit.

6. B: The passage refers to the nameless shoemaker's haggard eyes, his inability to focus on a question, his repetitive motions, and his inability to give his name. There is no indication of any art or gallery. The setting is Paris; the passage does not indicate that. Thus choice A is incorrect. The man being described is not identified as British or as a member of government, so choice C is incorrect. The man is making shoes, not hospital calls; therefore, choice D is incorrect. Although the man is making shoes by hand, there is no sign that he is a fashion designer. Choice E is also not correct.

7. A: The man gives his name as One Hundred and Five, North Tower, an address, not a personal name. The reference to a tower suggests a prison. Option B is an incorrect choice; the man has not apparently been out of the North Tower in many years. Nor is option C correct because the man is not precisely homeless. Nothing in the passage tells the reader when the man left home, so option D can be eliminated. There is also no reference to his marriage or lack of it in this selection, making number E incorrect.

8. D: The man does not laugh in this passage. Choice A is clearly stated in the passage. He has lapses in conversation with Mr. Lorry. It is also clear in the passage that the man has no remembrance of a given personal name, so choice B can be eliminated. The repeated motion of his hands when they do not hold the shoe is a telling sign of derangement, so choice C is incorrect. Choice E is not accurate; the man speaks in short, choppy sentences until his final sentence, a collection of short sentences strung together by *and*.

9. E: The man is working on a lady's walking-shoe when his visitors arrive and states that he had learned the trade, which was not his original manner of work, at his own request since arriving at the prison. He even expresses some pride in the quality of his work, which is based on a pattern because he has never seen the current mode of shoe. There is no indication that he is engaged in carving wood, blowing glass, smiting, or dressmaking. All of the other choices are clearly false.

10. B: Defarge is somehow the man's keeper and is concerned with his well-being. The first choice suggests unkindness, which is clearly not the case—Defarge is neutral at best. That option can be eliminated. He does not appear to be a family member, so choice C can be eliminated as well. These is also no suggestion of cruelty nor of a profession nor of a definite setting, leaving choice D untenable. A man in this setting is unlikely to have any money. Choice E thus makes no sense.

11. C: Since both authors are explaining in the passages how the same story may come to be in different cultures, it is clear they both accept that there are often common elements in fairy tales from different cultures.

12. A: The author of Passage 2 claims that the essence and nature of fairy tales is their representation of basic human experience. It is this assertion that leads the author to believe that the same story could develop independently in different places.

13. E: The author does not mention the movement of food in the passage.

14. B: The author never mentions witches in the passage.

15. C: The second paragraph of the passage notes that "up to one-third of people with peanut allergies have severe reactions." Since one-third is approximately 33%, (C) is the correct choice.

16. E: The second paragraph of the passage notes that in 2008, Duke experts stated that they expect to offer treatment in five years. Five years from 2008 is 2013.

17. B: The last sentence in paragraph five lists the cuisines in which one should watch for peanuts. Italian is not listed.

18. A: The second sentence of the first paragraph states that peanut allergy is the most common cause of food-related death.

19. C: The passage implies that it is not always easy to know which foods have traces of peanuts in them and that it's important to make sure you know what you're eating. This is hard or impossible if you share someone else's food.

20. E: Paragraph two gives examples of symptoms of peanut allergies and, more specifically, examples of symptoms of anaphylaxis. A running or stuffy nose is given as a symptom of the former, but not of the latter.

21. E: In the first paragraph, Miss Lucas states that "so very fine a young man, with family, fortune, every thing in his favour, should think highly of himself. If I may so express it, he

has a *right* to be proud." Basically, she feels he deserves to be proud because he is physically attractive, comes from a good family, has money, and is successful. The best choice is (E).

22. A: This question is asking you to make an inference about Elizabeth's feeling towards the gentleman. In paragraph 2, Elizabeth is "mortified" by the gentleman's actions towards her. From this statement, you can make the inference that she was offended by his actions.

23. C: A theme is a message or lesson conveyed by a written text. The message is usually about life, society or human nature. This particular excerpt is exploring pride as it relates to human nature. Mary's observations on pride are the best summary of the theme of this passage. "By all that I have ever read, I am convinced that it is very common indeed, that human nature is particularly prone to it." The best answer choice is (C).

24. D: Paragraph 3 gives the answer to this question. According to Mary, pride is an opinion of yourself, and vanity is what we want others to think of us.

Section 4

1. B: The sentence as written uses the wrong verb tense. The verb "to improve" should match the subject and be in the form "improve," rather than "improving."

2. C: A fast reader is singular so the use of "they" in the underlined portion is incorrect. The only answer choices that don't use "they" are (C) and (E). Choice (E) changes the meaning of the sentence, so (C) is correct.

3. E: As written, the sentence suggests that Barack Obama's campaign ran for president. Answer (E) clarifies that Obama himself ran for president.

4. B: The underlined portion refers to the time when her grandmother came to live with the speaker. The choices that refer to a specific time are (B), (D), and (E). Of those choices, (B) is the clearest and least awkward.

5. C: The expression requires the use of "seemed" plus an infinitive. Choice (C) is therefore correct.

6. E: "Whoever" is correct here because it is actually the subject of the sentence: "whoever...had contributed."

7. D: The subject of the sentence is singular: my aunt. The information about other relatives is purely parenthetical. A singular subject needs a singular verb, making choice (D) correct.

8. D: The subject of this sentence is the person(s) who audition(s) actresses for a lead role, not the actresses. Choice (D) clarifies the meaning and the subject of the sentence.

9. A: The sentence is correct.

10. D: Energetic here should be in adverb form because it modifies worked, so only answers (D) and (E) could be correct. "To complete" is more accurate than "for completing."

11. B: The underlined portion of the sentence needs to parallel the rest of the sentence. The living room is "for entertaining" – the version of the underlined portion that matches this form is "for relaxing in."

12. C: There should be an apostrophe before the *s* at the end of Barbara Schneider's name to show possession. The retirement reception belongs to her, so the correct way to write it should be: *Barbara Schneider's.*

13. A: The subject and verb do not agree. *Substance* is singular, so the verb should be *is* instead of *are*. If the subject had been plural, as in *substances*, the verb *are* would have been correct.

14. A: The correct word should be *laid* rather than *lied*. When you put something flat down into a horizontal position, you use and conjugate the verb *lay*. On the other hand, the verb *lie* is used and conjugated when someone is actually in or moving towards being horizontal.

15. D: The word *myself* is a reflexive pronoun. It should not be used as a substitute for the personal object pronoun *me*. In this sentence *me* is the correct pronoun to use.

16. B: In this sentence, *all together* is incorrect and should be replaced with the adverb *altogether*. In this context, *altogether* is used as a synonym for <u>entirely</u> or <u>completely</u>. The two words *all together* signify that more than one person is working together to do one task or action.

17. D: Although *pretty bad* is commonly used in speech, it is incorrect for formal writing. The word *bad* should be replaced with the adverb *badly*.

18. E: There is no error in this sentence

19. D: There is a problem with the parallel in the series given for this sentence. Each part of the series should follow the beginning of the sentence "our company philosophy is to strive to...". In answer choice D, *and an excellent product* does not follow. There needs to be another verb so that each of the parts in the series follow the same structure, as in *USE resources wisely, TREAT each employee with respect, and <u>(insert verb here)</u> an excellent product.* Some choices for verbs that would make sense might be CREATE, MANUFACTURE, MAKE, or any number of other verb choices.

20. B: While it is true that *either* and *or* go together just as *neither* and *nor* do, in this case the sentence structure is incorrect with the placement of the word *either*. When *either* is

followed by an object and verb, *or* must also be followed by an object and verb. In this sentence, you could correct the problem by moving the word *either* as such: *The boy could either take the goldfish given as a prize to the winners or choose the gift certificate instead.*

21. D: The error is in punctuation. The period should come inside of the quotation mark, as follows: "...recycling bin."

22. C: The subject, *class*, does not agree with the verb *are*. The sentence should correctly read: The class of 8ᵗʰ graders **is** not happy about the field trip cancellation.

23. A: The use of the word *if* here is incorrect. It cannot stand alone at the beginning of a sentence without later using the word *then* to finish the thought. In this sentence, *although* or *while* would be better choices to replace the ill-used *if*.

24. D: The word *worse* is used when comparing two things. This sentence is comparing more than to, so the superlative word *worst* should be used.

25. D: In this case, we have a problem with a misplaced modifier. *Wearing only his socks* is a statement about the teenager. The problem is that the placement of this statement in the sentence makes it seem as though the dog is the one with the sock issue. A modifier should be placed as close as possible to the subject, as follows: The teenager, wearing only his socks, ran as fast as he could to catch his dog. In this manner the sentence is more clear and makes logical sense.

26. D: The pronoun (*his*) does not agree with the subject (*children*).

27. D: The apostrophe, which indicates the possessive form of the plural word "babies," should be removed.

28. B: A comma is needed after the last word of dialogue ("over") and before the quotation mark.

29. A: A comma is needed after the first item in a series (here, after "twirled"). An optional comma could also be placed after "danced," but the first comma is required.

30. A: The sentence is declarative, rather than interrogative, despite the implied question that is asked. It, therefore, requires a period as end mark. Choice B is not correct; the apostrophe is necessary to indicate possessive. Choice C, likewise, is incorrect; it does not solve the problem, and it creates a problem of agreement. Option D is not correct; it offers a false homonym choice, which is not the problem and only compounds the error. Choice E is incorrect as well; the sentence as written contains an error to be remedied.

31. C: The sentence contains a disagreement between the compound subject, which is considered plural, and the singular verb. Changing *is* to *are* solves the problem. Choice A is incorrect; the comma is needed for items in a series. Choice B is not correct; the word is correctly spelled as written. Choice D, likewise, is incorrect; it offers only a cosmetic change, not a solution to the problem of subject-verb agreement. Choice E is incorrect as well; the sentence as written clearly contains an error to be remedied.

32. D: The problem in the sentence as written is one of subject-verb agreement and colloquial or substandard English. *Some* indicates that more than one apartment complex is being discussed. It, therefore, is necessary to change both the subject and verb to plural. Choice A is incorrect; the sentence as written clearly contains an error to be remedied. Choice B is not correct; choosing an alternative spelling for the homonym does not solve the problem. Choice C is incorrect as well; it creates instead a different subject-verb agreement problem. Choice E is incorrect as well; it merely creates new problems.

33. E: The question tests students on sentence reconstruction, placing the independent clause, rather than the dependent clause, first. The first words of the dependent clause, *if pets*, must, therefore, come first. Choice A is incorrect; building a phrase around these two words is grammatically impossible. Choice B is also not correct; one cannot create a clause

from such a beginning. Option C is incorrect as well; beginning with the verb is not a good choice. Option D is not correct; the clause requires the conditional word *if* to begin.

34. B: The problem is one of correct usage of two words often confused, *affect* and *effect*. *Affect* is the verb meaning to influence and is required here. *Effect* is the noun referring to the influence. Answer A is incorrect; there is a problem to address in the sentence. Option C is also incorrect; it creates a subject-verb agreement problem. Option D is not correct; it does not address the word choice, and it creates a subject-verb agreement problem. Choice E is incorrect as well; changing *someone* to *anyone* does not solve the problem.

35. A: *Irregardless* is unacceptable English, though it is often used. The word does not truly exist. The correct term is *regardless*. Choice B is not correct; the word *licensing* is correctly spelled as it is written in the sentence. Option C is also incorrect; the sentence is declarative and thus requires a period as the end mark rather than a question mark. Option D is not correct; the sentence does not contain extra commas. The first separates the dependent clause; the others are needed for items in a series. Choice E is incorrect as well; the sentence contains an error to be corrected.

Section 5

1. C: Each kitten eats 3 cans of food per day (or 1 1/2 cans twice a day), which would be 9 cans a day for all kittens combined, or 63 cans for the week (9 x 7 = 63). Since the owner left 60 cans, 3 more are needed.

2. E: Carina's take-home money totaled $92, which was 40% of the total sales price. The total sales price can be calculated by dividing $92 by 0.40 (or multiplying 92 by 100/40), which results in $230.

3. E: Just as flipping a coin any number of times could result in the same outcome (heads or tails) each time, ordering randomly (if such a thing is possible) is no guarantee that all

flavors will eventually be ordered. This is different from problems in which people select a jelly bean out of a pot and remove it from consideration for the next selection; because jelly beans are removed from consideration, that scenario ensures that all jelly beans will eventually be chosen.

4. A: In any triangle, the sum of all angles must equal 180 degrees. Answer choice A (45 degrees), when added to the measures of the other two angles (45 degrees and 90 degrees), produces the required total of 180 degrees. Answer choices B, D, and E would produce a total greater than 180 degrees, while answer choice C would produce a total of less than 180 degrees. The answer can be calculated by subtracting the two known angles (45 degrees and 90 degrees) from the desired total (180 degrees). The resulting answer, 45 degrees, is the measure of the remaining angle and the answer to the problem.

5. C: If it takes four "z"s to reach the equivalent of one "y," then y must be larger than z. Choices B and E can be eliminated because they are equivalent statements; saying that y is larger than z is the same as saying that z is smaller than y, and since there can be only one correct answer to the problem, neither B nor E can be the correct solution. A is incorrect (that is, the statement is true) because 3x must be equivalent to 4z, since both are equivalent to y. Because this statement is true, answer choice D (that z is smaller than x) must also be true, since we now know that it takes four "z"s to reach the equivalent of only three "x"s.

6. C: The whole pizza is a circle, and since one side of a slice (measured from the center of the circle to the outside) is 5.5 inches long, 5.5 can be determined to be the radius of the circle. The area of a circle is calculated by multiplying pi (3.14) by the square of the radius (or the radius times itself), which in this case is 5.5 x 5.5 = 30.25. So, 3.14 x 30.25 = 94.985, which rounds to 95 square inches.

7. C: Three percent is calculated by multiplying the amount of the certificate of deposit by 0.03, and adding this interest to the base amount (or by multiplying the base amount by 1.03). So, after the first year, the total amount will be $500 + ($500 x 0.03), or $500 x 1.03,

which is $515. In the second year, the new base amount is $515, and $515 + ($515 x 0.03), or $515 x 1.03, comes out to $530.45. In the third year, the new base amount is $530.45, and $530.45 + ($530.45 x 0.03), or $530.45 x 1.03, comes out to $546.36. Therefore, after three years, the total amount is more than $45 greater than the amount he started with.

8. B: To calculate the GPA, first multiply the number of As x 4 (4 x 4 = 16), the number of Bs by 3 (2 x 3 = 6), and the number of Cs by 2 (1 x 2 = 2). The subtotals are then added together (16 + 6 + 2 = 24). One also needs the total number of courses: since she earned an A in four courses, a B in two courses, and a C in one course, she must have taken seven courses total (4 + 2 + 1 = 7). One then divides the weighted GPA determined above by the number of courses to calculate the GPA: 24 divided by 7 = 3.43.

9. (24) First solve for b. If 3a + 5b = 98 and a = 11, then b = 13. Therefore, a + b is 11 + 13. The final answer is 24.

10. (30) The answer is found by dividing the volume of the rectangle (15 x 9 x 6) by the volume of the square (3 x 3 x 3). 810 divided by 27 is 30.

11. (35) A rectangle's area is length times width. Here, length is 5x and width is x so $5x^2$ = 245 and x^2 = 49. Therefore, x = 7 and the longest side is 35 inches.

12. (8) Rate = distance/time. Distance is 14. Time is 1 hour and 45 minutes, or 1 ¾, or 7/4. 14/7/4 = 14 x 4/7 = 8.

13. (16) To solve this problem, first set up the equation: (4 + 7 + 9 + x)/4 = 9. Multiply both sides by four to solve: 20 + x = 36. Therefore, x = 16.

14. (25) If the ratio of pennies to nickels is 2:6, the ratio of the pennies to the combined coins is 2:2+6, or 2:8. This is ¼ or, expressed as a percentage, 25%.

15. (8) The largest prime factor of 42 is 7 and the smallest is 1. The sum of the two is 8.

16. (5) Use long division to determine how many times 12 goes into 137 (11 times) and see what remains. There is a remainder of 5.

17. (55) Larry gave away ¼ + 1/5 = 5/20 + 4/20 = 9/20 of his candy, so he had 11/20 left. 11/20 = 55/100 = 55%.

18. (75) 18 people did not complete the climb. 18/24 = ¾ = 75%.

Section 6

1. D: The only choice in which the first word of the pair fits the context of the sentence is (D), so all other choices can be eliminated.

2. C: The first blank in this sentence needs to be something that would be embarrassing to the subject of the sentence. Chicanery, gaffe, and effrontery meet this requirement. Of those three choices, choice (C) has the second word, reclusive, that most compellingly describes a potential behavior or reaction someone might exhibit after being publicly embarrassed.

3. B: The blank in this sentence needs to describe something that the calls did to the realtor. The only word that fits this need is inundated. The agent was inundated, or swamped, with calls.

4. C: "Wrong answer" is a clue that indicates a negative word. *Belittled* means to *criticize*. All the other answer choices have a positive connotation and, therefore, do not fit the intended meaning of the sentence.

5. A: *Deforestation* would have a negative effect on the rainforest: therefore, *perished* is the only word that makes sense in the context of the sentence.

6. C: "Easygoing" is the word clue here. Find the word that indicates a similar personality trait. Demeanor and personality work best here. If someone is *easygoing*, you most likely do not want to *destroy* them. *Befriend* works best in the second blank, making Choice C the correct answer.

7. A: Death is usually associated with sadness and grief, resulting in melancholy. Both choices A and B have words that seem to fit the first blank answer space. However, a monument is not built to criticize the deceased, but to memorialize or praise them. Therefore, Choice A is the best answer.

8. D: Misbehavior does not usually exhilarate or embroil (excite or involve). It can depress or infuriate those who observe it. Use the clue "calm down" to narrow the remaining choices down to the word *infuriate*. Generally, a person does not need to calm down when they are already depressed. *Infuriated* is the right word choice here.

9. C: The first paragraph states that the main purpose of DST it to make better use of daylight.

10. A: Energy conservation is discussed as a possible benefit of DST, not a negative effect of it.

11. D: The first paragraph states that DST involves setting clocks forward one hour in the spring and one hour backward in the fall.

12. B: The last sentence in paragraph four notes that agricultural and evening entertainment interests have historically been opposed to DST.

13. D: The passage gives examples of both good and bad effects extra daylight can have on health.

14. E: The sixth paragraph notes that DST is observed in only some regions of Brazil.

15. C: The last paragraph of the passage notes that DST can lead to peculiar situations, and relays an anecdote about the effect of DST on the birth order of twins.

16. C: If $30,000,000 is gained over 7 weeks, each week has a gain of 1/7 of that, or $4,200,000.

17. B: In the second paragraph, the author asserts that Benjamin Franklin suggested DST as a way to save candles.

18. B: Tip number 2 best answers this detail question. The tip recommends that those who drink whole milk gradually switch to fat-free milk. Since the question asks about ways to reduce saturated fat and calories, using skim milk in the place of water does not address the issue being raised.

19. A: The author uses headings to organize the passage. While the headings are bold print, such font is not used to organize the passage (i.e. notify the reader of what information is forthcoming), but rather to draw the reader's eyes to the headings.

20. C: Tip number 2 bests answers this detail question. Reduced fat milk contains 2% fat.

21. B: Statement I and Statement II are both true statements about calcium rich foods. Canned fish, including salmon with bones, is recommended as a calcium rich food. Cheese is mentioned as a lactose-free alternative within the milk group. Statement III is false. According to the passage, condensed cream soups should be made with milk, not water.

22. D: The best choice for this question is choice (D). The other options would clarify information for minor details within the passage and would provide little new information for the reader. However, food recommendations for those who do not consume milk products are listed under a separate heading, and lactose intolerance is the only reason listed. The reader can deduce that this is a main idea in the passage and the definition of "lactose intolerance" would help explain this main idea to the reader.

23. E: The author's style is to give facts and details in a bulleted list. Of the options given, you are most likely to find this style in a health textbook. A tourist guidebook would most likely make recommendations about where to eat, not what to eat. An encyclopedia would list and define individual foods. A friendly letter would have a date, salutation, and a closing.

Section 7

1. D: Isolate a: $a = 8b + 6 + 16$. Thus, $a = 8b + 22$. Next add 3 to both side of the equation: $a + 3 = 8b + 22 + 3 = 8b + 25$.

2. D: Angles around a point add up to 360 degrees. Add the degrees of the given angles: $72°$ $+ 110° + 58° = 240°$. Then subtract from $360° - 240° = 120°$. Remember to divide $120°$ in half, since the question is asking for the degree measure of one angle, angle d.

3. B: Translate this word problem into a mathematical equation. Let Janice's weight $= x$. Let Elaina's weight $= x + 23$. Let June's weight $= x + 14$. Add their weights together and subtract 25 pounds:

$= x + x + 23 + x + 14 - 25$

$= 3x + 37 - 25$

$= 3x + 12$.

4. B: Add the 14 blue, 6 red, 12 green and 8 purple buttons to get a total of 40 buttons. If 25 buttons are removed, there are 15 buttons remaining in the bag. If the chance of drawing a red button is now $1/3$, divide 15 into thirds to get 5 red buttons remaining in the bag. The original total of red buttons was 6; so $6 - 5 = 1$: one red button was removed, choice (B).

5. D: This equation is asking you to multiply three algebraic expressions. When multiplying more than two expressions, multiply any two expressions (using the foil method), then multiply the result by the third expression. Start by multiplying:

$(y + 1)(y + 2) = (y \times y) + (y \times 2) + (1 \times y) + (1 \times 2)$

$= y^2 + 2y + y + 2$

$= y^2 + 3y + 2$

Then multiply the result by the third expression:

$(y^2 + 3y + 2)(y + 3) = (y^2 + 3y + 2)(y) + (y^2 + 3y + 2)(3)$

$= (y^3 + 3y^2 + 2y) + (3y^2 + 9y + 6)$

$= y^3 + 3y^2 + 2y + 3y^2 + 9y + 6$

$= y^3 + 3y^2 + 3y^2 + 9y + 2y + 6$

$= y^3 + 6y^2 + 11y + 6$

6. D: The area of a parallelogram is base X height or $A = bh$, where b is the length of a side and h is the length of an altitude to that side. In this problem,

$A = 6 \times 4$; $A = 24$. Remember, use the length of BE, not the length of CD for the height.

7. B: Use the Pythagorean Theorem to solve this problem: $a^2 + b^2 = c^2$ where c is the hypotenuse while a and b are the legs of the triangle.

$5^2 + 12^2 = c^2$

$25 + 144 = 169$

$\sqrt{169} = 13$.

8. C: To solve this problem, first calculate how many gallons each toilet uses in 375 flushes:

3.2 X 375 = 1,200 gallons

1.6 X 375 = 600 gallons

The problem is asking for the difference, so find the difference between the regular toilet and the low-flow toilet:

1,200 – 600 = 600 gallons. Note that you could also find the difference in water use for one flush, and then multiply that amount by 375:

3.2 – 1.6 = 1.6

1.6 X 375 = 600.

9. E: Use the formula for probability to solve this problem:

Probability = Number of Desirable Outcomes / Number of Possible Outcomes

Because there are effectively multiple events – the roll of each die is its own event – you must multiply all the possible outcomes for each die. Thus, to determine the number of possible outcomes, multiply the number of sides on dice exponentially by the number dice:

$6^5 = (6 \times 6 \times 6 \times 6 \times 6) = 7{,}776$

There is one desirable outcome: rolling all sixes. Probability = $^1/_{7{,}776}$

10. B: Remember to use the order of operations when simplifying this equation. The acronym *PEMDAS* will help you remember the correct order: Parenthesis, Exponentiation, Multiplication/Division, Addition/Subtraction.

$4(6 – 3)^2 – (-2)$

First, simplify the parentheses: $4 \times 3^2 – (-2)$

Next, simplify the exponent: $4 \times 9 – (-2)$

Then multiply: $36 – (-2)$

Finally, subtract: $36 – (-2) = 36 + 2 = 38$

The PEMDAS method is used to simplify multiple equations in this practice test.

11. B: Angles that form a straight line add up to 180 degrees. Such angles are sometimes referred to as being "supplementary."

$60 + 2x = 180$

$2x = 120$

$x = 60$

12. E: To solve for *n*, you have to isolate that variable by putting all of the other terms of the equation, including coefficients, integers, and variables on the other side of the equal sign. Add *p* to each side of the equation:

$4n – p = 3r$

$4n – p (+ p) = 3r (+ p)$

$4n = 3r + p$

Divide each term by 4:

$4n/4 = 3r/4 + p/4$

$n = 3r/4 + p/4$

13. E: An equilateral triangle has three sides of equal length. If each side is 4 inches long, the perimeter of the triangle is 12 inches. A square has four sides of equal length. Since its perimeter also must equal 12 inches, divide 12 by 4: $12 \div 4 = 3$,

14. C: Find the common denominator of $^3/_8$ and $^{13}/_{24}$.

$^3/_8 \times ^3/_3 = ^9/_{24}$

$^{13}/_{24} \times ^1/_1 = ^{13}/_{24}$

The value in the triangle must be greater than $^9/_{24}$ and less than $^{13}/_{24}$. Choice (C), $^5/_{12}$, when expressed as the equivalent fraction $^{10}/_{24}$, is correct.

15. A: The sum of the measures of the angles in a triangle equals 180°. Use the numbers given in the figure to make the following equation:

$6x + 8x + 4x = 180$

$18x = 180$

$x = 10$

16. D: Use the formula for circumference:

Circumference = $\pi \times$ diameter (π is approximately equal to 3.14).

To give the best estimate, round to the nearest whole number:

3.14 rounds to 3

12.2, the diameter, rounds to 12

$3 \times 12 = 36$

Section 8

1. C: An obstacle could be insuppressible, mountainous, or insurmountable, so any of these choices could fit the first blank. Choice D is incorrect because licentious doesn't fit the context of the first blank answer space. However, retention and indolence do not fit in the context of the second blank answer space, so they can be ruled out. Choice C is the best answer and makes the sentence meaningful

2. B: The goal is to go around the world in a hot air balloon. Circumscribe means to limit or restrict and does not fit the sentence meaning. Circulate means to distribute and makes no sense in context. Circumambulate means to walk around but it is unlikely that anyone would "ambulate" around the world. Circumnavigate means to travel completely around, and reflects the sentence's intended meaning . Circumnavigate is the best answer.

3. D: "Bad decision" relates to the weather conditions. Adverse means unfavorable, and therefore makes Choice D the best answer. Affable is a word that means very agreeable or personable and doesn't work here. Onerous or burdensome is closer in meaning but not as relevant as the word adverse. Meanwhile, the weather is never malleable, that is, able to be shaped the way we want it.

4. B: "Predictable" is the clue. Banal means to be common place or predictable. It can also be boring, capable of putting the students to sleep.

5. A: Ethereal means to be light or spiritual. Ethereal music could be mysterious and float through the trees. Ethereal is often used to describe music that touches the soul, making that word the best choice.

6. D: We're looking for a word capable of making a bad situation worse. Exacerbate means to increase in severity. It is the only answer choice that makes sense and imparts meaning to the sentence.

7. D: Answer choice (D) best summarizes the main topic discussed here. While choices (C) and (E) are both facts given about Tubman in the passage, they are not the main focus. Choices (A) and (B) are not discussed in the passage.

8. A: The author uses phrases like Tubman "was determined to gain her freedom" and "worried that she and the other slaves on the plantation were going to be sold" as he or she describes Tubman's life as a slave. The reader can deduce that author included these descriptions to illustrate why Harriet Tubman wanted to escape slavery, choice (A). The other answer choices are either insignificant details or not explained in the passage.

- 197 -

9. B: Paragraph 3 describes why Harriet Tubman suffered from seizures. An overseer threw a heavy weight and hit her in the head. The weight nearly crushed her skull. She suffered from seizures for the rest of her life. The best answer choice is (B).

10. C: Clue words such as "as a child" and "later," as well as the use of dates, indicates that this passage is arranged in chronological order.

11. A: Paragraph 4 explains how Araminta Ross became known as Harriet Tubman. She married John Tubman and took his last name. She also changed her first name to her mother's name.

12. C: A stanza consists of a grouping of lines, set off by a space, that usually has a set pattern of meter and rhyme. This poem has six stanzas.

13. E: Personification is a metaphor in which a thing or abstraction is represented as a person. Personification is used throughout this poem. However, of the answer choices given, line 11 is the best choice. The author personifies spring as a female.

14. A: The fifth stanza gives clues to whom "we" refers.

"Not one would mind, neither bird nor tree

If mankind perished utterly"

"We" is referencing mankind, choice (A).

15. B: This is an example of a rhymed verse poem. The last two words of each line rhymes in every stanza. A sonnet is a poem of fourteen lines following a set rhyme scheme and logical structure. Often, poets use iambic pentameter when writing sonnets. A free verse poem is written without using strict meter or rhyme. A lyric poem is a short poem that expresses personal feelings, which may or may not be set to music. An epic poem is a long narrative poem, usually about a serious subject. It often contains details of heroic deeds and events significant to a culture or nation.

16. A: Answer choice A gives the best summary of the poem, demonstrated by the phrases about things in nature not caring about war or the extinction of humanity.

17. D: Answer choice (D) best summarizes what this passage is mainly about.

18. E: Answer choice (E) is the best title for the passage because it best summarizes all the topics covered in the passage. The other answer choices are details mentioned in the passage, but are not the main focus of the passage.

19. A: The last paragraph of the passages answers this detail question.

20. C: The third paragraph of the passage answers this detail question.

Section 9

1. C: "Kids" is the subject of the sentence. As written, the sentence states that "they," which refers back to the subject and thus refers to kids, are displayed near checkout lines. Choice (C) corrects this confusion and clarifies that "snacks" are displayed near checkout lines.

2. C: The subject of the sentence is "I," so only Choices (C) or (E) could be correct. Choice (E) is awkward, so Choice (C) is the better option.

3. E: The correct usage here is "our" rather than "us."

4. C: The original sentence is redundant and wordy.

5. C: The syntax of the original sentence is fine, but a comma after *said* but before the open-quotation mark is required.

6. E: In the original sentence, the modifier is placed too far away from the word it modifies.

7. E: The verb structure should be consistent in a sentence with parallel structures.

8. A: The singular pronoun *her* is appropriate since the antecedents are joined by *or*. Also, the subjunctive verb form is required to indicate something indefinite.

9. B: The combination of *hardly* and *not* constitutes a double negative.

10. C: The plural demonstrative adjective *these* should be used with the plural noun *sorts*.

11. A: This sentence contains a number of parallel structures that must be treated consistently.

12. A: In this sentence, *whose* is the appropriate possessive pronoun to modify *opinion*.

13. E: This question is about parallel structure. If fighting "was" a popular sport in the past, then it "is" in the present. Choice E has the proper parallel structure.

14. D: The original sentence contains incorrect pronoun reference. It implies that "Johnny Rotten's first number 1 song" was "born John Joseph Lydon." The correct answer should show that it was Johnny Rotten who was born as John Joseph Lydon. Choice D corrects the error.

Practice Test #3

Practice Questions

Section 1
Essay

Time – 25 minutes

Consider the issue presented below:

A study conducted by a non-profit foundation examined teenagers' socializing on the Internet. The study found that most teenagers turn on their computers as soon as they return home from school every day, and that they use Facebook and similar sites, as well as instant messaging, to stay in touch with their circle of friends almost constantly throughout the day. Since many parents believe that internet socializing is a waste of time, the teenagers were subject to many restrictions, but they usually found ways to circumvent these rules.

Assignment:

Should internet socializing by teenagers be restricted? Write an essay developing your point of view on this issue. Support your position with evidence from your reading, experience, and personal observations.

Time -- 25 minutes

20 Questions

For this section, solve each problem and decide which of the choices given is the best.

1. If $10x + 2 = 7$, what is the value of $2x$?

(A) 0.5
(B) -0.5
(C) 1
(D) 5
(E) 10

2. A long distance runner does a first lap around a track in exactly 50 seconds. As she tires, each subsequent lap takes 20% longer than the previous one. How long does she take to run 3 laps?

(A) 180 seconds
(B) 182 seconds
(C) 160 seconds
(D) 72 seconds
(E) 150 seconds

A number N is multiplied by 3. The result is the same as when N is divided by 3. What is the value of N?

(A) 1
(B) 0
(C) -1
(D) 3
(E) -3

4. The letter H exhibits symmetry with respect to a horizontal axis, as shown in the figure, as everything below the dashed line is a mirror image of everything above it. Which of the following letters does NOT exhibit horizontal symmetry?

(A) C
(B) D
(C) E
(D) I
(E) Z

5.

y	-4	31	4	68	12
x	-2	3	0	4	2

Which of the following equations satisfies the five sets of numbers shown in the above table?

(A) $y = 2x^2 + 7$

(B) $y = x^3 + 4$

(C) $y = 2x$

(D) $y = 3x + 1$

(E) $y = 6x$

6. In a rectangular x,y coordinate system, what is the intersection of two lines formed by the equations $y = 2x + 3$ and $y = x - 5$?

(A) (5, 3)
(B) (8, 13)
(C) (-4, 13)
(D) (-8, -13)
(E) (2, -7)

7. A function *f(x)* is defined by *f(x)* = 2*x*² + 7. What is the value of 2*f(x)* – 3?

    (A) $4x^2 + 11$

    (B) $4x^4 + 11$

    (C) $x^2 + 11$

    (D) $4x^2 + 14$

    (E) $2x^2 + 14$

8. John buys 100 shares of stock at $100 per share. The price goes up by 10% and he sells 50 shares. Then, prices drop by 10% and he sells his remaining 50 shares. How much did he get for the last 50?

    (A) $5000

    (B) $5500

    (C) $4900

    (D) $5050

    (E) $4950

9. The sides of a triangle are equal to integral numbers of units. Two sides are 4 and 6 units long, respectively; what is the minimum value for the triangle's perimeter?

    (A) 10 units

    (B) 11 units

    (C) 12 units

    (D) 13 units

    (E) 9 units

10. The two shortest sides of a right triangle are 6 and 8 units long, respectively. What is the length of the perimeter?

    (A) 10 units
    (B) 18 units
    (C) 24 units
    (D) 14 units
    (E) 36 units

11. What is the area of an isosceles triangle inscribed in a circle of radius r if the base of the triangle is the diameter of the circle?

   (A) r^2

   (b) $2r^2$

   (c) πr^2

   (d) $2\pi r$

   (e) $2\pi + 1$

12. A regular deck of cards has 52 cards. What is the probability of drawing three aces in a row?

   (A) 1 in 52
   (B) 1 in 156
   (C) 1 in 2000
   (D) 1 in 5525
   (E) 1 in 132600

13.

Lemons	35%
Sugar	20%
Cups	25%
Stand improvements	5%
Profits	15%

Herbert plans to use the earnings from his lemonade stand according to the table above, for the first month of operations. If he buys $70 worth of lemons, how much profit does he take home?

   (A) $15
   (B) $20
   (C) $30
   (D) $35.50
   (E) $40

14. A teacher has 3 hours to grade all the papers submitted by the 35 students in her class. She gets through the first 5 papers in 30 minutes. How much faster does she have to work to grade the remaining papers in the allotted time?

(A) 10%
(B) 15%
(C) 20%
(D) 25%
(E) 30%

15. A sailor judges the distance to a lighthouse by holding a ruler at arm's length and measuring the apparent height of the lighthouse. He knows that the lighthouse is actually 60 feet tall. If it appears to be 3 inches tall when the ruler is held 2 feet from his eye, how far away is it?

Eye   Ruler   Lighthouse

(A) 60 feet
(B) 120 feet
(C) 240 feet
(D) 480 feet
(E) 960 feet

16. If p and n are positive consecutive integers such that $p > n$, and $p + n = 15$, what is the value of n?

(A) 5
(B) 6
(C) 7
(D) 8
(E) 9

17. What is the area of a square inscribed in a circle of radius r?

(A) r^2
(B) $2r^2$
(C) $2r^3$
(D) $2\pi r$
(E) $4r^2$

18. Forty students in a class take a test that is graded on a scale of 1 to 10. The histogram in the figure shows the grade distribution, with the *x*-axis representing the grades and the *y*-axis representing the number of students obtaining each grade. If the mean, median, and modal values are represented by *n, p,* and *q*, respectively, which of the following is true?

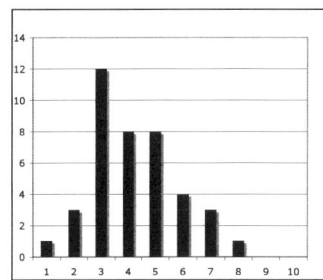

    (A) n > p > q
    (B) n > q > p
    (C) q > p > n
    (D) p > q > n
    (E) q > n > p

19. Referring again to the figure for Question 18, if the top 10% of students are to receive a grade of A, what is the minimum test score required to get an A?

    (A) 10

    (B) 9

    (C) 8

    (D) 7

    (E) 6

20. If *x* and *y* are positive integers, which of the following expressions is equivalent to $(xy)^{7y} - (xy)^{y}$?

    (A) $(xy)^{6y}$

    (B) $(xy)^{7y-1}$

    (C) $(xy)^{y}[(xy)^{7} - 1]$

    (D) $(xy)^{y}[(xy)^{6y} - 1]$

    (E) $(xy)^{7y}$

Section 3.

Time – 25 minutes

24 Questions

> *Questions 1-5*: Each sentence below has one or more blanks. Beneath each sentence are five words or sets of words labeled A through E. Choose the word or set of words that best fits the meaning of the sentence as a whole.

1. Because land is limited and the population is constantly growing, real estate _____ typically _____ over time.

    (A) development ... falters
    (B) values ... increase
    (C) brokers ... compromise
    (D) agents ... magnify
    (E) properties ... classify

2. Infants and toddlers may sometimes have _____ sleep patterns due to growth spurts and rapid changes in their physical development.

    (A) cohesive
    (B) natural
    (C) erratic
    (D) fanciful
    (E) mistaken

3. The maintenance workers handle quite a range of _____: irrigation repair, plumbing, and general maintenance.

    (A) visitors
    (B) flowers
    (C) attractions
    (D) responsibilities
    (E) distractions

4. Natural fibers like organic cotton and bamboo are _____ and _____ without the use of harsh chemicals.

    (A) manufactured ... deployed
    (B) woven ... filtered
    (C) commissioned ... forgotten
    (D) pilfered ... used
    (E) grown ... processed

5. _____ mattresses contain many toxic substances, such as flame-retardants, adhesives and chemical foams, which are not present in natural latex rubber.

    (A) Conventional
    (B) Queen-sized
    (C) White
    (D) Maximum
    (E) Significant

Questions 6-10 are based upon the following two passages:

> *Passage 1:* Ever since Henry Ford created the Model T and established the first assembly line, the love affair between Americans and the automobile has been unparalleled. From coast to coast, from driveway to highway, it seems that almost everyone in the country takes to the roads on weekends to "see the USA," as the old advertising jingle once intoned. People climb into sedans and coupes, trucks and SUVs, as individuals, couples, and whole families go off on sightseeing excursions, or to visit friends and family. This romance with the car has led to the development of a great industry, produced great technical advances, and has been responsible for the creation of the world's greatest highway system. The interstate highways, built during the Eisenhower administration, now link our cities and manufacturing centers, providing America with a great economic advantage. Although automobiles are found in every other country as well, America's relation to the car is truly unique.

> *Passage 2:* Los Angeles provides us with a great example of how the automobile has undermined the development of public transportation in the

- 209 -

USA. The Los Angeles basin is spread out over a wide area completely paved and cut by a grid of streets and avenues, and today it is crisscrossed by freeways that run in every possible direction. It is said that in order to sell more cars and fuel, the automobile and oil industries actively sought to suppress the development of public transportation, such as trams and light rail in the mid twentieth century. The number of cars in the basin went up five-fold from 1950 to 1990, while the population tripled and mass transit languished. The result is that today the roads are constantly clogged with too many cars, most of them occupied by only the driver. With fuel prices soaring, the cost of commuting to work and of routine business operations, such as shipping and deliveries, is out of control. Ringed by mountains that trap exhaust emissions, the basin is often the site of some of the world's worst air pollution. The driver's eyes may be assaulted by garish billboards, but the beautiful, far-off mountains remain hidden behind the smog.

6. The purpose of Passage 1 is to

    (A) Compare two hypotheses
    (B) Resolve a controversy
    (C) Refute the thesis of Passage 2
    (D) Describe a social phenomenon
    (E) Support a ruling

7. The purpose of Passage 2 is to

    (A) Refute a hypothesis
    (B) Analyze a social problem
    (C) Support a hypothesis
    (D) Compare two trends
    (E) Assign blame for a problem

8. The word "languish" on Line 23 indicates that mass transit in Los Angeles

    (A) Wasn't used much
    (B) Grew more slowly than elsewhere
    (C) Was a slow way to travel
    (D) Was inconvenient
    (E) Grew more slowly than it should have

9. The author of Passage 1

(A) Fully discusses the impact of the automobile
(B) Is an apologist for the automobile culture
(C) Likes to visit friends in his car
(D) Voted for Eisenhower
(E) Drives on interstate highways

10. These two passages have in common that they

(A) Examine only one side of an issue
(B) Compare various aspects of the impact of automobiles
(C) They carefully analyze the impact of cars
(D) Suggest ways of dealing with cars
(E) Compare cars to mass transit

Questions 11-17 are based on the following passage.

Zakov arrived at the prison shortly before noon, having dropped Ludmilla off at the train station beforehand. He was relieved to find that Gorkhi had gone, for he found the chief to be a bit bombastic, and was disposed to conduct the interrogation without him if he could. He was fortunate in that one of
5   Gorkhi's men recognized him and let him in to see the prisoner.

He found the student sitting on the floor of a damp cell. The only illumination came from a small window set high in the concrete wall. Nasadev raised red-rimmed eyes when the door opened, amid a clatter of keys and bolts, and Zakov found himself again amazed at the lad's
10   homeliness, rendered even more pathetic by features wet and swollen from weeping. Somewhat discomfited by his own reaction, he forced a smile.

The young man attempted to rise, but was hindered by the shackles about his ankles.

"Please, remain seated," offered Zakov quickly, and joined him on the
15   earthen floor. "Ludmilla delivered your note. Just what kind of trouble are you in?"

"They are saying that I killed Olga," the youth replied, his face contorted in a grimace. "As if I could! I adored her," he cried. "But things look rather bleak for me, the way they found my knife. Only you can help me,
20   sir. I know your reputation. Please help me, sir! Not for myself, but for my family. This will destroy them..." His tears welled up again, and he sniffled and dabbed vainly at his cheeks with his dirty sleeve.

Zakov looked at him sympathetically. Ludmilla had told him the student was pathetic, and she was right: the ordinary face, the weak chin,
25   now damp with tears and perspiration, made him seem a most unlikely suitor. He must have been deeply hurt by Olga's rejection. And she, delicate, spirited and appealing, must have found his attentions tedious and annoying, the more so since he had neither fortune nor prospects. Had she derided him, mocked him, gone too far setting trial to his devotion until he killed her?
30   "What made the police suspect you?" he asked.

- 212 -

"They talked to some of the other students, and my name came up."
Nasadev was almost whining. "One of them found a letter I had written, but
never sent. He told the others. It made me angry, but I guess it was foolish of
me to think that such a girl could ever like someone like me. But she was nice
35   to me, nonetheless. She told me about the play she was writing, and how she
hoped to go to Moscow."

Zakov found that his heart went out to the poor, infatuated youth. But
pity was not enough to resolve the charges the student faced.

"So the other students mentioned your name," he continued. "That
40   explains why the police spoke to you, but it's not enough for them to bring
charges. What else happened?"

Nasadev replied plaintively, fixing Zakov with an imploring look. "We
had a quarrel. In the park. The day before they found her. Someone must
have heard us and they told the police. They came and searched my room in
45   the dormitory, found my diary, some other letters I had written."

"What was the quarrel about?"

Nasadev hesitated, would not meet Zakov's eye. "I had asked her to
marry me. I know it was crazy...how could I support her? But I was afraid
she would stop seeing me, that someone else would come along and I would
50   lose her."

"And what did she say?" Zakov knew the answer already, but he had
to ask.

"She turned me down. She didn't laugh at me, but she turned me
down. And that was in my diary, too." Nasadev was practically inaudible.

55   Zakov stayed a while longer, asked a few more questions. A deep
sadness seemed to fill his heart as he regarded the small cell and its single
miserable occupant. Finally, with a shiver, he called for Gorkhi's man to open
the door and he left.

11. Zakov thought that Gorkhi, the police chief, was

   (A) considerate
   (B) pretentious
   (C) enthusiastic
   (D) moderate
   (E) uncooperative

12. The passage suggests that Nasadev's cell

   (A) was modern
   (B) had only a bed in it
   (C) was spacious
   (D) was unfurnished
   (E) smelled badly

13. Nasadev's frame of mind during the interview can best be described as

   (A) resigned
   (B) courageous
   (C) determined
   (D) desperate
   (E) calculating

14. Zakov's attitude toward Nasadev appears to be one of

   (A) disgust
   (B) magnanimity
   (C) sympathy
   (D) malice
   (E) anger

15. Nasadev's look, when he replies to Zakov's question (Line 42) implies that he is

   (A) begging for help
   (B) about to collapse
   (C) looking for words
   (D) exhausted
   (E) unable to think clearly

16. When the student tells Zakov that Olga's rejection of his proposal was in the diary found by the police (Line 54), his voice

(A) whines
(B) is hard to hear
(C) contains a signal
(D) breaks
(E) is a whisper

17. By the time Zakov leaves, he

(A) has proved Nasadev's guilt
(B) is angry at Gorkhi
(C) has found a possible motive for Nasadev to have committed the murder
(D) has proved Nasadev's innocence
(E) is late for a meeting with Ludmilla

Questions 18-24 are based on the following passage.

Living things such as animals and plants consist of immense clusters of atoms organized into compartments called cells. A man consists of nearly ten octillion (ten followed by 27 zeros) atoms. This huge collection of atoms is capable of consciousness, joy and suffering, the ability to distinguish

5   between good and evil, and many other complex emotional behaviors. The organism itself is characterized by an almost limitless variety of traits. Most remarkably, all living things are formed in a manner that allows them to survive and to reproduce in some existing environment.

There are two schools of thought that seek to explain this remarkable

10   habituation of organisms and their environments. Transcendentalists invoke preternatural forces, to which they assign responsibility for the design of complex organisms that are uniquely adapted to equally complex environments. Mechanists, in contrast, submit that life can be understood without recourse to such forces. They hold that complex biological

15   structures are simply highly evolved chemical or physical phenomena. The foremost proponent of the mechanist viewpoint was Darwin, who painted a picture of the evolution of modern organisms through gradual changes

between ancestors and offspring, changes that took place over billions of years of evolutionary history.

20   Darwin posited natural selection as the driving mechanism for these changes. Natural selection is the differential reproduction of organisms that are more or less adapted to the environments they inhabit. It is strictly a biological phenomenon, since it depends upon reproduction. It requires a mechanism for the generation of diversity, which is provided by the

25   molecular process of mutation. In addition, it requires that selected traits be heritable. In the years since it was first described, natural selection has been successful in explaining an enormous catalog of biological observations and has become one of the fundamental pillars of modern biology.

        Although Darwin is its best-known proponent, the mechanist school

30   of thought has its roots in the earlier work of the seventeenth century scholar René Descartes, the same man who gave us the Cartesian coordinate system used in mathematics. The Cartesian approach to biology was a strictly reductionist one that sought to describe life completely in terms of the chemical and physical processes that make up living organisms. Ultimately,

35   this approach would reduce all of biology to the status of a specialized branch of chemistry. And it must be said, there have been some outstanding successes based upon this approach. The elucidation of the role of nucleic acids in the transmission of hereditary traits is a prime example.

        Many molecular biologists have come to believe that once the study of

40   biological chemistry has progressed sufficiently, even the most complex biological phenomena will be able to be predicted based upon simple physicochemical interactions. But while the importance of molecular biology is beyond argument today, there are those who doubt that all of biology can be deduced from simple laws of chemistry and physics. Such doubts need

45   not have recourse to transcendental explanations, but point instead to the increasing complexity of biological organization. The biosphere is organized into a hierarchy of levels: molecular, cellular, organismic, populational,

ecosystemic. Each of these levels is characterized by laws and principles of

its own. Thus, the psychological axioms that govern the interactions of living

50   things at the levels of organisms and populations are simply not relevant to

the laws of chemistry, which describe the molecular and cellular levels. In

this view, while simple chemical principles may underlie all of biology, they

are insufficient to explain the interactions that take place at higher levels. In a

sense, the laws that govern biology have evolved, as well as the organisms

55   and systems that they describe.

18. The organism referred to in Line 10 is

(A) Man
(B) Any huge collection of atoms
(C) Any living collection of atoms
(D) Things capable of distinguishing between good and evil
(E) Living things made of ten octillion atoms

19. Which pairing best represents the two schools of thought described in the second

paragraph of the text?

(A) Large and small
(B) Moral and amoral
(C) Complex and simple
(D) Theoretical and practical
(E) Supernatural and chemical

20. The best synonym for the word "posit" used in Line 20 is

(A) Position
(B) Postulate
(C) Assume
(D) Claim
(E) Reject

21. The purpose of the third paragraph is to

(A) Prove that evolution is correct
(B) Describe a process that is necessary for the theory of evolution to be correct
(C) Discuss biology and reproduction
(D) Repeat some things that Darwin said
(E) Refute claims made by transcendentalists

22. According to the text, René Descartes was

(A) The first mechanist
(B) The foremost mechanist
(C) A chemist
(D) A reductionist
(E) A teacher

23. A strict reductionist would believe that

(A) Psychological axioms can be explained by chemistry and physics
(B) Ecosystems are characterized by laws and principles of their own
(C) Transcendental explanations are required to understand psychology
(D) Living organisms are made up of physical processes
(E) Darwin and Descartes worked together

24. The overall purpose of the passage is best described as

(A) A defense of Darwin's theory
(B) Drawing a contrast between Darwin and Descartes
(C) A description of the role of mathematics in biology
(D) Showing the context of evolutionary theory in biology
(E) Showing the limits of natural selection

Section 4.

Time – 25 minutes

35 Questions

Questions 1-11: A portion of each of the following sentences is underlined. Following the text there are five ways of phrasing the underlined material. Choice A is the original text; the other four choices are different. Select the choice that produces the best sentence.

1. When are the Federal government, the State and the city going to realize that they cannot raise its rates and taxes year after year?

    (A) that they cannot raise its rates and taxes
    (B) that they cannot raise it's rates and taxes
    (C) that they can not raise its rates and taxes
    (D) that rates and taxes can not be raised by them
    (E) that they cannot raise their rates and taxes

2. Since she moved into her own place, Janet has been doing her own cooking.

    (A) has been doing
    (B) does
    (C) did
    (D) is doing
    (E) will do

3. To help install the software, instructions provided by the manufacturer.

    (A) instruction provided by the manufacturer.
    (B) instruction manuals provided by the manufacturer.
    (C) manufacturer-provided instructions.
    (D) instructions were provided by the manufacturer.
    (E) instructions was provided by the manufacturer.

4. A daily routine of physical exercise is not only good for one's health, <u>and also improves one's mental outlook.</u>

    (A) and also improves one's mental outlook.
    (B) but also improves one's mental outlook.
    (C) as it also improves one's mental outlook.
    (D) and improves one's mental outlook, too.
    (E) and would foster an improved mental outlook, as well.

5. King Lear is one of Shakespeare's greatest <u>plays it explores the nature of human suffering and kinship</u>.

    (A) plays it explores the nature of human suffering and kinship.
    (B) plays as it explores the nature of human suffering and kinship.
    (C) plays who explores the nature of human suffering and kinship.
    (D) plays; it explores the nature of human suffering and kinship.
    (E) plays when it explores the nature of human suffering and kinship.

6. Given the price of going to a movie, <u>a ticket usually costs</u> around $10, more and more people are renting films to watch at home.

    (A) a ticket usually costs
    (B) which is usually
    (C) which usually costs
    (D) which can be usually
    (E) a ticket costs

7. Composers of modern popular music can feature syncopated rhythms, multiple-part harmonies, <u>and used electronic instrument orchestration.</u>

    (A) and used electronic instrument orchestration.
    (B) and they use electronic instrument orchestration.
    (C) and orchestration using electronic instruments.
    (D) as well as using electronic instrument orchestration.
    (E) with electronic instrument orchestration.

8. As the price of gasoline increased during the past ten years, American car manufacturers should have realized that a drop in the demand for gas-guzzling vehicles <u>was likely and would probably happen</u>.

    (A) was likely and would probably happen.
    (B) was likely and would probably happen in the future.
    (C) would be likely and would probably happen soon.
    (D) was a likely thing.
    (E) was likely.

9. As more and more of the younger generation moves to Tokyo to find work, <u>the remaining population of Japan's rural towns gets older and older.</u>

    (A) the remaining population of Japan's rural towns gets older and older.
    (B) the average population of Japan's rural towns gets older and older.
    (C) the population of Japan's rural towns continues to get older.
    (D) the population remaining in Japan's rural towns gets older and older.
    (E) the remaining population of Japan's rural towns gets older.

10. When the team got off the plane, <u>they were met by a throng of adoring fans</u>.

    (A) they were met by a throng of adoring fans.
    (B) they were met by many adoring fans,
    (C) it was met by a throng of adoring fans.
    (D) they encountered a throng of adoring fans.
    (E) it meets a throng of adoring fans.

11. One of Shakespeare's favorite forms was the sonnet, <u>it is a fourteen line poem</u> written in iambic pentameter.

    (A) it is a fourteen line poem
    (B) a fourteen-line poem
    (C) it is a fourteen-line poem
    (D) these were fourteen-line poems
    (E) it was a fourteen line poem

Questions 12-29: The following sentences test your ability to recognize grammar and usage errors. Each sentence contains either one error or no error at all. No sentence contains more than one error. The error, if there is one, is underlined. If the sentence contains an error, select the underlined part that must be changed to make the sentence correct. If the sentence is correct, select choice E.

12. It was (A) <u>really cold out</u>, and (B) <u>her and I</u> were (C) <u>freezing because</u> (D) <u>we had on</u> only light jackets. (E) <u>No error</u>.

13. (A)<u>With the construction</u> of the Aswan Dam, (B)<u>sediments normally carried</u> by the Nile were no longer (C)<u>able to fertilize</u> the lower Nile Valley, and farm production (D)<u>fell off drastically</u>. (E) <u>No error</u>.

14. It always made Daniel (A)<u>really angry</u> when (B)<u>he fails</u> to get (C)<u>better than a</u> ninety percent score on (D)<u>one of his</u> tests. (E) <u>No error</u>.

15. Kevlar vests (A)<u>are very effective</u> (B)<u>at reducing</u> projectile velocity, (C)<u>thereby</u> reducing casualties (D)<u>among troops</u> and law enforcement officers. (E) <u>No error</u>.

16. Every morning (A)<u>at about eight</u>, the (B)<u>sound of</u> car horns (C)<u>blaring in</u> the streets (D)<u>indicate</u> the beginning of the rush hour. (E) <u>No error</u>.

17. Two of the pathology students (A)<u>had gotten</u> into an argument about (B)<u>which tissue</u> was (C)<u>the better</u> indicator of the (D)<u>time of death</u>. (E) <u>No error</u>.

18. When Charles Lindbergh (A)<u>flew</u> his plane – the Spirit of Saint Louis – (B)<u>nonstop across</u> the Atlantic in 1927, he (C)<u>had been</u> the first person (D)<u>to do so</u>. (E) <u>No error</u>.

19. The specification (A)<u>called for</u> 17-gauge steel, but (B)<u>the only</u> (C)<u>kinds</u> we (D)<u>have available</u> is lighter than that. (E) <u>No error</u>.

20. <u>Me and him</u> used to be the (B)<u>best of friends</u>, until he started (C)<u>hanging out</u> with the people from North Avenue (D)<u>and acting</u> like a fool. (E) <u>No error</u>.

21. John (A)<u>worked</u> out in his basement gym (B)<u>every morning</u>, then he (C)<u>takes</u> a shower, has breakfast, and goes to work (D)<u>in his car</u>. (E) <u>No error</u>.

22. The construction crew (A) were hanging (B) nets under the scaffolding to protect (C) passers-by from (D) the danger of falling materials. (E) No error.

23. (A)Most of the 200,000 drivers (B) who cross the bridge (C) every day (D) has to wait more than ten minutes at the toll booths. (E) No error.

24. Luis said that (A)he and his (B)team of volunteers provided (C)about 100 pounds of food to each of the families (D)that came to the shelter for help. (E) No error.

25. (A)During the Renaissance, (B) both the visual arts and literature (C) did enjoy a great (D) infusion of new themes and technical advances. (E) No error.

26. Dodson is a (A) terrific talent (B) whose agent says that he can (C) turn a team around and (D) whose said to be looking for a ten year contract at five million dollars. (E) No error.

27. It never (A) ceases to amaze me how people can be so gullible (B) that they spend thousands of hard-earned dollars (C) on psychics, palmists, and other forms of (D) chicanery. (E) No error.

28. (A)Over the winter, the general managers and their (B) staffs work hard (C) in order to meet the needs of (D) they're teams for the next season. (E) No error.

29. There was never (A) the slightest doubt (B)but that he would accept the offer, which was (C)tantamount to a (D)doubling of his previous salary. (E) No error.

- 223 -

Questions 30-35: The following passage is an early draft of an essay. Some parts of the passage need to be rewritten. Read the passage and select the best answers for the questions that follow. Some questions are about particular sentences or parts of sentences and ask you to improve sentence structure or word choice. Other questions ask you to consider organization and development. In choosing answers, follow the requirements of standard written English.

Questions 30-35 refer to the following passage:

(1)One of the pioneer sculptors of the nineteenth century was Honore Daumier (1810-1879). (2)He is well-known particularly for caricature heads that were created between 1830 and 1832. (3)His later works anticipate the work of Rodin, what with their highly cut-out surfaces offset by studied, flowing poses.

(4)Although Daumier was one of the first modern sculptors, his work did not serve as an influence to later artists. (5)This is because nearly all of the other artists of the time hardly ever got to see any of it. (6)This is also true of the sculpture of Degas, who was known as a painter rather than a sculptor, and whose sculpture also was not widely exhibited at the time. (7)And yet, Degas was clearly the greatest sculptor of the era. (8)His bronze casts of dancers and horses retain the layered feeling of the wax models that were their first versions. (9)His more complex scenes seem like crosses between sculpture and painting. (10)When looked at more closely, they display a feeling of mass that the painted canvas cannot by itself convey. (11)It is the interplay between the separate masses in these scenes that involves the viewer and gives them their sense of intrigue.

30. Which is the best version of the underlined part of sentence 2 (reproduced below)?

He is well-known particularly for caricature heads that were created between 1830 and 1832.

    (A) (as it is now)
    (B) He is well known, particularly
    (C) He is particularly well known
    (D) He is well known particularly
    (E) He was well-known particularly

31. Which is the best version of the underlined part of sentence 3 (reproduced below)?

His later works anticipate the work of Rodin, what with their highly cut-out surfaces offset by

studied, flowing poses.

    (A) (as it is now)
    (B) of Rodin, what with highly cut-out surfaces
    (C) of Rodin; what with highly cut out surfaces
    (D) of Rodin, with highly cut-out surfaces
    (E) of Rodin, with cut-out surfaces

32. In context, which is the best revision of sentence 5 (reproduced below)?

This is because nearly all of the other artists of the time hardly ever got to see any of it.

    (A) (as it is now)
    (B) This is because it was almost never exhibited at the time.
    (C) His work was hardly ever exhibited.
    (D) This is because they hardly ever saw any of it.
    (E) This is because it was hardly ever seen by the other artists.

33. In context, which is the best way to revise sentence 6 (reproduced below)?

This is also true of the sculpture of Degas, who was known as a painter rather than a sculptor,

and whose sculpture also was not widely exhibited at the time.

    (A) Add "In addition," to the beginning of the sentence.
    (B) Delete the words ", and whose sculpture was also not widely exhibited at the time."
    (C) Change the words "sculpture of Degas" to read "work of Degas".
    (D) Change "This is also true" to "This was also true".
    (E) Delete the words "rather than a sculptor".

34. Which sentence is best inserted after sentence 7?

(A) A large body of his sculpted works can be found in museums today.
(B) His paintings were famous even before the time of his death.
(C) He wrote several books and articles about art that were read by his contemporaries.
(D) He made sculptures out of bronze, stone, and even wood.
(E) You can see pictures of his work in many books.

35. Which is best added to the beginning of sentence 10?

(A) Increasingly,
(B) And yet,
(C) Beneath this,
(D) However,
(E) It follows that

Time – 25 minutes

18 Questions

For this section, solve each problem and decide which of the choices given is the best.

Questions 1-4: please refer to the following Venn diagrams. Venn diagrams are sets of overlapping or non-overlapping circles that show the relationships between sets of objects.

A.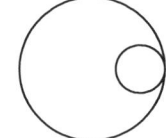

B.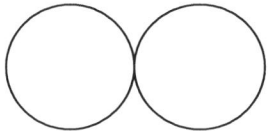

C.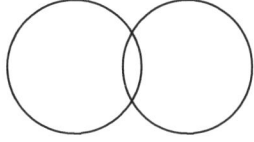

D.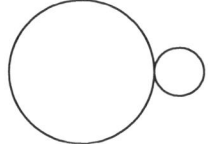

E.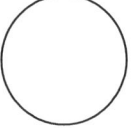

1. A class contains an equal number of boys and girls. All the children are wearing socks. Most of the girls wear white socks, but only a few of the boys do. Which of the diagrams best represents the sets of boys wearing white socks and girls wearing white socks?

    (A) A
    (B) B
    (C) C
    (D) D
    (E) E

2. Please refer to the class described in Question 1. Which of the diagrams best describes the sets of girls wearing white socks and girls wearing socks of other colors?

    (A) A
    (B) B
    (C) C
    (D) D
    (E) E

3. Please refer to the class described in Question 1. Which diagram best describes the sets of boys wearing socks and boys wearing white socks?

    (A) A
    (B) B
    (C) C
    (D) D
    (E) E

4. Please refer to the class described in Question 1. Which of the diagrams best describes the set of girls wearing socks?

    (A) A
    (B) B
    (C) C
    (D) D
    (E) E

5. If $x^2 - 4 = 45$, then x could be equal to

  (A) 9
  (B) 5
  (C) 3
  (D) -4
  (E) -7

6. The average of 3 numbers $x, y,$ and z is 23. The average of three numbers $a, b,$ and c is

also 23. What is the average of all six numbers $a, b, c, x, y,$ and z?

  (A) 11.5
  (B) 23
  (C) 34.5
  (D) 46
  (E) 5.25

7. Determine the area of a rectangle with a length of 7 feet and a height of 9 feet.

  (A) 81 ft.2
  (B) 63 ft.2
  (C) 32 ft.2
  (D) 31.5 ft.2
  (E) 16 ft.2

8. If the statement "All of Joan's daughters have brown eyes" is true, which of the following

statements must also be true?

  (A) If Lupe has blue eyes, then she is not Joan's daughter.
  (B) If Sandra has brown eyes, then she is Joan's daughter.
  (C) If Carmella is not Joan's daughter, then she does not have brown eyes.
  (D) If Laura is Joan's daughter, then she has blue eyes.
  (E) If Walter is Joan's son, then he has brown eyes.

For Questions 9-18: Use the grids on the answer sheet page where you have answered Questions 1-8.

9. What is the value of the product of the first two prime numbers that are larger than 10 divided by the largest prime number smaller than 30?

10. Determine the perimeter of a rectangle with a length of 5 inches and a height of 7 inches.

11. Determine which figure has a greater area: Figure A, which is a circle with a diameter of 9 inches, or Figure B, which is a circle with a radius of 5 inches.

12. In the system of equations below, what is the value of $2x + y$?

$$2x + y + 7a = 50$$
$$2x + y + 5a = 40$$

13. In the system of equations below, what is the value of y?

$$x^2 + y^2 = 24$$
$$2x^2 + 3y^2 = 52$$

14. A commuter survey counts the people riding in cars on a highway in the morning. Each car contains only one man, only one woman, or both one man and one woman. Out of 25 cars, 13 contain a woman and 20 contain a man. How many contain both a man and a woman?

15. In the graph shown below, what is the slope of a line through the origin that will intercept the line $y = f(x)$ at a point where $y = 2$?

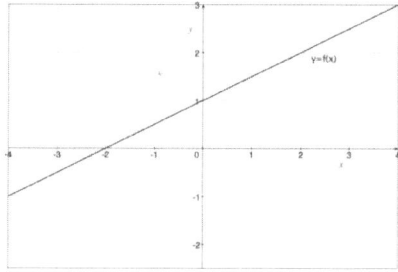

16. If x is a negative integer and $5 < |x - 3| < 7$, what is the value of $|x|$?

17. There are 400 fish in a tank. 150 are blue, 150 are red, and the remainder are brown. Tranh dips a net into the tank and pulls out one fish. The probability of pulling out any single fish is the same. What is the probability, in percent, that the fish he pulls out is brown?

18. Five less than three times a number is equal to 58. What is the number?

Section 6

Time -- 25 minutes

23 Questions

Questions 1-8: Each sentence below has one or more blanks, each blank indicating that something has been omitted. Beneath each sentence are five words or sets of words labeled A through E. Choose the word or set of words that, when inserted in the sentence, best fits the meaning of the sentence as a whole.

1. A surge protector siphons off _____ voltage in electric circuits that can be _____ to electronic devices.

    (A) electric .. salutary
    (B) excess .. harmful
    (C) capable .. damaging
    (D) considerable .. refractory
    (E) malignant .. repentant

2. Anne felt that taking vitamin supplements daily would have a _____ effect, that is, it would promote health and well-being.

    (A) cognitive
    (B) mercurial
    (C) salubrious
    (D) loquacious
    (E) acrimonious

3. Hanley's race car produced a _____ amount of noise, more than any of the other vehicles.

    (A) prodigal
    (B) redundant
    (C) quantitative
    (D) prodigious
    (E) frivolous

4. Most of us did not feel that Carmen was cut out to be a trial lawyer, given her _____ for

_____ any kind of confrontation.

    (A) ambition .. influencing
    (B) regard .. negotiating
    (C) habit .. protesting
    (D) penchant .. avoiding
    (E) feeling .. analyzing

5. Samantha had a _____ appetite and went through all the food we had brought in one

night.

    (A) fragile
    (B) minute
    (C) voracious
    (D) fastidious
    (E) misogynous

6. She had many reasons for choosing to _____ a year of her life putting her _____

variety of skills to work for others.

    (A) donate .. immense
    (B) lose .. single
    (C) summarize .. cavernous
    (D) fashion .. industrial
    (E) sanitize .. vigorous

7. Anthony was a _____ individual, whose _____ eyes always gave the impression

that he had recently lost something dear to him.

    (A) gleeful .. laughing
    (B) hot-headed .. flashing
    (C) tall .. glinting
    (D) lugubrious .. mournful
    (E) malevolent .. squinting

8. He could not understand Della's _____, her constant locking of doors and windows as if

to protect herself from some _____ threat.

    (A) paranoia .. unspecified
    (B) glee .. manifest
    (C) actions .. global
    (D) kindness .. imminent
    (E) candor .. qualified

Questions 9-10 are based on the following passage.

The grey clouds had been threatening rain all morning. Farnham shuffled down the street from the lounge, staring absently at the ground before him, his colorless clothes blending into the background of dirty concrete and broken stone walls. Those who saw him could barely conceal their reaction to his countenance: eyes would narrow or be averted, nostrils would sniff suspiciously, shoulders would be raised as if the rain had already begun to fall. He was a regular on these sidewalks, stumbling home in the colorless morning after a night made still more somber by its strained and failed reach for animation.

9. Farnham's walk is described as a "shuffle" (Line 2) or "stumble" (Line 6). These words establish which aspect of his personality?

    (A) His sense of humor
    (B) His resiliency
    (C) His short temper
    (D) His melancholy
    (E) His restraint

10. The reaction to Farnham of people who saw him on the street, described in Lines 3-5, indicates that they were

    (A) commiserative
    (B) sympathetic
    (C) mistrustful
    (D) altruistic
    (E) affectionate

Questions 11-12 are based on the following passage.

Physically, at least, Hal seemed a most unlikely burglar. He looked more suited to the life of a professional athlete, the practitioner of some brutal contact sport. His legs were the trunks of ancient trees and his white shirts – he always wore white shirts – spread across is belly like the winter snow on an Alberta meadow. And yet, at night, he moved across the glistening rooftops on cat's feet, a passing shadow, dropping unseen to the topmost landing of fire escape or outside stairway. There, by starlight, his soft hands found whatever open window had been left unguarded and, in a

matter of seconds, he would disappear inside.

11. The reference to tree trunks (Line 3) shows that

(A) Hal's legs were brown
(B) Hal's legs were made of wood
(C) Hal's wore pants the color of bark
(D) Hal's legs were very large
(E) Hal's skin was wrinkled

12. Line 6 describes Hal as moving on cat's feet. This means that

(A) he had fur-lined shoes
(B) he moved very quietly
(C) he stepped on a cat
(D) he was disguised
(E) he moved on all fours

Questions 13-23 are based on the following passages.

Passage 1

One of the major challenges facing the renewable fuel industry is the

variability in the pricing of traditional fossil fuels such as petroleum and coal.

Those seeking to develop alternative energy sources such as wind and solar

power and, especially, electric cars face an uncertain marketplace in which

the price of their chief competitors, gasoline and oil, is virtually impossible to

predict. This makes investing in renewable alternatives a risky business: at

what price must alternative fuels be offered in order to gain a share of the

market? Government can stabilize this situation – and encourage the

development of green energy sources – by taxing petroleum-based fuels to

establish a minimum price at the pump.

Recently, we have seen the price of gasoline, and of other fossil fuels,

driven to new highs. This price increase has been driven by increasing

demand, as millions of consumers in places like China and India have

increased their buying power and joined Americans and Europeans behind

the steering wheels of automobiles. The price of a barrel of oil has risen, creating a favorable investing environment for the development of green alternatives like electric cars. But, although the long-term trend for the price of oil is definitely upwards, it seems that every time the price peaks something happens to drive it back down. This might be an economic recession that reduces demand, a release of stockpiled oil by the government to increase supply, or simply a price manipulation by the oil companies themselves. Whatever the cause, these price reductions sour the picture for companies working on renewable energy sources, and their research and development programs often falter and stop. What can be done to forestall this boom-and-bust cycle and provide a stable investing environment to encourage the development of renewable energy?

One possibility is to use the government's power of taxation to establish a minimum price for gasoline at the pump. Under such a scheme, a variable excise tax would be triggered whenever the price of gasoline were to fall below a minimum amount, for example $3 a gallon. The amount of this tax would vary, so as to keep the price at the minimum, and the proceeds could be returned to consumers by reducing the overall income tax, or by providing tax credits to those who would be most impacted by the higher gasoline price: truck and taxi drivers, or businesses involved in the delivery of various products. And, with a stable price at the pump, companies developing electric and hybrid vehicles would be encouraged to continue their efforts with a clear view of potential profits ahead.

Passage 2

Various proposals have been put forth to encourage the development of renewable energy sources, especially in the realm of transportation, where fossil fuel-burning cars release damaging pollutants into the atmosphere while rendering the country increasingly dependent on foreign suppliers. Recently, demand from emerging economies in India, China, and even Latin America has driven the price of gasoline to new highs, adding another reason to encourage the development of alternative energy sources. Consumers are

- 236 -

suffering from high energy prices, and they are asking, "What can the government do to keep prices under control while protecting the environment?"

We would all love to see the advent of the electric car, or of an auto that burns U.S.-produced ethanol without producing any environmental pollutants. But development has been slow. Small companies with novel approaches spring up whenever the price of oil goes up, but they seem to falter whenever it comes back down. And the major car companies, with few exceptions, have not placed a sustained effort behind the development of vehicles that burn alternatives to oil. Indeed, American car companies seem to fill their showrooms with gas-guzzlers, and their investments in electric or hybrid vehicles have not sufficed to move these programs forward rapidly. It seems that we need a policy that can encourage American ingenuity to develop forms of transportation, be they fuels or vehicles, while providing the American consumer with affordable pricing at the pump.

The government can do this without interfering with the working of the free market. After all, free market capitalism has been the driving force for innovation in this country since its inception. Any form of price manipulation, however laudable its goals, tends to have the opposite effect of that intended. Fortunately, government has at its disposal a powerful tool to encourage innovation without directly interfering in the market.

This tool is the tax credit. Tax credits reduce the amount of tax that companies have to pay on their profits, in exchange for their investments in new technologies. By providing tax credits to companies that invest in the development of electric vehicles, alternative fuels, or other forms of green energy, government could encourage the development of those products without overtly interfering in the marketplace. Consumers would ultimately benefit from a greater choice of transportation and fuel alternatives, and the goal of developing environmentally clean energy sources would be served.

13. The authors of both passages are in agreement that

    (A) taxes should be used to reduce the use of oil.
    (B) businesses working on renewable energy should get a tax break.
    (C) a tax strategy should be used to encourage development of renewable energy
        sources.
    (D) prices of traditional fossil fuels should be kept high.
    (E) fuel prices should be manipulated.

14. A main point of disagreement between the two authors is whether or not

    (A) demand from China is driving up fuel prices.
    (B) consumers should be protected from high fuel prices.
    (C) it is desirable to develop an electric car.
    (D) high fuel prices should be maintained at the pump.
    (E) companies providing renewable energy should make a profit.

15. The author of Passage 2 would probably consider the proposal in Passage 1 as

    (A) another good way to help develop renewable energy sources.
    (B) interference in the free market that is unlikely to succeed.
    (C) useful only for developing electric cars and not for meeting other energy needs.
    (D) an example of why tax policies are never a good way of guiding an industry.
    (E) something that would work together with his own proposal.

16. In Line 23, "sour the picture" most nearly means

    (A) manipulate prices
    (B) lower fuel prices
    (C) increase profits from existing fuels
    (D) cause irate consumers to deface walls
    (E) make future profits seem less likely

17. The purpose of the first paragraph in Passage 1 is to

    (A) complain about low prices.
    (B) establish that electric cars are good for the environment.
    (C) introduce a proposal.
    (D) show that companies developing new technologies must be able to expect a profit.
    (E) give a detailed argument in favor of a variable fuel tax.

18. The author of Passage 1 would probably say that the tax credit proposed in Passage 2

(A) is as good as the proposal in Passage 1.
(B) does not address the issue of maintaining a price structure that supports future profits.
(C) should be offered to the consumer, instead.
(D) would be too expensive.
(E) would encourage consumers to burn more gasoline.

19. The main purpose of the third paragraph of Passage 2 (Lines 64-68) is to

(A) argue against a potential alternative strategy.
(B) give a short history of free-market capitalism.
(C) distinguish low prices from price manipulation.
(D) show how the government can encourage innovation.
(E) point out errors made in the past.

20. Which of the following techniques is used by the authors of both passages?

(A) Citing well-known authorities in support of their proposals.
(B) Describing a problem and then describing a possible solution and how it would work.
(C) Attacking people who disagree with their proposals.
(D) Wrapping their proposal in patriotic arguments.
(E) Belittling the ability of government to deal with economic problems.

21. The main purpose of the last paragraph of Passage 1 (Lines 28-38) is to

(A) show that the variable excise tax is the only way to foster renewable fuel development.
(B) show that truck drivers would not suffer under the variable tax proposal.
(C) offer one solution to the problem of uncertain profits slowing development of alternative fuels.
(D) establish a price of $3 a gallon for gasoline.
(E) argue that only government can encourage development of renewable energy sources.

22. The main purpose of the last paragraph of Passage 2 (Lines 69-76) is to

(A) explain what a tax credit is.
(B) offer a solution to the problem of slow development of alternative energy source.
(C) argue in favor of electric vehicles.
(D) give consumers a choice of taxes to pay.
(E) summarize the arguments made in the preceding paragraphs of the passage.

23. Which best characterizes the overall relationship between the two passages?

    (A) Both argue for similar approaches to encourage renewable energy development.
    (B) Passage 2 rejects the proposal made in Passage 1.
    (C) Passage 1 rejects the proposal made in Passage 2.
    (D) The proposal made in Passage 1 includes the one made in Passage 2.
    (E) The proposal made in Passage 2 includes the one made in Passage 1

Time – 20 minutes

16 Questions

For this section, solve each problem and decide which of the choices given is the best.

1. If $= (6a)x^2 = 30$, then $ax^2 =$

(A) 6
(B) 5
(C) 30
(D) $\dfrac{\sqrt{30}}{6}$
(E) 3

2. In a game played with toothpicks, players A and B take turns removing toothpicks from a row on a table. At each turn, each player must remove 1, 2, or 3 toothpicks from the row. The object is to force the other player to remove the last toothpick. If there are 6 toothpicks in the row, which of the following moves ensures a win?

(A) Remove 1
(B) Remove 2
(C) Remove 3
(D) Remove 1 or 2
(E) There is no way to ensure a win

3. Which equation is represented by the graph shown below?

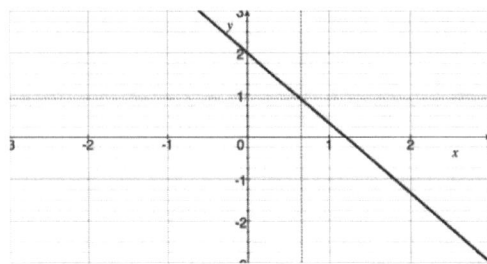

(A) $y = \dfrac{5}{3}x + 2$

(B) $y = -\dfrac{5}{3}x - 2$

(C) $y = -\dfrac{5}{3}x + 2$

(D) $y = \dfrac{5}{3}x - 2$

(E) $y = 5x + 2$

4. Determine the volume of a rectangular box with a length of 5 inches, a height of 7 inches, and a width of 9 inches.

(A) 445.095 in.3

(B) 315 in.3

(C) 45 in.3

(D) 35 in.3

(E) 21 in.3

5. What is the greatest integer value of y for which $5y - 20 < 0$?

(A) 5
(B) 4
(C) 3
(D) 2
(E) 1

6. A water sprinkler covers a circular area with a radius of 6 feet. If the water pressure is increased so that the radius increases to 8 feet, by approximately how much is the area covered by the water increased?

(A) 2 square feet
(B) 4 square feet
(C) 36 square feet
(D) 64 square feet
(E) 88 square feet

7. The graph below, not drawn to scale, shows a straight line passing through the origin. Point P1 has the (x,y) coordinates (-5,-3). What is the x-coordinate of point P2 if its y-coordinate is 3?

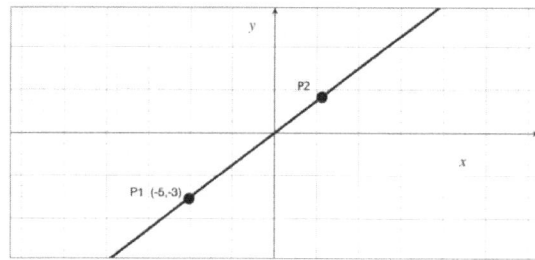

(A) 0.8
(B) 1
(C) 5
(D) 3
(E) 8

8. If $ax^2 + by = 0$, which of the following must be true?

(A) $ax^2 = by$
(B) $ax^2 = \sqrt{by}$
(C) $ax = b\sqrt{y}$
(D) $ax^2 = -by$
(E) $ax = b\sqrt{y}$

9. Equal numbers of dimes and pennies are placed in a single row on a table. Which of the following must be true?

    (A) Every dime will be next to a penny.
    (B) If there are two dimes at one end of the row, two pennies must be next to one another.
    (C) If there is a dime at one end of the row, there must be a penny at the other end.
    (D) Every penny will be between two dimes.
    (E) If there are two pennies together anywhere in the row, there must be dimes at both ends.

10. A satellite in a circular orbit rotates around the Earth every 120 minutes. If the Earth's radius is 4000 miles at sea level, and the satellite's orbit is 400 miles above sea level, approximately what distance does the satellite travel in 40 minutes?

    (A) 1400 miles
    (B) 9210 miles
    (C) 4400 miles
    (D) 4120 miles
    (E) 8000 miles

11. Which of the following equations best describes the straight line in the graph below? Note that a and b are non-zero constants.

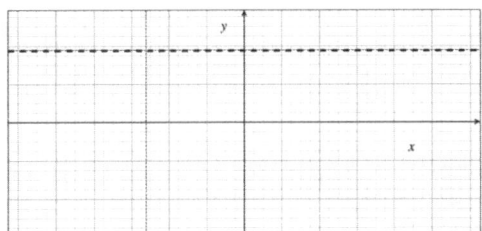

    (A) $y = x$
    (B) $x = a$
    (C) $y = ax + b$
    (D) $y = b$
    (E) $x = 0$

12. A ticket agency finds that demand for tickets for a concert in a 25,000-seat stadium falls if the price is raised. The number of tickets sold, N, varies with the dollar price, p, according to the relationship $N = 25000 - 0.1p^2$. What is the lowest price at which they will sell no tickets at all?

(A) $10
(B) $25
(C) $50
(D) $500
(E) $1000

13. Refer to the equation in Question 12, which gives the relationship between ticket price and number of tickets sold. No matter how many tickets are sold, the cost of putting on the concert is $500,000. Which of the following equations can be used to calculate the profit Q made for any ticket price?

(A) $Q = 25,000p - 0.1p^3$
(B) $Q = 25,000p - 0.1p^3 - 500,000$
(C) $Q = 25,000p - 0.1p^3 - 500,000p$
(D) $Q = p(25,000 - 0..1p) - 500,000$
(E) $Q = p^2(25,000 - 0.1) - 500,000$

14. The right circular cylinder shown in the figure above has a height of 10 units and a radius of 1 unit. Points O and P are the centers of the top and bottom surfaces, respectively. A slice is cut from the cylinder as shown, so that the angle at the top, O, is 60 degrees, and the angle at the bottom, P, is 60 degrees. What is the volume of the slice?

(A) 31.4 units
(B) 5.23 units
(C) 10.47 units
(D) 7.85 units
(E) 15.7 units

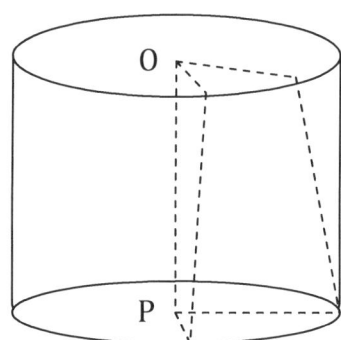

- 245 -

15. For the number set {7, 12, 5, 16, 23, 44, 18, 9, Z}, which of the following values could be equal to Z if Z is the median of the set?

    (A) 14
    (B) 11
    (C) 12
    (D) 17
    (E) 21

16. If Q is divisible by 2 and 7, which of the following is also divisible by 2 and 7?

    (A) $Q + 2$
    (B) $Q + 7$
    (C) $Q + 28$
    (D) $Q + 9$
    (E) $Q + 11$

Time – 20 minutes

19 Questions

Questions 1-6:

Each sentence below has one or more blanks, each blank indicating that something has been omitted. Beneath each sentence are five words or sets of words labeled A through E. Choose the word or set of words that, when inserted in the sentence, best fits the meaning of the sentence as a whole.

1. Jeremy was considered _____ child by his teachers because he was noisy and often stubbornly defiant.

    (A) a model
    (B) a capricious
    (C) an obstreperous
    (D) a saturnine
    (E) a brooding

2. Nesting from sea level to 2000 feet, willow flycatchers favor open or bushy areas over heavily _____ habitats.

    (A) closeted
    (B) timbered
    (C) rainy
    (D) mountainous
    (E) moribund

3. Solar flare activity is notoriously variable: _____ flare-ups may continue for days, only to be followed by lengthy periods of _____.

    (A) huge..discharge
    (B) prolix..irruption
    (C) violent..quiescence
    (D) magma..dissolution
    (E) moderate..continuance

4. A man of questionable morals, he had such a reputation for _____ that I gave _____ to nothing that he told me.

    (A) duplicity..credence
    (B) sapience..payment
    (C) incisiveness..doubt
    (D) rapaciousness..contrition
    (E) confidence..gramercy

5. After the election, the winning candidate took a _____ tone in his remarks about his _____ rival.

    (A) cathartic..malignant
    (B) conciliatory..defeated
    (C) verbose..barnstorming
    (D) laudatory..victorious
    (E) deprecatory..ululating

6. When she was angry, she would sit quietly at the back of the room, _____ at everyone.

    (A) nictating
    (B) flinching
    (C) ruminating
    (D) glowering
    (E) canvassing

Questions 7-19 are based on the following passage.

        The first photographs were based on the work of the German chemist Johann Heinrich Schulze who, in 1727, discovered that silver nitrate darkened upon exposure to light. The first "photograms" were images made by exposing silver nitrate on paper or metal surfaces. During the nineteenth
5   century, a number of researchers worked to combine this effect with various lenses in order to capture and reproduce images from different sources. The first process for making commercial images was ultimately announced in 1839 by Louis Jacques Mandé Daguerre, a French painter whose name became attached to the product, the daguerreotype.
10   The daguerreotype quickly became popular in Victorian England, where it was used, principally, for portraits. Today, as photography moves beyond the chemical capture of images onto paper and into the digital era,

other applications abound: landscapes, interiors, sports and journalism, to name but a few. And yet, the portrait remains one of the major applications for the technology.

In portraiture, as in other types of photography, the nature and characteristics of light are of the utmost importance. To the photographer, light is a living thing, dynamic and animated. But, whereas in sports or journalism, for example, the photographer must make do with the light conditions he finds when it is time to shoot, light can usually be controlled for a portrait shot. And, good lighting can make all the difference in the world in a portrait, conveying mood, revealing detail, establishing the photographer's style, even making a "mistake" seem like a bit of *panache*. Understanding light is the creative equivalent of a get-out-of-jail-free card. So much so that the professional portrait photographer expends a great deal of time and money on lights and equipment that will put him in charge.

The various lighted areas of a photograph are described as *highlights, mid-tones,* and *shadows. Specular* highlights are the brightest spots: direct reflections from the studio lights or strobes. In a portrait they are typically seen in the eyes or on the tip of the nose. From these bright portions, *diffused* highlights spread gradually into the mid-tones. At the other side of the mid-tonal range, there will be *transition areas* where the available light fades gradually into the dark shadows. If these transitions are abrupt, narrow areas, the lighting is said to be *hard light.* Hard light can give a stark effect to portraits and might be used for a craggy-faced coal miner, for example, or for black-and-white shots. Broader transitions produce *soft lighting*, and lead to a gentler mood. This type of lighting is more suitable for a wedding portrait, for example.

A wide variety of devices are available for producing and modifying the light in a photographic studio. Studio lighting has the advantage of being reproducible, so the skilled photographer can get the same results every time. Modern lighting usually consists of flash units, also called *strobes,* rather than the hot, power-hungry floodlights that used to be the norm. While this equipment can be elaborate and expensive, it doesn't have to be. A poor carpenter blames his tools, but with practice, one can get great results from a simple setup comprised of two or three lights. Studio lighting setups vary with the preferences of the photographer, but they all have a number of elements in common.

The main light that shines on the subject is called the *key light*. The camera exposure is determined by the amount of light the key throws upon the subject. The key is usually positioned off to one side of the camera, and will throw shadows across the face from the subject's nose and eyebrows. One or more *fill lights* may be used to lighten these shadowed areas and reduce image harshness. Fill lights are adjusted to throw half as much light, or less, onto the subject compared to the key. A *kicker* may be positioned to illuminate the back of the model, creating a halo effect and making the subject stand out from the background. Finally, there may be *background lights* to illuminate the background directly.

Studio photographers often use *modifiers* of one type or another to diffuse and soften the light emanating from these sources. Modifiers make the light source effectively larger, reducing shadows and broadening transition areas. The best-known light modifier is the photographer's white umbrella, which can be used to reflect light from the source onto the model, but many other types of modifiers exist. The simplest is a large piece of white cardboard, called a *fill card*. As with lights, the choice of modifiers is a matter of individual preference, and every studio photographer has his favorite combinations of lights and modifiers for achieving different effects.

Although the basic principles remain the same, the practice of photography has come a long way since the days of the daguerreotype.

7. The main purpose of this passage is

(A) give a history of photography
(B) to show that different photographers have different styles
(C) to compare portraiture with other forms of photography
(D) to contrast modern photography with the daguerreotype
(E) to give an overview of photographic portrait lighting

8. The main purpose of the first three paragraphs is to

(A) explain how daguerreotypes were made
(B) describe the different kinds of photography
(C) provide context for the discussion of portrait lighting
(D) contrast chemical and digital photography
(E) show why sports photography may not have good lighting

9. In Line 3, the word "photogram" is between quotation marks because

(A) it is something that Johann Heinrich Schulze said.
(B) it is a coined term not in common use today.
(C) it is a German word.
(D) the author wants to place emphasis upon it.
(E) it was a way of sending messages with silver nitrate at that time.

10. The phrase "light is a living thing" (Line 18) is an example of

(A) a metaphor.
(B) a simile.
(C) an exaggeration.
(D) an anthropomorphism.
(E) poetic license.

11. The word "mistake" (Line 23) is between quotation marks because

(A) it is something that someone said.
(B) it is a slang expression.
(C) it describes something that may not really be an error.
(D) all photographers make mistakes sometimes.
(E) the author doesn't want to offend anyone.

12. The phrase "Understanding light is the creative equivalent of a get-out-of-jail-free card"

(Lines 24) is an example of

    (A) a metaphor.
    (B) a simile.
    (C) an attribution.
    (D) poetic license.
    (E) hybrid vigor.

13. The main purpose of paragraph 4 is to

    (A) show the relationship between lighting and mood.
    (B) explain the difference between hard and soft light.
    (C) tell the reader what kind of lighting to use for a wedding portrait.
    (D) define a number of terms used to describe lighting features on photographs.
    (E) tell the reader where specular highlights are found.

14. The word "specular" (Line 28) is in italics because

    (A) it is a term that is being defined in the sentence.
    (B) it is a foreign word.
    (C) it is misspelled.
    (D) it is a slang expression.
    (E) it is a double-entendre.

15. The sentence (Line 43) that describes floodlights as hot and power-hungry implies that

flash units, or strobes,

    (A) are also hot and power-hungry.
    (B) are more modern than floodlights.
    (C) are more expensive than floodlights.
    (D) are not hot or power-hungry.
    (E) are more easily combined.

16. In Lines 56-57, the words "model" and "subject"

    (A) refer to the same thing.
    (B) contrast two different things that may be photographed.
    (C) contrast the front and back of the person being photographed.
    (D) are both conjunctions.
    (E) both refer to the background.

17. The main purpose of paragraph 6 is to

   (A) describe how to set the camera exposure.
   (B) tell the reader where to position a key light.
   (C) define the different types of studio lights.
   (D) distinguish between floodlights and strobes.
   (E) explain how to get a halo effect.

18. The main purpose of paragraph 7 is to

   (A) tell the reader how to use an umbrella.
   (B) explain the use of white cardboard in photography
   (C) show how to make strobes brighter.
   (D) tell the reader that different photographers have individual preferences in lighting
       equipment.
   (E) describe ways to soften the light that comes from studio strobes or floodlights.

19. After reading this passage, readers should understand

   (A) why portraits were popular in Victorian England.
   (B) the complexity of photographic portrait lighting.
   (C) why camera equipment is so expensive.
   (D) exactly how to position lights for portrait photography.
   (E) how to light a scene for landscape photography.

Section 9

Time – 10 minutes

14 Questions

> *Questions 1-14*: A portion of each of the following sentences is underlined.
>
> Following the text there are five ways of phrasing the underlined material.
>
> Choice A is the original text; the other four choices are different. Select the
>
> choice that, in your judgment, produces the best sentence.

1. Home music production equipment has become so <u>sophisticated, and</u> amateur musicians can produce recordings that are competitive with the output of professional studios.

    (A) sophisticated, and
    (B) sophisticated, also
    (C) sophisticated that
    (D) sophisticated consequently
    (E) sophisticated wherefore

2. Since people who drive while intoxicated are responsible for many injuries and deaths, <u>severely punished</u> is what they deserve.

    (A) severely punished
    (B) severe punishment
    (C) severely punishment
    (D) severeness of punishment
    (E) severity in punishment

3. Tobacco use is still very high in China, where public health officials are urging the public to stop <u>smoking which has been linked to lung cancer.</u>

    (A) smoking which has been linked to lung cancer.
    (B) smoking because it has been linked to lung cancer.
    (C) smoking on account of its being linked to lung cancer.
    (D) smoking, which has been linked to lung cancer.
    (E) smoking when it has been linked to lung cancer.

4. Even professional chefs disagree <u>about what is the best way to</u> cook a steak.

(A) about what is the best way to
(B) about, what is the best way to
(C) about how to
(D) about what the best way is to
(E) about the best way to

5. Across the country there are hundreds of thousands, if not millions, <u>of potentially</u> <u>affected families</u> by the distress of this industry.

(A) of potentially affected families
(B) of potential families affected
(C) of families potentially affected
(D) of families affected potentially
(E) of affected families

6. A ski holiday can be ruined either because of warm weather, <u>but also because</u> someone is injured in a fall.

(A) but also because
(B) but also owing to
(C) or the cause is
(D) or because of
(E) but possible because

7. Drug therapies are replacing a lot of <u>medicines as we used to know it.</u>

(A) medicines as we used to know it.
(B) medicine as we used to know it.
(C) medicines as we used to know.
(D) therapies as we used to know it.
(E) other therapies as we used to know it.

8. If you teach a child to read, <u>he or her will</u> be able to pass a literacy test.

(A) he or her will
(B) they will
(C) it will
(D) he will
(E) he or she will

9. I am mindful of preserving executive powers not only for myself, but for my predecessors as well.

    (A) predecessors as well.
    (B) predecessors, too.
    (C) forebears as well.
    (D) predecessors additionally.
    (E) successors as well.

10. Spread by a rapidly mutating virus, millions of people come down with the flu every year.

    (A) millions of people come down with the flu every year.
    (B) the flu infects millions of people every year.
    (C) and millions of people come down with the flu every year.
    (D) this causes millions of people to catch the flu every year.
    (E) this is why millions of people come down with the flu every year.

11. French cooking, which is famous for its rich sauces, makes use of more butter than other European countries.

    (A) more butter than other European countries.
    (B) butter more than other European countries.
    (C) more butter than other European cooking.
    (D) butter, which is different from other European countries.
    (E) more butter than do other Europeans.

12. When Martha showed up at the reception, it was a sudden and unexpected surprise for everyone.

    (A) it was a sudden and unexpected surprise for everyone.
    (B) it was an unexpected surprise for everyone.
    (C) it surprised everyone unexpectedly.
    (D) it was a surprise for everyone.
    (E) everyone was unexpectedly and suddenly surprised.

13. Traditional Southeast Asian cooking, augmented by Chinese, Indian, and European influences, <u>were the foundation of</u> Thai cuisine.

    (A) were the foundation of
    (B) were the foundation for
    (C) have been the foundation of
    (D) are the foundation of
    (E) was the foundation of

14. Although he originally wanted an afternoon event, it was eventually decided by Liam to have the party in the evening, when more people could come.

    (A) it was eventually decided by Liam to have the party in the evening,
    (B) Liam's eventual decision was to have the party in the evening,
    (C) Liam eventually decided to have the party in the evening,
    (D) Liam decided to eventually have the party in the evening,
    (E) Liam's eventual decision was having the party in the evening.

Answer Key

1. C: To determine this, you must solve the given equation for x. Since $10x + 2 = 7$, we have

$x = \dfrac{7-2}{10} = \dfrac{5}{10} = 0.5$, and $2x = 1$. Alternately, $10x = 5$; divide both sides by 5 to get $2x = 1$.

2. B: If the first lap takes 50 seconds, the second one takes 20% more, or

$T_2 = 1.2 \times T_1 = 1.2 \times 50 = 60$ seconds, where T_1 and T_2 are the times required for the first and second laps, respectively. Similarly, $T_3 = 1.2 \times T_2 = 1.2 \times 60 = 72$ seconds, the time required for the third lap. Add the times for the three laps: 50 + 60 + 72 = 182.

3. B: Zero is the only number that gives the same result when multiplied or divided by a factor. In each case, the answer is zero.

4. E: All of the other capital letters shown are symmetrical with respect to a horizontal axis drawn through the middle as in the H shown in the figure. Only Z is not symmetrical in this respect.

5. B: The easiest pair to test is the third: $y = 4$ and $x = 0$. Substitute these values in each of the given equations and evaluate. Choice B gives 4 = 0 + 4, which is a true statement. None of the other answer choices is correct this number set.

6. D: At the point of intersection, the y-coordinates are equal on both lines so that $2x + 3 = x - 5$. Solving for x, we have $x = -8$. Then, evaluating y with either equation yields $y = 2(-8) + 3 = -16 + 3 = -13$ or $y = -8 - 5 = -13$

7. A: Evaluate as follows: $2f(x) - 3 = 2(2x^2 + 7) - 3 = 4x^2 + 14 - 3 = 4x^2 + 11$.

8. E: The stock first increased by 10%, that is, by $10 (10% of $100) to $110 per share. Then, the price decreased by $11 (10% of $110) so that the sale price was $110-$11 = $99 per share, and the sale price for 50 shares was 99 x $50 = $4950.

9. D: The sides of a triangle must all be greater than zero. The sum of the lengths of the two shorter sides must be greater than the length of the third side. Since we are looking for the minimum value of the perimeter, assume the longer of the two given sides, which is 6, is the longest side of the triangle. Then the third side must be greater than 6 – 4 = 2. Since we are told the sides are all integral numbers, the last side must be 3 units in length. Thus, the minimum length for the perimeter is 4+6+3 = 13 units.

10. C: The hypotenuse must be the longest side of a right triangle, so it must be the lengths of the other two sides that are given as 6 and 8 units. Calculate the length of the hypotenuse, H, from the Pythagorean Theorem: $H^2 = S_1^2 + S_2^2 = 6^2 + 8^2 = 36 + 64 = 100$, which yields $H = 10$ and the perimeter equals 10+6+8 = 24.

11. A: The area of a triangle equals half the product of base times height. Since the base passes through the center, we have base = 2 r and height = r, so that the area A is

$$A = \frac{r \times 2r}{2} = r^2$$

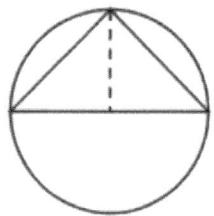

12. D: The probability of getting three aces in a row is the product of the probabilities for each draw. For the first ace, that is 4 in 52, since there are 4 aces in a deck of 52 cards. For the second, it is 3 in 51, since 3 aces and 51 cards remain; and for the third, it is 2 in 50. So the overall probability, P, is $P = \frac{4}{52} \times \frac{3}{51} \times \frac{2}{50} = \frac{24}{132600} = \frac{1}{5525}$.

13. C: If $70, the amount used to buy more lemons, represents 35% of Herbert's earnings, then 1% corresponds to $\dfrac{\$70}{35} = \$2$, and 15% corresponds to $2 X 15 = $30.

14. C: She has been working at the rate of 10 papers per hour. She has 30 papers remaining and must grade them in the 2.5 hours that she has left, which corresponds to a rate of 12 papers per hour. $\dfrac{12}{10} = 120\%$ of her previous rate, or 20% faster.

15. D: The ratio of the ruler's height to the distance from eye to ruler, which is the tangent of the angle subtended at the eye by the ruler's height, must be the same as the ratio of the lighthouse's height to its distance, which is the tangent of the same angle. Since 3 inches is ¼ foot, we have $\dfrac{1/4}{2} = \dfrac{60}{D}$, and solving for D gives $D = \dfrac{2 \times 60}{1/4} = 4 \times 120 = 480$ feet.

16. C: This can be solved as two equations with two unknowns. Since the integers are consecutive with $p > n$, we have $p - n = 1$, so that $p = 1 + n$. Substituting this value into $p + n = 15$ gives $1 + 2n = 15$, or $n = \dfrac{14}{2} = 7$.

17. B: The square is one whose diagonal corresponds to the diameter of the circle. This allows calculation of the side a by the Pythagorean Theorem, where the diameter is $d = 2r$: $d^2 = 4r^2 = a^2 + a^2$. Thus, $4r^2 = 2a^2$, and the area of the square $a^2 = 2r^2$.

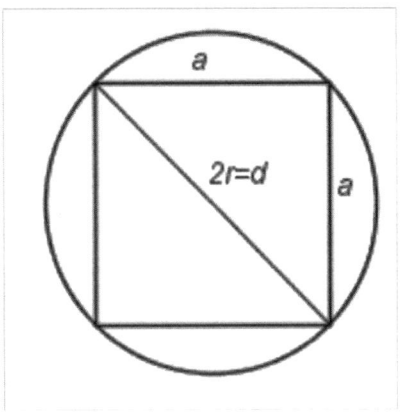

18. A: The mean, or average of the distribution can be computed by multiplying each grade by the number of students obtaining it, summing, and dividing by the total number of students. Here, $n = 4.2$. The median is the value for which an equal number of students have received higher or lower grades. Here, $p = 4$. The mode is the most frequently obtained grade, and here, $q = 3$.

19. D: 10% of the tested population of 40 students is 4 students. Four students got grades of 7 or higher.

20. D: Remember that when you multiply like bases, you add the exponents, and when you divide like bases, you subtract the exponents.

$$(xy)^{7y} - (xy)^y = (xy)^y[(xy)^{7y-y} - 1] = (xy)^y[(xy)^{6y} - 1]$$

Section 3

1. B: The word "because" at the beginning of the sentence indicates that a reason is being given for the condition described in the second clause. Answer B logically completes the sentence: increasing demand for a limited resource leads to an increase in its value.

2. C: The second part of the sentence suggests that growth spurts and rapid physical changes disturb sleep patterns, so they are not likely to be "natural." Of the remaining choices, only "erratic" makes sense, and it provides a good description of a disturbed pattern.

3. D: The list that follows clearly describes tasks for which maintenance workers may be responsible as part of their jobs.

4.E: The sentence describes the advantages of natural organic fibers for the consumer. Choice E describes the steps required to bring them to market.

5. A: The sentence contrasts the properties of typical, or "conventional", mattresses with natural ones. The properties listed obviously have no connection with mattress size or color.

6. D: The passage describes the impact of the automobile on the social fabric of the country. Choices (A) and (E) make no sense, because the passage does not compare the automobile to anything, nor does it make mention of any ruling. Choices (B) and (C) are also inappropriate, because no controversy is mentioned, nor is there any mention of the problems brought up in Passage 2.

7. B: The passage describes a series of problems caused by the prevalence of automobiles in Los Angeles. Choices (A) and (C) make no sense, because no hypothesis is presented. Choice (D) is incorrect because two trends are not compared. (E) is inappropriate because, although the automobile and oil companies are blamed for suppressing mass transit, the main thrust of the passage is to describe many of the negative aspects of the prevalent automobile culture.

8. E: The growth of mass transit is being compared to the growth in population and in the number of automobiles. There is no mention of transit development elsewhere or in particular locales.

9. B: An apologist is a person who makes a defense of an idea or belief. (A) is obviously wrong since Passage I presents only positive aspects of the automobile culture. (C), (D), and (E) cite minor details of the passage that are of limited significance.

10. A: Passage A presents only positive aspects, and Passage 2 is thoroughly negative about the effects of automobiles. As a result, neither can be characterized as a careful analysis, and neither proposes any solutions to a problem. Nor are there any comparisons, although in Passage 2 there is an implicit suggestion that mass transit causes fewer of the problems mentioned.

11. B: Gorkhi is described in line 6 as a bit bombastic. A bombastic individual is one who is overbearing and pretentious.

12. D: Line 13 tells us that Zakov found the student on the floor.

13. D: Nasadev is described as whining, with his eyes red from crying, and concerned that his troubles will affect his family.

14. C: Zakov tries to understand how the student must have felt about Olga's rejection. His "heart went out" to the student, and later, when he leaves, he feels a deep sadness for him.

15. A: The student regards Zakov with an imploring look. To implore is to beg.

16. B: The passage describes his voice as "practically inaudible", which means "unable to be heard", but does not describe it as a whisper.

17. C: Olga's rejection of the student provides a reasonable motive, but there is nothing in the passage to suggest that Zakov had proof of Nasadev's guilt or innocence.

18. A: While the discussion is not restricted to man or to other higher-order living things that distinguish good from evil, the context of the line in question is specifically discussing man.

19. E: The text contrasts transcendental models, which invoke preternatural, or supernatural, forces, with mechanistic, or physicochemical, models.

20. The best answer is (B). To posit means to propose or to postulate something in the context of a hypothesis, which may be proven wrong. To claim or to assume means to hold that something is true without considering that it may be shown to be wrong.

21. B: The paragraph discusses aspects of natural selection, a process upon which the theory of evolution depends. In the process, it makes mention of biology and reproduction, but these are not the main point of the paragraph. Nor does it, by itself, seek to prove the correctness of the theory or refute any claims.

22. D: The text tells us that Descartes' approach to biology was "strictly reductionist". Although it says that the roots of mechanist thought lay in Descartes' work, it does not claim that he was the first to expound that school of thought.

23. A: The final paragraph contrasts the reductionist view that all living phenomena can be explained by chemistry and physics with a different perspective that higher-order aspects of living things are subject to laws and principles of their own. So the reductionist would reject answers (B) and (C). Note that answer (D) is incorrect because living things are not made of processes, although processes may take place within them.

24. D: The passage describes various aspects of evolutionary theory, its history, its relation to other schools of thought, in order to show how it fits into the overall picture of modern biological thinking.

Section 4

1. E: The subject of the sentence comprises three items (the federal government, the state and the city) and is therefore plural. The sentence discusses raising the rates and taxes of all three.

2. A: The past progressive form indicates that Janet began doing something in the past, and continues to do so today.

3. D: The original lacks a verb, as do choices B and C. Choice E mismatches a plural subject and singular verb.

4. B: The expression "not only...but also" is used to compare two conditions that are mutually reinforcing.

5. D: The original is a run-on sentence. Choice D correctly separates two related independent clauses with a semi-colon. Choices B and E change the meaning, and choice C incorrectly uses the pronoun "who" for the inanimate "play."

6. B: The pronoun "which" refers to the price. The original and choice E are run-on sentences. In choice C, "cost" is redundant with "price," and choice D is awkwardly phrased.

7. C: Which establishes a list separated by series commas. The original changes the verb tense in mid-sentence, choices B and D are awkwardly phrased, and choice E changes the meaning slightly and is not appropriate following a comma.

8. E: The original is redundant, since "likely" and "would probably happen" mean the same thing. The same holds for choices B and C. Choice D is awkward and less succinct than the preferred choice E.

9. B: Which specifies that it is the average population age that is increasing. All of the other choices simply indicate that the people in these towns are getting older, not that the average age is changing.

10. C: Which the pronoun "it" matches the word "team" for which it stands, and which is singular, not plural.

11. B: Which simply defines the word "sonnet" in a dependent clause.

12. B: Which should be changed to read "she and I."

13. E: The sentence is correct.

14. B: Which should be changed to read "he failed", to match the tense of the verb at the beginning of the sentence.

15. E: The sentence is correct.

16. D: Which should be changed to "indicate", since the subject "sound" is singular.

17. E: The sentence is correct.

18. C: Which should be changed to "was."

19. C: Which should be changed to "kind" to match the singular verb "is", which follows.

20. A: Which should be changed to "He and I", since it is the subject of the verb.

21. A: Which should be changed to the past tense "worked", to match the tense of the other verbs in the sentence.

22. A: Which should be changed to "was" to match the subject "crew", which is singular.

23. D: Which should be changed to "have" to match the subject "Most", which is plural.

24. E: The sentence is correct.

25. C: Which should be changed to "enjoyed", the simple past tense.

26. D: Which should be changed to "who's", the contraction of "who is".

27. E: The sentence is correct.

28. D: Which should be changed to the possessive, "their".

29. B: The word "but" should be eliminated.

30. C: Which the adverb "particularly" clearly modifies the adjectival phrase "well known". Choices B and E subtly change the meaning. Choice D corrects the spelling of the original, but is a more awkward phrasing.

31. D: Which eliminates the slang expression "what with". Choice E subtly changes the meaning.

32. B: Choices A and E awkwardly repeat the word "artist." Choice C fails to make the connection with the preceding sentence, establishing itself as the explanation for Daumier's lack of influence, and choice D fails to explain why other artists did not see Daumier's work.

33. B: Since the sentence begins with "This is also true," the phrase in choice B is redundant with the preceding sentence (see Question 32). None of the other choices address this.

34. A: Which expands upon the previous sentence by explaining why he is considered the greatest sculptor of the era.

35. D: The word "however" shows that the sentence will provide a contrast to the preceding sentence. Choice B does this as well, but repeats the same expression used two sentences before.

Section 5

1. D: One set is bigger than the other, and there is no overlap, since boys cannot be girls.

2. D: One set is bigger than the other, and there is no overlap, since girls wearing white socks are not wearing another color.

3. A: The set of boys wearing white socks is completely contained within the larger set of boys wearing socks.

4. E: The set of "girls wearing socks" makes no distinction between the colors of socks, and so is best represented as a single circle.

5. E: $x^2 = 49$. When you take the square root of a number, the answer is the positive and negative values of the root. Therefore, $x = 7$ and $x=-7$. Only -7 is an answer choice.

6. B: If the averages are equal, then we have $\dfrac{x+y+z}{3} = \dfrac{a+b+c}{3}$, so that it must be true that $(x+y+z) = (a+b+c)$. Therefore the average of all six numbers is

$$\frac{(x+y+z)+(a+b+c)}{6} = \frac{2(x+y+z)}{6} = \frac{x+y+z}{3} = 23.$$

7. B: as the area of a rectangle can be determined by using the formula A = B * h or the formula A = l * w. This means that the area of a rectangle is equal to the length of the base of the rectangle multiplied by the height or width of the rectangle. Therefore, the area of the rectangle described in this question is equal to 7 inches * 9 inches or 63 in2. The other choices offered for this question are incorrect because they do not use the correct formula. (A) is incorrect because it simply offers the rectangle's height squared rather than using the appropriate formula. (C) is incorrect because it offers the perimeter of the rectangle rather than the area. (D) is incorrect because it offers the area of a triangle with a base of 7 inches and a height of 9 inches, and (E) is incorrect because it is simply the sum of the length and width.

8. A: If Lupe's eyes are blue, they are not brown and therefore she cannot be Joan's daughter. Choice B is not necessarily true since not all brown-eyed females are Joan's daughters. Choice C is not necessarily true, because some females who are not Joan's daughters may nevertheless have brown eyes. Choice D is the opposite of the given

statement. And Choice E is not necessarily true because the given statement says nothing about Joan's sons, only her daughters.

9. The correct answer is 4.93. When gridding an answer that does not come out even, you must either enter the entire fraction, or as many decimal places as the answer field allows. The first two prime numbers larger than 10 are 11 and 13, and their product is 143. The largest prime number smaller than 30 is 29. The fraction will not fit in the answer field, so you must convert it to a decimal and round to the appropriate number of places: $\frac{143}{29} = 4.93$

10. The correct answer may be gridded as 24 in. The perimeter of a rectangle can be determined by using the formula P = 2 * (Side 1 + Side 2). This means that the perimeter of a rectangle can be determined by adding the length of the base of the rectangle to the height of the rectangle and multiplying by 2. Therefore, the perimeter of the rectangle described in this question is equal to 2 * (5 inches + 7 inches), or 24 inches. The other choices for this question are incorrect because they do not use the correct formula. (A) is incorrect because it simply offers the rectangle's height squared rather than using the appropriate formula. (B) is incorrect because it offers the area of the rectangle rather than the perimeter. (D) is incorrect because it offers the area of a triangle with a base of 5 inches and a height of 7 inches, and (E) is incorrect because it is simply the sum of the length and width.

11. The correct answer: Figure A has a greater area than figure B. A circle with a radius of 5 inches has a greater area than a circle with a diameter of 9 inches. This is because the area of a circle can be determined by using the formula A = π * r2 and the radius of a circle is equal to half of the circle's diameter. Applying these common geometric formulas to the problem, this means that the radius of figure A is 4.5 inches and the radius of figure B, which is stated within the question, is 5 inches. Therefore, the area of figure A is equal to 3.14 * 4.52 or 63.585 and the area of figure B is equal to 3.14 * 52 or 78.5.

12. The correct answer is 15. Subtracting the second equation from the first, we have $2x + y + 7a - 2x - y - 5a = 50 - 40$, which simplifies to $2a = 10$, or $a = 5$. Substitute this value into either of the original equations. The first equation yields $2x + y + 35 = 50$, so that $2x + y = 15$. The second equation gives the same answer: $2x + y + 25 = 40 \Rightarrow 2x + y = 15$.

13. The correct answer is 2. Rearranging the first equation gives $x^2 = 24 - y^2$. Now, substituting this value into the second equation gives $2(24 - y^2) + 3y^2 = 52 \Rightarrow$ $48 - 2y^2 + 3y^2 = 52$. Rearranging once again gives $y^2 = 4$, or $y = \pm 2$. The grid does not allow for negative numbers, so grid in 2.

14. The correct answer is 8. The total $20 + 13 = 33$, but only 25 cars have been scored. Therefore $33 - 25$, or 8 cars must have had both a man and a woman inside.

15. The correct answer is 1. At $y = 2$, we see that $x = 2$ for the plotted line. The equation for a straight line is of the form $y = ax + b$, where a is the slope and b is the y-intercept at $x=0$. If the new line passes through the origin, then $b = 0$, and the slope a must be 1 for y to equal 2 when x equals 2.

16. The correct answer is 3. By definition, $x - 3 = 6$ and $x - 3 = -6$. Since x is defined as a negative integer, solve $x - 3 = -6 \Rightarrow x = -3$. The question asks for $|x|$, therefore $|x| = 3$.

17. The correct answer is 25. Three quarters of the fish, or 300, are red or blue, leaving only 100, or 25% brown fish. Since the probability of pulling out any single fish is the same, he has a 25% of getting a brown fish.

18. The correct answer is 21. The sentence in the question is translates to $3x - 5 = 58$. Therefore, $x = \dfrac{58 + 5}{3} = 21$.

Section 6

1. B: Choice A makes no sense because "salutary" means "designed for improvement", and thus would require no protection. The other choices make no sense.

2. C: The definition of "salubrious", which means "promoting health", is given in the sentence.

3. D: "Prodigious" means "a great deal." Of the other choices, note that "quantitative" means "pertaining to the measurement of quantity" and that the sentence does not deal with measurement.

4. D: Since trial lawyers are regularly involved in confrontation, Carmen seems unsuited because she has a tendency (penchant) for avoiding such interactions.

5. C: "Voracious" means "craving or consuming large quantities."

6. A: In choice B, one cannot have a "single variety", and the other choices do not make sense.

7. D: The words "lugubrious" and "mournful", which have similar meanings, are appropriate for a description of someone who seems to have just suffered a loss.

8. A: A "paranoia" is an unjustified fear, so it makes sense that the threat was unspecified. The other choices are inconsistent with the locking of doors and response to a threat.

9. D: The overall tone of the passage is one of bleakness and melancholy, and these words describe a walk that is slow, hesitant, and generally disheartened.

10. C: The actions described are defensive and indicate a lack of trust.

11. D: The passage describes Hal as a very large man suited to contact sports, and this metaphor indicates that he had massive legs the size of tree trunks.

12. B: Cats are known to move very quietly. Here, Hal's massive size is being contrasted with his ability to move as quietly as a cat.

13. C: The author of Passage 1 suggests a tax at the pump to keep prices high, while the author of Passage 2 proposes a tax reduction for businesses developing renewable energy technology. Choice A is the opposite of what is proposed in Passage 1, and choice B is not mentioned in Passage 1. Choices D and E are the opposite of what is proposed in Passage 2.

14. D: The author of Passage 1 wants to maintain high fuel prices, while the author of Passage 2 wants to keep prices "under control" (Line 43). Choice B is incorrect because both authors want to protect the consumer: in Passage 2 by keeping prices low, and in Passage 1 by returning the surcharge to taxpayers (Lines 28-29).

15. B: The author of Passage 2 argues that price manipulations don't work (Lines 59-60). Thus, he/she would not consider it an alternative or complement to his/her own strategy. Choice D is wrong because Passage 2 itself is suggesting a tax policy.

16. E: The point of Passage 1 is that lower prices make it seem likely that new technologies will have to be sold at lower prices to compete, and therefore be less profitable.

17. C: The first paragraph introduces the proposal by describing the problem faced by new technology developers. The detailed argument (Choice E) is made later in the passage.

18. B: The tax credit makes it easier for companies to conduct research today, but does not maintain a stable price or profit structure for the future. So the proposal does not address the main concern of Passage 1.

19. A: This paragraph brings up price manipulation as an alternative strategy and argues against it.

20. B: Both passages describe the slow progress in developing renewable fuels and then describe their own proposals for addressing this.

21. C: The first line of the paragraph (Line 24) states that the author is about to describe "one possibility" for dealing with the issue. Although the paragraph shows how truck drivers could be protected from high prices (Lines 28-30) that is not the main point, so Choice B is wrong. And the $3 price for gasoline is offered only as an example in Line 26, so Choice D is also wrong.

22. B: The paragraph describes how the tax credit might encourage further research and development into alternative energy. Although it explains how tax credits work (Lines 63-64), this is ancillary to the main purpose.

23. B: The author of Passage 2 explicitly rejects the price manipulation suggested in Passage 1 (Lines 59-61).

Section 7

1. B: $(6a) x^2$ is equivalent to $6 \times ax^2$, so that ax^2 is simply 1/6th of this, or $\frac{30}{6} = 5$.

2. A: Since a player cannot remove fewer than 1 or more than 3 toothpicks per turn, it follows that leaving 2, 3 or 4 toothpicks in a row allows a winning response, and that leaving 5 toothpicks forces the next player to leave 2, 3, or 4.

3. C: The line in the graph has a negative slope and a positive y-axis intercept, so the factor multiplying the variable x, or the slope, must be negative, and the constant, or y-intercept, must be positive.

- 273 -

4. B: As the volume of a rectangular box can be determined using the formula $V = l * w * h$. This means that the volume of a rectangular box can be determined by multiplying the length of the base of the box by the width of the box and multiplying that product by the height of the box. Therefore, the volume of the box described in this question is equal to $5 * 7 * 9$, or 315 in³. (A) is incorrect because it provides the volume of a cylinder with a diameter of 9 inches and a height of 7 inches. (C) is incorrect because it provides the area of a rectangle with a base of 5 inches and a width of 9 inches. (D) is incorrect because it states the area of a rectangle with a base of 5 inches and a width of 7 inches, and (E) is incorrect because it states the *sum* of the length, width, and height rather than the *product* of length, width, and height.

5. C: If $5y - 20 < 0$, then $5y < 20$ and $y < 4$. Since y must be an integer, the answer must be 3, the largest integer that is less than 4. Choice B is wrong because, in this case, $5y - 20 = 0$, which is not less than 0.

6. E: The circular area covered by the sprinkler is πr^2, so the difference is obtained as $\pi \times 8^2 - \pi \times 6^2 = \pi(64 - 36) = 28\pi = 87.92$.

7. C: Since the line is straight, the slope is the same throughout. Thus, if 5 y-units are traversed in going from $x = -3$ to $x = 0$ (where y increases from -5 to 0, to reach the origin), then 5 y-units will be traversed in going from $x = 0$ to $x = 3$.

8. D: Which is obtained by moving the second term to the right of the equality and changing its sign.

9. B: Since there are equal numbers of each coin in the row, if two of one type are next to each other, two of the other type must also be next to each other someplace within the row, or else at each end of the row. Since the two dimes take up one end of the row, the two pennies must be together.

10. B: The radius, R, of the satellite's orbit is the sum of the Earth's radius plus the satellite's orbital altitude, or R = 4400 miles. The circumference of the circular orbit is therefore $C = 2\pi r = 2\pi(4400) = 8800\pi$ miles. Since 40 minutes is one third of the satellite's 120-minute orbital time, it traverses one third of this distance in that time. So the distance,

$$D = \frac{40}{120} \times 2\pi \times 4400 = 9210.66$$ miles, using 3.14 for π.

11. D: The line in the graph has a constant value of y, one that does not change regardless of the value of x. This is a special case of the equation for the straight line, $y = mx + b$, for which m = 0.

12. D: When no tickets are sold, N = 0, and $0 = 25000 - 0.1p^2$, so that $0.1p^2 = 25000$, and

$$p^2 = \frac{25000}{0.1} = 250{,}000 = 2500 \times 100 = 50^2 \times 10^2,$$ so that $p = 50 \times 10 = 500$.

13. B: Profit equals (tickets sold) x (price) – cost. The number of tickets sold is given by the equation in Question 12. Multiplying this expression by price, p, gives $25{,}000p - 0.1p^3$, and subtracting cost gives the expression in Choice B.

14. B: The total volume of the cylinder is given by $V = h\pi r^2 = 10\pi \times 1 = 31.4$, when $\pi = 3.14$. Since the slice is a straight, 60-degree slice, its volume is one sixth of this ($\frac{60}{360} = \frac{1}{6}$), or 5.23.

15. A: The median of a set of numbers is one for which the set contains an equal number of greater and lesser values. Besides Z, there are 8 numbers in the set, so that 4 must be greater and 4 lesser than Z. The 4 smallest values are 5, 7, 9, and 12. The 4 largest are 16, 18, 23, and 44. So Z must fall between 12 and 16.

16. C: If Q is divisible by both 7 and 2, it must be a multiple of 14, which is the least common multiple of both 2 and 7. Therefore, if one adds another multiple of 14 to Q, it will also be divisible by both 2 and 7. Of the choices given, only 28 is a multiple of 14.

1. C: *Obstreperous* is defined as noisy, clamorous, or difficult to control. *Saturnine* or *brooding* children are moody. *Capricious* ones are simply hard to predict.

2. B: A *timbered* area is one with a lot of forest cover, here contrasted to the open or shrub-covered landscape favored by the birds. Since their favored elevation has already been specified, choice D is incorrect. The other choices make no sense.

3. C: *Quiescence* means calm: here, periods of violent eruptions are followed by periods with little or no flare activity.

4. A: *Duplicity* indicates lack of truthfulness, and *credence* is belief in what one is told.

5. B: A *conciliatory* tone is one that seeks to reconcile with someone. Choice D is incorrect because the rival could not have been victorious since the sentence describes activities of the winning candidate.

6. D: To *glower* is to stare in a sullen, disapproving manner.

7. E: After introducing its topic, the bulk of the passage describes the features that light produces on a photograph and the kinds of lighting that are used to produce these features.

8. C: The paragraphs describe the origins of photography and the early popularity of the portrait, then sets the stage for the description of lighting methods by indicating the importance of good lighting for the portrait.

9. B: The quotation marks are used to show that the word was invented to describe the results of Schulze's process, but was later replaced by other terms to describe the outputs of photographic methods, and is no longer in use.

10. A: Light is being compared to a living thing, with characteristics of dynamism and animation, explicitly stating that a comparison is being made. (Light IS a living thing.) This is the definition of a metaphor, as opposed to a simile, in which the comparison shows two things to be similar, usually through the use of the preposition "like" or "as." (Light IS LIKE a living thing.)

11. C: The word is used here to describe something a photographer may do that is different from common methods, but that may be an element of his or her personal style. The point is that by showing technical competence with good lighting technique, the "mistake" may be presented as a deliberate flaunting of convention.

12. A: By using the noun "equivalent" to characterize the comparison, the author makes it explicit. Thus, it is a metaphor and not a simile. A simile is similar ("like" or "as") but not exact.

13. D: While all the other choices describe information that is included in the paragraph, its main purpose is to define a large number of terms.

14. A: The author uses this technique throughout the passage: placing a term in italics and using it in a sentence that describes what it means.

15. D: The sentence contrasts floodlights with strobes and implies that strobes, being more modern, do not share these negative characteristics of floodlights.

16. A: Both words refer to the person being photographed. The author uses them in this manner to avoid repeating the same word twice in one sentence.

17. C: The paragraph runs through the different kinds of lights used for portraiture, presenting the name of each in italics and in a sentence that describes or defines it.

18. E: The paragraph describes several ways of modifying the output of studio lights to "diffuse and soften" their output.

19. B: The passage describes the different types of studio portrait lights, modifiers, and the lighting features that they produce on a photograph. It does not go into detail on positioning (Choice D).

Section 9

1. C: The dependent clause shows a consequence of the condition described in the first clause, and is not separated by a comma when introduced by a correlative conjunction ("so...that").

2. B: Where the noun "punishment" is modified by the adjective "severe."

3. D: The absence of the comma in the original version suggests that only some smoking has been linked to lung cancer, and that it is only that smoking which nutritionists are urging the public to stop. The comma makes it clear that all smoking is linked to cancer. Choice E is similar to the original. Choice B requires a comma to separate the independent clause. Choice C is awkwardly phrased.

4. E: Which is far more succinct than choice D. The original version is slang usage. Choice C does not explicitly state that the disagreement is about the best practice.

5. C: Which links the verb "affected" to the cause of the effect, i.e., the distress of the industry, for maximum clarity.

6. D: Which makes use of the correlative conjunction "either...or" to link two equivalent portions of a sentence. Note that "either...also", "either...owing to", and "either...but" do not make sense.

7. B: The pronoun "it" used at the end of the sentence must refer to a singular noun. The word "medicine" in Choice B refers to the practice of medicine, and is singular. Note that there are many other ways to fix this sentence by replacing "it" with "them", for example, but they are not offered as choices.

8. E: Note that "he" and "she" are both subjects of the verb "to be able", and so must be in the subjective case. The objective "her" is suited to be the object of a verb.

9. E: A predecessor is someone who has come before you, and you cannot preserve anything for them. A successor is one who comes afterwards.

10. B: The adjectival clause that begins the sentence describes the flu virus, not the millions of people who are infected each year.

11. C: The original compares cooking with countries, which is illogical.

12. D: A surprise is always unexpected, and generally sudden, so the original version is redundant. Choice D conveys the same information succinctly.

13. E: The subject of the sentence is the word "cooking", which is singular and calls for a singular verb.

14. C: Which is the simplest, most straightforward phrasing.

Secret Key #1 - Time is Your Greatest Enemy

To succeed on the SAT, you must use your time wisely. Most students do not finish at least one section. The table below shows the time challenge you are faced with:

SECTION	Total amount of time allotted
Critical Reading	70 min
Mathematics	70 min
Writing (multiple choice)	25 min
Writing (essay)	25 min

As you can see, the time constraints are brutal. To succeed, you must ration your time properly. The reason that time is so critical is that every question counts the same toward your final score. If you run out of time on any passage, the questions that you do not answer will hurt your score far more than earlier questions that you spent extra time on and feel certain are correct.

Success Strategy

Pace Yourself
Wear a watch to the SAT Test. At the beginning of the test, check the time (or start a chronometer on your watch to count the minutes), and check the time after each passage to make sure you are "on schedule."

If you find that you are falling behind time during the test, begin skipping difficult questions (unless you know it at a quick glance). Once you catch back up, you can continue working each problem. If you have time at the end, go back then and finish the questions that you left behind.

Remember that on most sections you have slightly more than a minute per question, which makes it easy to keep track of your time. If you are spending more than a minute per question, skip it and move on. It is better to end with more time than you need than to run out of time. You can always go back and work the problems that you skipped. Besides, they were difficult or you wouldn't have skipped them. The difficult questions are the ones you are most likely to miss anyway, so it isn't a big loss. If you have time left over, as you review the skipped questions, start at the earliest skipped question, spend at most another minute, and then move on to the next skipped question.

Always mark skipped questions in your workbook, NOT on the Scantron. Last minute guessing will be covered in the next chapter.

Lastly, sometimes it is beneficial to slow down if you are constantly getting ahead of time. You are always more likely to catch a careless mistake by working more slowly than quickly, and among very high-scoring students (those who are likely to have lots of time left over), careless errors affect the score more than mastery of material.

Estimation
For some math questions, estimate. Calculation takes time, and you should avoid it whenever possible. You can usually eliminate three obviously wrong choices quite easily. For example, suppose a graph shows that an object has traveled 48 meters in 11 seconds, and you are asked to find its speed. You are given these choices:

a. 250 m/s
b. 42 m/s
c. 4.4 m/s
d. 1.2 m/s
e. 0.8 m/s

You know that 48 divided by 11 will be a little over 4, so you can pick out C as the answer without ever doing the calculation.

Scanning
For critical reading sections, don't waste time reading, enjoying, and completely

- 281 -

understanding the passage. Simply scan the passage to get a rough idea of what it is about. You will return to the passage for each question, so there is no need to memorize it. Only spend as much time scanning as is necessary to get a vague impression of its overall subject content.

Secret Key #2 - Guessing is not Guesswork

You probably know that guessing can be either a good or bad idea on the SAT, because there is a penalty for giving the wrong answer. Quick answer: If you have no idea of the answer, i.e. you can't even eliminate a single answer choice, then guessing is a bad idea. If you can eliminate one answer choice, guessing is a maybe, but very dangerous unless done correctly and as part of an overall strategy. If you eliminate two or more answer choices, then guessing becomes a good idea.

Most students do not understand the impact that proper guessing can have on their score. Unless you score above 2000 or so, guessing will contribute about 180-240 points to your final score.

Monkeys Take the SAT

If you have only four answer choices, then you have approximately a 25% chance of getting it correct. What most students don't realize is that to insure a 25% chance, you have to guess randomly. If you put 20 monkeys in a room to take the SAT, assuming they answered once per question and behaved themselves, on average they would get 25% of the questions correct. Put 20 high school students in the room, and the average will be much lower among guessed questions. Why?

1. SAT intentionally writes deceptive answer choices that "look" right. A student has no idea about a question, so picks the "best looking" answer, which is often wrong. The monkey has no idea what looks good and what doesn't, so will consistently be lucky about 25% of the time.
2. Students will eliminate answer choices from the guessing pool based on a hunch or intuition. Simple but correct answers often get excluded, leaving a 0% chance of being correct. The monkey has no clue, and often gets lucky with the best choice.

This is why the process of elimination endorsed by most test courses is flawed and detrimental to your performance- students don't guess, they make an ignorant stab in the dark that is usually worse than random.

The SAT "Guessing" Penalty

SAT penalizes you for wrong answers, not guessing. This penalty, in theory, has no effect on your score. Its purpose is to discourage students from randomly guessing, by eliminating the benefit associated with it. Let's take a look at these penalties more closely.

All Question Types except Grid-In
For all question types except grid-in, guessing, on average, will hurt your score if you can't eliminate any choices. If you can eliminate one choice, there is neither a penalty nor benefit to guessing. If you can eliminate more than one choice, then guessing is beneficial. We know that you should NOT guess in cases where you can't eliminate any choices, and that you SHOULD guess when you can eliminate two or more choices, but what about when you can only eliminate one choice?

The effect of not guessing when you can eliminate only one choice effectively reduces the *variability* of your score, i.e. if you took the SAT 3 times without guessing on questions where you could eliminate exactly one choice, your scores would be closer together than if you had guessed on questions where you could not eliminate choices. If you are using Secret Key #4 in this manual to maximize your score (i.e. taking the SAT multiple times and the "cherry picking" your best score to send to colleges), then you want to maximize the variance, as your highest score would, on average, be higher with greater variance. If you are taking the SAT only once, we do not recommend guessing when you can eliminate only one answer choice.

Grid-In Questions

There's no penalty for guessing here but your chances of guessing it right are almost zero. Guess, but do it quickly to make time for more questions.

Success Strategy

Let me introduce one of the most valuable ideas of this course- the $5 challenge:

You only mark your "best guess" if you are willing to bet $5 on it.
You only eliminate choices from guessing if you are willing to bet $5 on it.

Why $5? Five dollars is an amount of money that is small yet not insignificant, and can really add up fast (20 questions could cost you $100). Likewise, each answer choice on one question of the SAT will have a small impact on your overall score, but it can really add up to a lot of points in the end.

The process of elimination IS valuable.

If you eliminate wrong answer choices until only this many remain:	Chance of getting it correct:
1	100%
2	50%
3	33%

If you accidentally eliminate the right answer or go on a hunch for an incorrect answer, your chances drop dramatically: to 0%, not to mention the wrong answer penalty. By guessing among all the answer choices, you are GUARANTEED to have a shot at the right answer.

That's why the $5 test is so valuable- if you give up the advantage and safety of a pure guess, it had better be worth the risk.

What we still haven't covered is how to be sure that whatever guess you make is truly random. Here's the easiest way:

Always pick the first answer choice among those remaining.

Such a technique means that you have decided, **before you see a single test question**, exactly how you are going to guess- and since the order of choices tells you nothing about which one is correct, this guessing technique is perfectly random.

Let's try an example. A student encounters the following problem on a math section:

What is the cosine of an angle in a right triangle that is 3 meters on the adjacent side, 5 meters on the hypotenuse, and 4 meters on the opposite side?

A. 1
B. 0.6
C. 0.8
D. 0.75
E. 1.25

The student has a small idea about this question- he is pretty sure that cosine is opposite over hypotenuse, but he wouldn't bet $5 on it. He knows that cosine is "something" over hypotenuse, and since the hypotenuse is the largest number, he is willing to bet $5 on both choices A and E not being correct. So he is down to B, C, and D. At this point, he guesses B, since B is the first choice remaining.

The student is correct by choosing B, since cosine is adjacent over hypotenuse. He only eliminated those choices he was willing to bet money on, AND he did not let his stale memories (often things not known definitely will get mixed up in the exact opposite arrangement in one's head) about the formula for cosine influence his guess. He blindly chose the first remaining choice, and was rewarded with the fruits of a random guess.

This section is not meant to scare you away from making educated guesses or eliminating choices- you just need to define when a choice is worth eliminating. The $5 test, along with a pre-defined random guessing strategy, is the best way to make sure you reap all of the benefits of guessing.

Specific Guessing Techniques

Slang
Scientific sounding answers are better than slang ones. In the answer choices below, choice B is much less scientific and is incorrect, while choice A is a scientific analytical choice and is correct.

Example:
a.) To compare the outcomes of the two different kinds of treatment.
b.) Because some subjects insisted on getting one or the other of the treatments.

Extreme Statements
Avoid wild answers that throw out highly controversial ideas that are proclaimed as established fact. Choice A is a radical idea and is incorrect. Choice B is a calm rational statement. Notice that Choice B does not make a definitive, uncompromising stance, using a hedge word "if" to provide wiggle room.
Example:
a.) Bypass surgery should be discontinued completely.
b.) Medication should be used instead of surgery for patients who have not had a heart attack if they suffer from mild chest pain and mild coronary artery blockage.

Similar Answer Choices
When you have two answer choices that are direct opposites, one of them is usually the correct answer.
Example:

A.) Passage 1 described the author's reasoning about the influence of his childhood on his adult life.
B.) Passage 2 described the author's reasoning about the influence of his childhood on his adult life.

These two answer choices are very similar and fall into the same family of answer choices. A family of answer choices is when two or three answer choices are very similar. Often two will be opposites and one may show an equality.
Example:
A.) Operation I or Operation II can be conducted at equal cost
B.) Operation I would be less expensive than Operation II
C.) Operation II would be less expensive than Operation I
D.) Neither Operation I nor Operation II would be effective at preventing the spread of cancer.

Note how the first three choices are all related. They all ask about a cost comparison.

Beware of immediately recognizing choices B and C as opposites and choosing one of those two. Choice A is in the same family of questions and should be considered as well. However, choice D is not in the same family of questions. It has nothing to do with cost and can be discounted in most cases.

Hedging

When asked for a conclusion that may be drawn, look for critical "hedge" phrases, such as likely, may, can, will often, sometimes, etc, often, almost, mostly, usually, generally, rarely, sometimes. Question writers insert these hedge phrases to cover every possibility. Often an answer will be wrong simply because it leaves no room for exception. Avoid answer choices that have definitive words like "exactly," and "always".

Summary of Guessing Techniques

1. Eliminate as many choices as you can by using the $5 test. Use the common guessing strategies to help in the elimination process, but only eliminate choices that pass the $5 test.
2. Among the remaining choices, only pick your "best guess" if it passes the $5 test. If you eliminated two or more choices with the $5 test in step 1, then guess randomly by picking the first remaining choice.
3. If you can only eliminate one choice with the $5 test, and you are intentionally taking the SAT multiple times to "cherry pick" your best score, go ahead and guess. If you are taking the SAT only once, do not guess when you can only eliminate one choice.
4. Never guess when you can't eliminate any choices.

Secret Key #3 - Practice Smarter, Not Harder

Many test takers delay the test preparation process because they dread the awful amounts of practice time they think necessary to succeed on the test. We have refined an effective method that will take you only a fraction of the time.

There are a number of "obstacles" in the path to success. Among these are answering questions, finishing in time, and mastering test-taking strategies. All must be executed on the day of the test at peak performance, or your score will suffer. The test is a mental marathon that has a large impact on your future.

Just like a marathon runner, it is important to work your way up to the full challenge. So first you just worry about questions, and then time, and finally strategy:

Success Strategy

1. Find a good source for practice tests.
2. If you are willing to make a larger time investment, consider using more than one study guide. Often the different approaches of multiple authors will help you "get" difficult concepts.
3. Take a practice test with no time constraints, with all study helps, "open book." Take your time with questions and focus on applying strategies.
4. Take a practice test with time constraints, with all guides, "open book."
5. Take a final practice test without open material and with time limits.

If you have time to take more practice tests, just repeat step 5. By gradually exposing yourself to the full rigors of the test environment, you will condition your mind to the stress of test day and maximize your success.

Secret Key #4 - Prepare, Don't Procrastinate

Let me state an obvious fact: if you take the SAT three times, you will get three different scores. This is due to the way you feel on test day, the level of preparedness you have, and, despite SAT's claims to the contrary, some tests WILL be easier for you than others, especially on the passages in the critical reading sections.

Since your acceptance and qualification for scholarships will largely depend on your score, you should maximize your chances of success by taking the SAT at least twice and sending only the highest score to your colleges. We recommend taking the SAT three times to fully account for all variances in performance, preparedness, and test difficulty.

Also, most colleges will accept EITHER the SAT or ACT for admission. Take both and submit the one you do better on (if you really want to beat the system, take both twice!). An SAT/ACT equivalency table is located in the appendix.

Secret Key #5 - Test Yourself

Everyone knows that time is money. There is no need to spend too much of your time or too little of your time preparing for the test. You should only spend as much of your precious time preparing as is necessary for you to get the score you need.

Once you have taken a practice test under real conditions of time constraints, then you will know if you are ready for the test or not.

If you have scored extremely high the first time that you take the practice test, then there is not much point in spending countless hours studying. You are already there.

Benchmark your abilities by retaking practice tests and seeing how much you have improved. Once you consistently score high enough to guarantee success, then you are ready.

If you have scored well below where you need, then knuckle down and begin studying in earnest. Check your improvement regularly through the use of practice tests under real conditions. Above all, don't worry, panic, or give up. The key is perseverance!

Then, when you go to take the test, remain confident and remember how well you did on the practice tests. If you can score high enough on a practice test, then you can do the same on the real thing.

General Strategies

The most important thing you can do is to ignore your fears and jump into the test immediately. Do not be overwhelmed by any strange-sounding terms. You have to jump into the test like jumping into a pool—all at once is the easiest way.

Make Predictions

As you read and understand the question, try to guess what the answer will be. Remember that several of the answer choices are wrong, and once you begin reading them, your mind will immediately become cluttered with answer choices designed to throw you off. Your mind is typically the most focused immediately after you have read the question and digested its contents. If you can, try to predict what the correct answer will be. You may be surprised at what you can predict.

Quickly scan the choices and see if your prediction is in the listed answer choices. If it is, then you can be quite confident that you have the right answer. It still won't hurt to check the other answer choices, but most of the time, you've got it!

Answer the Question

It may seem obvious to only pick answer choices that answer the question, but the test writers can create some excellent answer choices that are wrong. Don't pick an answer just because it sounds right, or you believe it to be true. It MUST answer the question. Once you've made your selection, always go back and check it against the question and make sure that you didn't misread the question and that the answer choice does answer the question posed.

Benchmark

After you read the first answer choice, decide if you think it sounds correct or not. If it doesn't, move on to the next answer choice. If it does, mentally mark that answer choice. This doesn't mean that you've definitely selected it as your answer choice, it just means that it's the best you've seen thus far.

Go ahead and read the next choice. If the next choice is worse than the one you've already selected, keep going to the next answer choice. If the next choice is better than the choice you've already selected, mentally mark the new answer choice as your best guess. The first answer choice that you select becomes your standard. Every other answer choice must be benchmarked against that standard. That choice is correct until proven otherwise by another answer choice beating it out. Once you've decided that no other answer choice seems as good, do one final check to ensure that your answer choice answers the question posed.

Valid Information

Don't discount any of the information provided in the question. Every piece of information may be necessary to determine the correct answer. None of the information in the question is there to throw you off (while the answer choices will certainly have information to throw you off). If two seemingly unrelated topics are discussed, don't ignore either. You can be confident there is a relationship, or it wouldn't be included in the question, and you are probably going to have to determine what is that relationship to find the answer.

Avoid "Fact Traps"

Don't get distracted by a choice that is factually true. Your search is for the answer that answers the question. Stay focused and don't fall for an answer that is true but irrelevant. Always go back to the question and make sure you're choosing an answer that actually answers the question and is not just a true statement. An answer can be factually correct, but it MUST answer the question asked. Additionally, two answers can both be seemingly correct, so be sure to read all of the answer choices, and make sure that you get the one that BEST answers the question.

Milk the Question

Some of the questions may throw you completely off. They might deal with a subject you have not been exposed to, or one that you haven't reviewed in years. While your lack of knowledge about the subject will be a hindrance, the question itself can give you many clues that will help you find the correct answer. Read the question carefully and look for clues. Watch particularly for adjectives and nouns describing difficult terms or words that you don't recognize. Regardless of whether you completely understand a word or not, replacing it with a synonym, either provided or one you more familiar with, may help you to understand what the questions are asking. Rather than wracking your mind about specific detailed information concerning a difficult term or word, try to use mental substitutes that are easier to understand.

The Trap of Familiarity

Don't just choose a word because you recognize it. On difficult questions, you may not recognize a number of words in the answer choices. The test writers don't put "make-believe" words on the test, so don't think that just because you only recognize all the words in one answer choice that that answer choice must be correct. If you only recognize words in one answer choice, then focus on that one. Is it correct? Try your best to determine if it is correct. If it is, that's great. If not, eliminate it. Each word and answer choice you eliminate increases your chances of getting the question correct, even if you then have to guess among the unfamiliar choices.

Eliminate Answers

Eliminate choices as soon as you realize they are wrong. But be careful! Make sure you consider all of the possible answer choices. Just because one appears right, doesn't mean that the next one won't be even better! The test writers will usually put more than one good answer choice for every question, so read all of them. Don't worry if you are stuck between two that seem right. By getting down to just two remaining possible choices, your odds are now 50/50. Rather than wasting too much time, play the odds. You

are guessing, but guessing wisely because you've been able to knock out some of the answer choices that you know are wrong. If you are eliminating choices and realize that the last answer choice you are left with is also obviously wrong, don't panic. Start over and consider each choice again. There may easily be something that you missed the first time and will realize on the second pass.

Tough Questions

If you are stumped on a problem or it appears too hard or too difficult, don't waste time. Move on! Remember though, if you can quickly check for obviously incorrect answer choices, your chances of guessing correctly are greatly improved. Before you completely give up, at least try to knock out a couple of possible answers. Eliminate what you can and then guess at the remaining answer choices before moving on.

Brainstorm

If you get stuck on a difficult question, spend a few seconds quickly brainstorming. Run through the complete list of possible answer choices. Look at each choice and ask yourself, "Could this answer the question satisfactorily?" Go through each answer choice and consider it independently of the others. By systematically going through all possibilities, you may find something that you would otherwise overlook. Remember though that when you get stuck, it's important to try to keep moving.

Read Carefully

Understand the problem. Read the question and answer choices carefully. Don't miss the question because you misread the terms. You have plenty of time to read each question thoroughly and make sure you understand what is being asked. Yet a happy medium must be attained, so don't waste too much time. You must read carefully, but efficiently.

Face Value

When in doubt, use common sense. Always accept the situation in the problem at face value. Don't read too much into it. These problems will not require you to make huge leaps of logic. The test writers aren't trying to throw you off with a cheap trick. If you have to go beyond creativity and make a leap of logic in order to have an answer choice answer the question, then you should look at the other answer choices. Don't overcomplicate the problem by creating theoretical relationships or explanations that will warp time or space. These are normal problems rooted in reality. It's just that the applicable relationship or explanation may not be readily apparent and you have to figure things out. Use your common sense to interpret anything that isn't clear.

Prefixes

If you're having trouble with a word in the question or answer choices, try dissecting it. Take advantage of every clue that the word might include. Prefixes and suffixes can be a huge help. Usually they allow you to determine a basic meaning. Pre- means before, post- means after, pro - is positive, de- is negative. From these prefixes and suffixes, you can get an idea of the general meaning of the word and try to put it into context. Beware though of any traps. Just because con- is the opposite of pro-, doesn't necessarily mean congress is the opposite of progress!

Hedge Phrases

Watch out for critical hedge phrases, led off with words such as "likely," "may," "can," "sometimes," "often," "almost," "mostly," "usually," "generally," "rarely," and "sometimes." Question writers insert these hedge phrases to cover every possibility. Often an answer choice will be wrong simply because it leaves no room for exception. Unless the situation calls for them, avoid answer choices that have definitive words like "exactly," and "always."

Switchback Words

Stay alert for "switchbacks." These are the words and phrases frequently used to alert you to shifts in thought. The most common switchback word is "but." Others include "although," "however," "nevertheless," "on the other hand," "even though," "while," "in spite of," "despite," and "regardless of."

New Information

Correct answer choices will rarely have completely new information included. Answer choices typically are straightforward reflections of the material asked about and will directly relate to the question. If a new piece of information is included in an answer choice that doesn't even seem to relate to the topic being asked about, then that answer choice is likely incorrect. All of the information needed to answer the question is usually provided for you in the question. You should not have to make guesses that are unsupported or choose answer choices that require unknown information that cannot be reasoned from what is given.

Time Management

On technical questions, don't get lost on the technical terms. Don't spend too much time on any one question. If you don't know what a term means, then odds are you aren't going to get much further since you don't have a dictionary. You should be able to immediately recognize whether or not you know a term. If you don't, work with the other clues that you have—the other answer choices and terms provided—but don't waste too much time trying to figure out a difficult term that you don't know.

Contextual Clues

Look for contextual clues. An answer can be right but not the correct answer. The contextual clues will help you find the answer that is most right and is correct. Understand the context in which a phrase or statement is made. This will help you make important distinctions.

Don't Panic

Panicking will not answer any questions for you; therefore, it isn't helpful. When you first see the question, if your mind goes blank, take a deep breath. Force yourself to mechanically go through the steps of solving the problem using the strategies you've learned.

Pace Yourself

Don't get clock fever. It's easy to be overwhelmed when you're looking at a page full of questions, your mind is full of random thoughts and feeling confused, and the clock is ticking down faster than you would like. Calm down and maintain the pace that you have set for yourself. As long as you are on track by monitoring your pace, you are guaranteed to have enough time for yourself. When you get to the last few minutes of the test, it may seem like you won't have enough time left, but if you only have as many questions as you should have left at that point, then you're right on track!

Answer Selection

The best way to pick an answer choice is to eliminate all of those that are wrong, until only one is left and confirm that is the correct answer. Sometimes though, an answer choice may immediately look right. Be careful! Take a second to make sure that the other choices are not equally obvious. Don't make a hasty mistake. There are only two times that you should stop before checking other answers. First is when you are positive that the answer choice you have selected is correct. Second is when time is almost out and you have to make a quick guess!

Check Your Work

Since you will probably not know every term listed and the answer to every question, it is important that you get credit for the ones that you do know. Don't miss any questions through careless mistakes. If at all possible, try to take a second to look back over your answer selection and make sure you've selected the correct answer choice and haven't made a costly careless mistake (such as marking an answer choice that you didn't mean to mark). The time it takes for this quick double check should more than pay for itself in caught mistakes.

Beware of Directly Quoted Answers

Sometimes an answer choice will repeat word for word a portion of the question or reference section. However, beware of such exact duplication. It may be a trap! More than likely, the correct choice will paraphrase or summarize a point, rather than being exactly the same wording.

Slang

Scientific sounding answers are better than slang ones. An answer choice that begins "To compare the outcomes…" is much more likely to be correct than one that begins "Because some people insisted…"

Extreme Statements

Avoid wild answers that throw out highly controversial ideas that are proclaimed as established fact. An answer choice that states the "process should be used in certain situations, if…" is much more likely to be correct than one that states the "process should be discontinued completely." The first is a calm rational statement and doesn't even make a definitive, uncompromising stance, using a hedge word "if" to provide wiggle room, whereas the second choice is a radical idea and far more extreme.

Answer Choice Families

When you have two or more answer choices that are direct opposites or parallels, one of them is usually the correct answer. For instance, if one answer choice states "x increases" and another answer choice states "x decreases" or "y increases," then those two or three answer choices are very similar in construction and fall into the same family of answer choices. A family of answer choices consists of two or three answer choices, very similar in construction, but often with directly opposite meanings. Usually the correct answer choice will be in that family of answer choices. The "odd man out" or answer choice that doesn't seem to fit the parallel construction of the other answer choices is more likely to be incorrect.

Special Report: SAT/ACT Equivalency Table

ACT Composite Score	SAT Score (Critical Reading + Math)
36	1600
35	1560
34	1510
33	1460
32	1420
31	1380
30	1340
29	1300
28	1260
27	1220
26	1190
25	1150
24	1110
23	1070
22	1030
21	990
20	950
19	910
18	870
17	830
16	790
15	740
14	690
13	640
12	590
11	530

Special Report: Area, Volume, Surface Area Formulas

These are VERY valuable to memorize for the SAT Math.

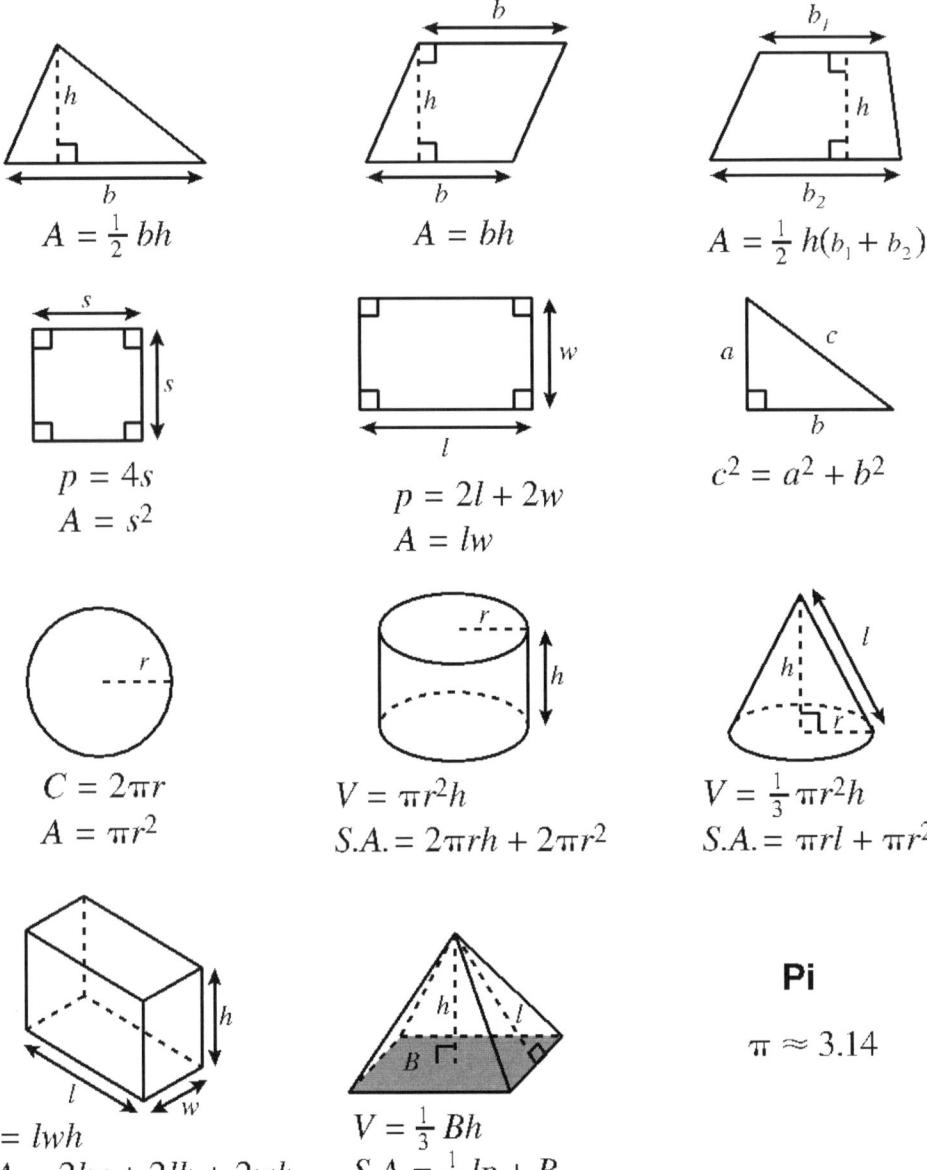

$$A = \tfrac{1}{2} bh$$

$$A = bh$$

$$A = \tfrac{1}{2} h(b_1 + b_2)$$

$$p = 4s$$
$$A = s^2$$

$$p = 2l + 2w$$
$$A = lw$$

$$c^2 = a^2 + b^2$$

$$C = 2\pi r$$
$$A = \pi r^2$$

$$V = \pi r^2 h$$
$$S.A. = 2\pi rh + 2\pi r^2$$

$$V = \tfrac{1}{3} \pi r^2 h$$
$$S.A. = \pi rl + \pi r^2$$

$$V = lwh$$
$$S.A. = 2lw + 2lh + 2wh$$

$$V = \tfrac{1}{3} Bh$$
$$S.A. = \tfrac{1}{2} lp + B$$

Pi

$$\pi \approx 3.14$$

Special Report: How to Overcome Your Fear of Math

If this article started by saying "Math," many of us would feel a shiver crawl up our spines, just by reading that simple word. Images of torturous years in those crippling desks of the math classes can become so vivid to our consciousness that we can almost smell those musty textbooks, and see the smudges of the #2 pencils on our fingers.

If you are still a student, feeling the impact of these sometimes overwhelming classroom sensations, you are not alone if you get anxious at just the thought of taking that compulsory math course. Does your heart beat just that much faster when you have to split the bill for lunch among your friends with a group of your friends? Do you truly believe that you simply don't have the brain for math? Certainly you're good at other things, but math just simply isn't one of them? Have you ever avoided activities, or other school courses because they appear to involve mathematics, with which you're simply not comfortable?

If any one or more of these "symptoms" can be applied to you, you could very well be suffering from a very real condition called "Math Anxiety."

It's not at all uncommon for people to think that they have some sort of math disability or allergy, when in actuality, their block is a direct result of the way in which they were taught math!

In the late 1950's with the dawning of the space age, New Math - a new "fuzzy math" reform that focuses on higher-order thinking, conceptual understanding and solving problems - took the country by storm. It's now becoming ever more clear that teachers were not supplied with the correct, practical and effective way in which they should be teaching new math so that students will understand the methods comfortably. So is it any wonder that so many students struggled so deeply, when their teachers were required to change their entire math systems without the foundation of proper training? Even if you have not been personally, directly affected by that precise event, its impact is still as rampant as ever.

Basically, the math teachers of today are either the teachers who began teaching the new math in the first place (without proper training) or they are the students of the math teachers who taught new math without proper training. Therefore, unless they had a unique, exceptional teacher, their primary, consistent examples of teaching math have been teachers using methods that are not conducive to the general understanding of the entire class. This explains why your discomfort (or fear) of math is not at all rare.

It is very clear why being called up to the chalk board to solve a math problem is such a common example of a terrifying situation for students - and it has very little to do with a fear of being in front of the class. Most of us have had a minimum of one humiliating experience while standing with chalk dusted fingers, with the eyes of every math student piercing through us. These are the images that haunt us all the way through adulthood. But it does not mean that we cannot learn math. It just means that we could be developing a solid case of math anxiety.

But what exactly is math anxiety? It's an very strong emotional sensation of anxiety, panic, or fear that people feel when they think about or must apply their ability to understand mathematics. Sufferers of math anxiety frequently believe that they are incapable of doing activities or taking classes that involve math skills. In fact, some people with math anxiety have developed such a fear that it has become a phobia; aptly named math phobia.

The incidence of math anxiety, especially among college students, but also among high school students, has risen considerably over the last 10 years, and currently this increase shows no signs of slowing down. Frequently students will even chose their college majors and programs based specifically on how little math will be compulsory for the completion of the degree.

The prevalence of math anxiety has become so dramatic on college campuses that many of these schools have special counseling programs that are designed to assist math anxious students to deal with their discomfort and their math problems.

Math anxiety itself is not an intellectual problem, as many people have been lead to believe; it is, in fact, an emotional problem that stems from improper math teaching techniques that have slowly built and reinforced these feelings. However, math anxiety can result in an intellectual problem when its symptoms interfere with a person's ability to learn and understand math.

The fear of math can cause a sort of "glitch" in the brain that can cause an otherwise clever person to stumble over even the simplest of math problems. A study by Dr. Mark H. Ashcraft of Cleveland State University in Ohio showed that college students who usually perform well, but who suffer from math anxiety, will suffer from fleeting lapses in their working memory when they are asked to perform even the most basic mental arithmetic. These same issues regarding memory were not present in the same students when they were required to answer questions that did not involve numbers. This very clearly demonstrated that the memory phenomenon is quite specific to only math.

So what exactly is it that causes this inhibiting math anxiety? Unfortunately it is not as simple as one answer, since math anxiety doesn't have one specific cause. Frequently math anxiety can result of a student's either negative experience or embarrassment with math or a math teacher in previous years.

These circumstances can prompt the student to believe that he or she is somehow deficient in his or her math abilities. This belief will consistently lead to a poor performance in math tests and courses in general, leading only to confirm the beliefs of the student's inability. This particular phenomenon is referred to as the "self-fulfilling prophecy" by the psychological community. Math anxiety will result in poor performance, rather than it being the other way around.

Dr. Ashcraft stated that math anxiety is a "It's a learned, almost phobic, reaction to math," and that it is not only people prone to anxiety, fear, or panic who can develop math anxiety.

The image alone of doing math problems can send the blood pressure and heart rate to race, even in the calmest person.

The study by Dr. Ashcraft and his colleague Elizabeth P. Kirk, discovered that students who suffered from math anxiety were frequently stumped by issues of even the most basic math rules, such as "carrying over" a number, when performing a sum, or "borrowing" from a number when doing a subtraction. Lapses such as this occurred only on working memory questions involving numbers.

To explain the problem with memory, Ashcraft states that when math anxiety begins to take its effect, the sufferer experiences a rush of thoughts, leaving little room for the focus required to perform even the simplest of math problems. He stated that "you're draining away the energy you need for solving the problem by worrying about it."

The outcome is a "vicious cycle," for students who are sufferers of math anxiety. As math anxiety is developed, the fear it promotes stands in the way of learning, leading to a decrease in self-confidence in the ability to perform even simple arithmetic.

A large portion of the problem lies in the ways in which math is taught to students today. In the US, students are frequently taught the rules of math, but rarely will they learn why a specific approach to a math problems work. Should students be provided with a foundation of "deeper understanding" of math, it may prevent the development of phobias.

Another study that was published in the Journal of Experimental Psychology by Dr. Jamie Campbell and Dr. Qilin Xue of the University of Saskatchewan in Saskatoon, Canada, reflected the same concepts. The researchers in this study looked at university students who were educated in Canada and China, discovering that the Chinese students could generally outperform the Canadian-educated students when it came to solving complex math problems involving procedural knowledge - the ability to know how to solve a math problem, instead of simply having ideas memorized.

A portion of this result seemed to be due to the use of calculators within both elementary and secondary schools; while Canadians frequently used them, the Chinese students did not.

However, calculators were not the only issue. Since Chinese-educated students also outperformed Canadian-educated students in complex math, it is suggested that cultural factors may also have an impact. However, the short-cut of using the calculator may hinder the development of the problem solving skills that are key to performing well in math.

Though it is critical that students develop such fine math skills, it is easier said than done. It would involve an overhaul of the training among all elementary and secondary educators, changing the education major in every college.

Math Myths

One problem that contributes to the progression of math anxiety, is the belief of many math myths. These erroneous math beliefs include the following:

Men are better in math than women - however, research has failed to demonstrate that there is any difference in math ability between the sexes.
There is a single best way to solve a math problem - however, the majority of math problems can be solved in a number of different ways. By saying that there is only one way to solve a math problem, the thinking and creative skills of the student are held back.

Some people have a math mind, and others do not - in truth, the majority of people have much more potential for their math capabilities than they believe of themselves.
It is a bad thing to count by using your fingers - counting by using fingers has actually shown that an understanding of arithmetic has been established.
People who are skilled in math can do problems quickly in their heads - in actuality, even math professors will review their example problems before they teach them in their classes.

The anxieties formed by these myths can frequently be perpetuated by a range of mind games that students seem to play with themselves. These math mind games include the following beliefs:

I don't perform math fast enough - actually everyone has a different rate at which he or she can learn. The speed of the solving of math problems is not important as long as the student can solve it.

I don't have the mind for math - this belief can inhibit a student's belief in him or herself, and will therefore interfere with the student's real ability to learn math.

I got the correct answer, but it was done the wrong way - there is no single best way to complete a math problem. By believing this, a student's creativity and overall understanding of math is hindered.

If I can get the correct answer, then it is too simple - students who suffer from math anxiety frequently belittle their own abilities when it comes to their math capabilities.
Math is unrelated to my "real" life - by freeing themselves of the fear of math, math anxiety sufferers are only limiting their choices and freedoms for the rest of their life.

Fortunately, there are many ways to help those who suffer from math anxiety. Since math anxiety is a learned, psychological response to doing or thinking about math, that interferes with the sufferer's ability to understand and perform math, it is not at all a reflection of the sufferer's true math skills and abilities.

Helpful Strategies

Many strategies and therapies have been developed to help students to overcome their math anxious responses. Some of these helpful strategies include the following:

Reviewing and learning basic arithmetic principles, techniques and methods. Frequently math anxiety is a result of the experience of many students with early negative situations, and these students have never truly developed a strong base in basic arithmetic, especially in the case of multiplication and fractions. Since math is a discipline that is built on an accumulative foundation, where the concepts are built upon gradually from simpler concepts, a student who has not achieved a solid basis in arithmetic will experience difficulty in learning higher order math. Taking a remedial math course, or a short math course that focuses on arithmetic can often make a considerable difference in reducing the anxious response that math anxiety sufferers have with math.

Becoming aware of any thoughts, actions and feelings that are related to math and responses to math. Math anxiety has a different effect on different students. Therefore it is very important to become familiar with any reactions that the math anxiety sufferer may have about him/herself and the situation when math has been encountered. If the sufferer becomes aware of any irrational or unrealistic thoughts, it's possible to better concentrate on replacing these thoughts with more positive and realistic ones.

Find help! Math anxiety, as we've mentioned, is a learned response, that is reinforced repeatedly over a period of time, and is therefore not something that can be eliminated instantaneously. Students can more effectively reduce their anxious responses with the help of many different services that are readily available. Seeking the assistance of a psychologist or counselor, especially one with a specialty in math anxiety, can assist the sufferer in performing an analysis of his/her psychological response to math, as well as learning anxiety management skills, and developing effective coping strategies. Other great tools are tutors, classes that teach better abilities to take better notes in math class, and other math learning aids.

Learning the mathematic vocabulary will instantly provide a better chance for understanding new concepts. One major issue among students is the lack of understanding of the terms and vocabulary that are common jargon within math classes. Typically math classes will utilize words in a completely different way from the way in which they are utilized in all other subjects. Students easily mistake their lack of understanding the math terms with their mathematical abilities.

Learning anxiety reducing techniques and methods for anxiety management. Anxiety greatly interferes with a student's ability to concentrate, think clearly, pay attention, and remember new concepts. When these same students can learn to relax, using anxiety management techniques, the student can regain his or her ability to control his or her emotional and physical symptoms of anxiety that interfere with the capabilities of mental processing.

Working on creating a positive overall attitude about mathematics. Looking at math with a positive attitude will reduce anxiety through the building of a positive attitude.

Learning to self-talk in a positive way. Pep talking oneself through a positive self talk can greatly assist in overcoming beliefs in math myths or the mind games that may be played. Positive self-talking is an effective way to replace the negative thoughts - the ones that create the anxiety. Even if the sufferer doesn't believe the statements at first, it plants a positive seed in the subconscious, and allows a positive outlook to grow.

Beyond this, students should learn effective math class, note taking and studying techniques. Typically, the math anxious students will avoid asking questions to save themselves from embarrassment. They will sit in the back of classrooms, and refrain from seeking assistance from the professor. Moreover, they will put off studying for math until the very last moment, since it causes them such substantial discomfort. Alone, or a combination of these negative behaviors work only to reduce the anxiety of the students, but in reality, they are actually building a substantially more intense anxiety.

There are many different positive behaviors that can be adopted by math anxious students, so that they can learn to better perform within their math classes.

Sit near the front of the class. This way, there will be fewer distractions, and there will be more of a sensation of being a part of the topic of discussion.

If any questions arise, ASK! If one student has a question, then there are certain to be others who have the same question but are too nervous to ask - perhaps because they have not yet learned how to deal with their own math anxiety.

Seek extra help from the professor after class or during office hours.

Prepare, prepare, prepare - read textbook material before the class, do the homework and work out any problems available within the textbook. Math skills are developed through practice and repetition, so the more practice and repetition, the better the math skills.

Review the material once again after class, to repeat it another time, and to reinforce the new concepts that were learned.

Beyond these tactics that can be taken by the students themselves, teachers and parents need to know that they can also have a large impact on the reduction of math anxiety within students.

As parents and teachers, there is a natural desire to help students to learn and understand how they will one day utilize different math techniques within their everyday lives. But when the student or teacher displays the symptoms of a person who has had nightmarish memories regarding math, where hesitations then develop in the instruction of students, these fears are automatically picked up by the students and commonly adopted as their own.

However, it is possible for teachers and parents to move beyond their own fears to better educate students by overcoming their own hesitations and learning to enjoy math.

Begin by adopting the outlook that math is a beautiful, imaginative or living thing. Of course, we normally think of mathematics as numbers that can be added or subtracted, multiplied or divided, but that is simply the beginning of it.

By thinking of math as something fun and imaginative, parents and teachers can teach children different ways to manipulate numbers, for example in balancing a checkbook. Parents rarely tell their children that math is everywhere around us; in nature, art, and even architecture. Usually, this is because they were never shown these relatively simple connections. But that pattern can break very simply through the participation of parents and teachers.

The beauty and hidden wonders of mathematics can easily be emphasized through a focus that can open the eyes of students to the incredible mathematical patterns that arise everywhere within the natural world. Observations and discussions can be made into things as fascinating as spider webs, leaf patterns, sunflowers and even coastlines. This makes math not only beautiful, but also inspiring and (dare we say) fun!

Pappas Method

For parents and teachers to assist their students in discovering the true wonders of mathematics, the techniques of Theoni Pappas can easily be applied, as per her popular and celebrated book "Fractals, Googols and Other Mathematical Tales." Pappas used to be a math phobia sufferer and created a fascinating step-by-step program for parents and teachers to use in order to teach students the joy of math.

Her simple, constructive step-by-step program goes as follows:

Don't let your fear of math come across to your kids - Parents must be careful not to perpetuate the mathematical myth - that math is only for specially talented "math types." Strive not to make comments like; "they don't like math" or "I have never been good at math." When children overhear comments like these from their primary role models they begin to dread math before even considering a chance of experiencing its wonders. It is important to encourage your children to read and explore the rich world of mathematics, and to practice mathematics without imparting negative biases.

Don't immediately associate math with computation (counting) - It is very important to realize that math is not just numbers and computations, but a realm of exciting ideas that touch every part of our lives -from making a telephone call to how the hair grows on someone's head. Take your children outside and point out real objects that display math concepts. For example, show them the symmetry of a leaf or angles on a building. Take a close look at the spirals in a spider web or intricate patterns of a snowflake.

Help your child understand why math is important - Math improves problem solving, increases competency and should be applied in different ways. It's the same as reading. You can learn the basics of reading without ever enjoying a novel. But, where's the excitement in that? With math, you could stop with the basics. But why when there is so much more to be gained by a fuller Understanding? Life is so much more enriching when we go beyond the basics. Stretch your children's minds to become involved in mathematics in ways that will not only be practical but also enhance their lives.

Make math as "hands on" as possible - Mathematicians participate in mathematics. To really experience math encourage your child to dig in and tackle problems in creative ways. Help them learn how to manipulate numbers using concrete references they understand as well as things they can see or touch. Look for patterns everywhere, explore shapes and symmetries. How many octagons do you see each day on the way to the grocery store? Play math puzzles and games and then encourage your child to try to invent their own. And, whenever possible, help your child realize a mathematical conclusion with real and tangible results. For example, measure out a full glass of juice with a measuring cup and then ask your child to drink half. Measure what is left. Does it measure half of a cup?

Read books that make math exciting:

Fractals, Googols and Other Mathematical Tales introduces an animated cat who explains fractals, tangrams and other mathematical concepts you've probably never heard of to children in terms they can understand. This book can double as a great text book by using one story per lesson.

A Wrinkle in Time is a well-loved classic, combining fantasy and science.

The Joy of Mathematics helps adults explore the beauty of mathematics that is all around.

The Math Curse is an amusing book for 4-8 year olds.

The Gnarly Gnews is a free, humorous bi-monthly newsletter on mathematics.

The Phantom Tollbooth is an Alice in Wonderland-style adventure into the worlds of words and numbers.

Use the internet to help your child explore the fascinating world of mathematics.

Web Math provides a powerful set of math-solvers that gives you instant answers to the stickiest problems.

Math League has challenging math materials and contests for fourth grade and above.

Silver Burdett Ginn Mathematics offers Internet-based math activities for grades K-6.

The Gallery of Interactive Geometry is full of fascinating, interactive geometry activities.

Math is very much like a language of its own. And like any second language, it will get rusty if it is not practiced enough. For that reason, students should always be looking into new ways to keep understanding and brushing up on their math skills, to be certain that foundations do not crumble, inhibiting the learning of new levels of math.

There are many different books, services and websites that have been developed to take the fear out of math, and to help even the most uncertain student develop self confidence in his or her math capabilities.

There is no reason for math or math classes to be a frightening experience, nor should it drive a student crazy, making them believe that they simply don't have the "math brain" that is needed to solve certain problems.

There are friendly ways to tackle such problems and it's all a matter of dispelling myths and creating a solid math foundation.

Concentrate on re-learning the basics and feeling better about yourself in math, and you'll find that the math brain you've always wanted, was there all along.

Special Report: How to Overcome Test Anxiety

The very nature of tests caters to some level of anxiety, nervousness or tension, just as we feel for any important event that occurs in our lives. A little bit of anxiety or nervousness can be a good thing. It helps us with motivation, and makes achievement just that much sweeter. However, too much anxiety can be a problem; especially if it hinders our ability to function and perform.

"Test anxiety," is the term that refers to the emotional reactions that some test-takers experience when faced with a test or exam. Having a fear of testing and exams is based upon a rational fear, since the test-taker's performance can shape the course of an academic career. Nevertheless, experiencing excessive fear of examinations will only interfere with the test-takers ability to perform and his/her chances to be successful.

There are a large variety of causes that can contribute to the development and sensation of test anxiety. These include, but are not limited to lack of performance and worrying about issues surrounding the test.

Lack of Preparation

Lack of preparation can be identified by the following behaviors or situations:

- Not scheduling enough time to study, and therefore cramming the night before the test or exam
- Managing time poorly, to create the sensation that there is not enough time to do everything
- Failing to organize the text information in advance, so that the study material consists of the entire text and not simply the pertinent information
- Poor overall studying habits

Worrying, on the other hand, can be related to both the test-taker and many other factors around him/her that will be affected by the results of the test. These include worrying about:

- Previous performances on similar exams, or exams in general
- How friends and other students are achieving
- The negative consequences that will result from a poor grade or failure

There are three primary elements to test anxiety: physical components, which involve the same typical bodily reactions as those to acute anxiety (to be discussed below); emotional factors, which have to do with fear or panic; and mental or cognitive issues, which concern attention spans and memory abilities.

Physical Signals

There are many different symptoms of test anxiety, and these are not limited to mental and emotional strain. Frequently there are a range of physical signals that will let a test taker know that he/she is suffering from test anxiety. These bodily changes can include the following:

- Perspiring
- Sweaty palms
- Wet, trembling hands
- Nausea
- Dry mouth
- A knot in the stomach
- Headache
- Faintness
- Muscle tension
- Aching shoulders, back and neck
- Rapid heart beat

- Feeling too hot/cold

To recognize the sensation of test anxiety, a test-taker should monitor him/herself for the following sensations:

- The physical distress symptoms as listed above
- Emotional sensitivity, expressing emotional feelings such as the need to cry or laugh too much, or a sensation of anger or helplessness
- A decreased ability to think, causing the test-taker to blank out or have racing thoughts that are hard to organize or control.

Though most students will feel some level of anxiety when faced with a test or exam, the majority can cope with that anxiety and maintain it at a manageable level. However, those who cannot are faced with a very real and very serious condition, which can and should be controlled for the immeasurable benefit of this sufferer.

Naturally, these sensations lead to negative results for the testing experience. The most common effects of test anxiety have to do with nervousness and mental blocking.

Nervousness

Nervousness can appear in several different levels:

- The test-taker's difficulty, or even inability to read and understand the questions on the test
- The difficulty or inability to organize thoughts to a coherent form
- The difficulty or inability to recall key words and concepts relating to the testing questions (especially essays)
- The receipt of poor grades on a test, though the test material was well known by the test taker

Conversely, a person may also experience mental blocking, which involves:

- Blanking out on test questions
- Only remembering the correct answers to the questions when the test has already finished

Fortunately for test anxiety sufferers, beating these feelings, to a large degree, has to do with proper preparation. When a test taker has a feeling of preparedness, then anxiety will be dramatically lessened.

The first step to resolving anxiety issues is to distinguish which of the two types of anxiety are being suffered. If the anxiety is a direct result of a lack of preparation, this should be considered a normal reaction, and the anxiety level (as opposed to the test results) shouldn't be anything to worry about. However, if, when adequately prepared, the test-taker still panics, blanks out, or seems to overreact, this is not a fully rational reaction. While this can be considered normal too, there are many ways to combat and overcome these effects.

Remember that anxiety cannot be entirely eliminated; however, there are ways to minimize it, to make the anxiety easier to manage. Preparation is one of the best ways to minimize test anxiety. Therefore the following techniques are wise in order to best fight off any anxiety that may want to build.

To begin with, try to avoid cramming before a test, whenever it is possible. By trying to memorize an entire term's worth of information in one day, you'll be shocking your system, and not giving yourself a very good chance to absorb the information. This is an easy path to anxiety, so for those who suffer from test anxiety, cramming should not even be considered an option.

Instead of cramming, work throughout the semester to combine all of the material which is presented throughout the semester, and work on it gradually as the course goes by, making sure to master the main concepts first, leaving minor details for a week or so before the test.

To study for the upcoming exam, be sure to pose questions that may be on the examination, to gauge the ability to answer them by integrating the ideas from your texts, notes and lectures, as well as any supplementary readings.

If it is truly impossible to cover all of the information that was covered in that particular term, concentrate on the most important portions, that can be covered very well. Learn these concepts as best as possible, so that when the test comes, a goal can be made to use these concepts as presentations of your knowledge.

In addition to study habits, changes in attitude are critical to beating a struggle with test anxiety. In fact, an improvement of the perspective over the entire test-taking experience can actually help a test taker to enjoy studying and therefore improve the overall experience. Be certain not to overemphasize the significance of the grade - know that the result of the test is neither a reflection of self worth, nor is it a measure of intelligence; one grade will not predict a person's future success.

To improve an overall testing outlook, the following steps should be tried:

Keeping in mind that the most reasonable expectation for taking a test is to expect to try to demonstrate as much of what you know as you possibly can.
Reminding ourselves that a test is only one test; this is not the only one, and there will be others.
The thought of thinking of oneself in an irrational, all-or-nothing term should be avoided at all costs.

A reward should be designated for after the test, so there's something to look forward to. Whether it is going to a movie, going out to eat, or simply visiting friends, schedule it in advance, and do it no matter what result is expected on the exam.

Test-takers should also keep in mind that the basics are some of the most important things, even beyond anti-anxiety techniques and studying. Never neglect the basic social, emotional and biological needs, in order to try to absorb information. In order to best achieve, these three factors must be held as just as important as the studying itself.

Study Steps

Remember the following important steps for studying:

Maintain healthy nutrition and exercise habits. Continue both your recreational activities and social pass times. These both contribute to your physical and emotional well being.
Be certain to get a good amount of sleep, especially the night before the test, because when you're overtired you are not able to perform to the best of your best ability.
Keep the studying pace to a moderate level by taking breaks when they are needed, and varying the work whenever possible, to keep the mind fresh instead of getting bored. When enough studying has been done that all the material that can be learned has been learned, and the test taker is prepared for the test, stop studying and do something relaxing such as listening to music, watching a movie, or taking a warm bubble bath.

There are also many other techniques to minimize the uneasiness or apprehension that is experienced along with test anxiety before, during, or even after the examination. In fact, there are a great deal of things that can be done to stop anxiety from interfering with lifestyle and performance. Again, remember that anxiety will not be eliminated entirely, and it shouldn't be. Otherwise that "up" feeling for exams would not exist, and most of us depend on that sensation to perform better than usual. However, this anxiety has to be at a level that is manageable.

Of course, as we have just discussed, being prepared for the exam is half the battle right away. Attending all classes, finding out what knowledge will be expected on the exam, and knowing the exam schedules are easy steps to lowering anxiety. Keeping up with work will remove the need to cram, and efficient study habits will eliminate wasted time. Studying should be done in an ideal location for concentration, so that it is simple to become interested in the material and give it complete attention. A method such as SQ3R (Survey, Question, Read, Recite, Review) is a wonderful key to follow to make sure that the study habits are as effective as possible, especially in the case of learning from a textbook. Flashcards are great techniques for memorization. Learning to take good notes will mean that notes will be full of useful information, so that less sifting will need to be done to seek out what is pertinent for studying. Reviewing notes after class and then again on occasion will keep the information fresh in the mind. From notes that have been taken summary sheets and outlines can be made for simpler reviewing.

A study group can also be a very motivational and helpful place to study, as there will be a sharing of ideas, all of the minds can work together, to make sure that everyone understands, and the studying will be made more interesting because it will be a social occasion.

Basically, though, as long as the test-taker remains organized and self confident, with efficient study habits, less time will need to be spent studying, and higher grades will be achieved.

There are many useful steps to become more self-confident. The first of these is "self talk." It has been shown through extensive research, that self-talk for students who suffer from test anxiety, should be well monitored, in order to make sure that it contributes to self confidence as opposed to sinking the student. Frequently the self talk of test-anxious students is negative or self-defeating, thinking that everyone else is smarter and faster, that they always mess up, and that if they don't do well, they'll fail the entire course. It is important to decreasing anxiety that awareness is made of self talk. Try writing any negative self thoughts and then disputing them with a positive statement instead. Begin self-encouragement as though it was a friend speaking. Repeat positive statements to help reprogram the mind to believing in successes instead of failures.

Helpful Techniques

Other extremely helpful techniques include:

- Self-visualization of doing well and reaching goals
- While aiming for an "A" level of understanding, don't try to "overprotect" by setting your expectations lower. This will only convince the mind to stop studying in order to meet the lower expectations.
- Don't make comparisons with the results or habits of other students. These are individual factors, and different things work for different people, causing different results.
- Strive to become an expert in learning what works well, and what can be done in order to improve. Consider collecting this data in a journal.
- Create rewards for after studying instead of doing things before studying that will only turn into avoidance behaviors.
- Make a practice of relaxing - by using methods such as progressive relaxation, self-hypnosis, guided imagery, etc - in order to make relaxation an automatic sensation.
- Work on creating a state of relaxed concentration so that concentrating will take on the focus of the mind, so that none will be wasted on worrying.
- Take good care of the physical self by eating well and getting enough sleep.
- Plan in time for exercise and stick to this plan.

Beyond these techniques, there are other methods to be used before, during and after the test that will help the test-taker perform well in addition to overcoming anxiety.

Before the exam comes the academic preparation. This involves establishing a study schedule and beginning at least one week before the actual date of the test. By doing this, the anxiety of not having enough time to study for the test will be automatically eliminated. Moreover, this will make the studying a much more effective experience, ensuring that the learning will be an easier process. This relieves much undue pressure on the test-taker.

Summary sheets, note cards, and flash cards with the main concepts and examples of these main concepts should be prepared in advance of the actual studying time. A topic should never be eliminated from this process. By omitting a topic because it isn't expected to be on the test is only setting up the test-taker for anxiety should it actually appear on the exam. Utilize the course syllabus for laying out the topics that should be studied. Carefully go over the notes that were made in class, paying special attention to any of the issues that the professor took special care to emphasize while lecturing in class. In the textbooks, use the chapter review, or if possible, the chapter tests, to begin your review.

It may even be possible to ask the instructor what information will be covered on the exam, or what the format of the exam will be (for example, multiple choice, essay, free form, true-false). Additionally, see if it is possible to find out how many questions will be on the test. If a review sheet or sample test has been offered by the professor, make good use of it, above anything else, for the preparation for the test. Another great resource for getting to know the examination is reviewing tests from previous semesters. Use these tests to review, and aim to achieve a 100% score on each of the possible topics. With a few exceptions, the goal that you set for yourself is the highest one that you will reach.

Take all of the questions that were assigned as homework, and rework them to any other possible course material. The more problems reworked, the more skill and confidence will form as a result. When forming the solution to a problem, write out each of the steps. Don't simply do head work. By doing as many steps on paper as possible, much clarification and therefore confidence will be formed. Do this with as many homework problems as possible, before checking the answers. By checking the answer after each problem, a reinforcement will exist, that will not be on the exam. Study situations should be as exam-like as possible, to prime the test-taker's system for the experience. By waiting to check the answers at the end, a psychological advantage will be formed, to decrease the stress factor.

Another fantastic reason for not cramming is the avoidance of confusion in concepts, especially when it comes to mathematics. 8-10 hours of study will become one hundred percent more effective if it is spread out over a week or at least several days, instead of doing it all in one sitting. Recognize that the human brain requires time in order to assimilate new material, so frequent breaks and a span of study time over several days will be much more beneficial.

Additionally, don't study right up until the point of the exam. Studying should stop a minimum of one hour before the exam begins. This allows the brain to rest and put things in their proper order. This will also provide the time to become as relaxed as possible when going into the examination room. The test-taker will also have time to eat well and eat sensibly. Know that the brain needs food as much as the rest of the body. With enough food and enough sleep, as well as a relaxed attitude, the body and the mind are primed for success.
Avoid any anxious classmates who are talking about the exam. These students only spread anxiety, and are not worth sharing the anxious sentimentalities.

Before the test also involves creating a positive attitude, so mental preparation should also be a point of concentration. There are many keys to creating a positive attitude. Should fears become rushing in, make a visualization of taking the exam, doing well, and seeing an A written on the paper. Write out a list of affirmations that will bring a feeling of confidence, such as "I am doing well in my English class," "I studied well and know my material," "I enjoy this class." Even if the affirmations aren't believed at first, it sends a positive message to the subconscious which will result in an alteration of the overall belief system, which is the system that creates reality.

If a sensation of panic begins, work with the fear and imagine the very worst! Work through the entire scenario of not passing the test, failing the entire course, and dropping out of school, followed by not getting a job, and pushing a shopping cart through the dark alley where you'll live. This will place things into perspective! Then, practice deep breathing and create a visualization of the opposite situation - achieving an "A" on the exam, passing the entire course, receiving the degree at a graduation ceremony.

On the day of the test, there are many things to be done to ensure the best results, as well as the most calm outlook. The following stages are suggested in order to maximize test-taking potential:

Begin the examination day with a moderate breakfast, and avoid any coffee or beverages with caffeine if the test taker is prone to jitters. Even people who are used to managing caffeine can feel jittery or light-headed when it is taken on a test day.

Attempt to do something that is relaxing before the examination begins. As last minute cramming clouds the mastering of overall concepts, it is better to use this time to create a calming outlook.

Be certain to arrive at the test location well in advance, in order to provide time to select a location that is away from doors, windows and other distractions, as well as giving enough time to relax before the test begins.
Keep away from anxiety generating classmates who will upset the sensation of stability and relaxation that is being attempted before the exam.

Should the waiting period before the exam begins cause anxiety, create a self-distraction by reading a light magazine or something else that is relaxing and simple.

During the exam itself, read the entire exam from beginning to end, and find out how much time should be allotted to each individual problem. Once writing the exam, should more time be taken for a problem, it should be abandoned, in order to begin another problem. If there is time at the end, the unfinished problem can always be returned to and completed.

Read the instructions very carefully - twice - so that unpleasant surprises won't follow during or after the exam has ended.

When writing the exam, pretend that the situation is actually simply the completion of homework within a library, or at home. This will assist in forming a relaxed atmosphere, and will allow the brain extra focus for the complex thinking function.

Begin the exam with all of the questions with which the most confidence is felt. This will build the confidence level regarding the entire exam and will begin a quality momentum. This will also create encouragement for trying the problems where uncertainty resides.

Going with the "gut instinct" is always the way to go when solving a problem. Second guessing should be avoided at all costs. Have confidence in the ability to do well.

For essay questions, create an outline in advance that will keep the mind organized and make certain that all of the points are remembered. For multiple choice, read every answer, even if the correct one has been spotted - a better one may exist.

Continue at a pace that is reasonable and not rushed, in order to be able to work carefully. Provide enough time to go over the answers at the end, to check for small errors that can be corrected.

Should a feeling of panic begin, breathe deeply, and think of the feeling of the body releasing sand through its pores. Visualize a calm, peaceful place, and include all of the sights, sounds and sensations of this image. Continue the deep breathing, and take a few minutes to continue this with closed eyes. When all is well again, return to the test.

If a "blanking" occurs for a certain question, skip it and move on to the next question. There will be time to return to the other question later. Get everything done that can be done, first, to guarantee all the grades that can be compiled, and to build all of the confidence possible. Then return to the weaker questions to build the marks from there.

Remember, one's own reality can be created, so as long as the belief is there, success will follow. And remember: anxiety can happen later, right now, there's an exam to be written!

After the examination is complete, whether there is a feeling for a good grade or a bad grade, don't dwell on the exam, and be certain to follow through on the reward that was promised...and enjoy it! Don't dwell on any mistakes that have been made, as there is nothing that can be done at this point anyway.

Additionally, don't begin to study for the next test right away. Do something relaxing for a while, and let the mind relax and prepare itself to begin absorbing information again.

From the results of the exam - both the grade and the entire experience, be certain to learn from what has gone on. Perfect studying habits and work some more on confidence in order to make the next examination experience even better than the last one.

Learn to avoid places where openings occurred for laziness, procrastination and day dreaming.

Use the time between this exam and the next one to better learn to relax, even learning to relax on cue, so that any anxiety can be controlled during the next exam. Learn how to relax the body. Slouch in your chair if that helps. Tighten and then relax all of the different muscle groups, one group at a time, beginning with the feet and then working all the way up to the neck and face. This will ultimately relax the muscles more than they were to begin with. Learn how to breathe deeply and comfortably, and focus on this breathing going in and out as a relaxing thought. With every exhale, repeat the word "relax."

As common as test anxiety is, it is very possible to overcome it. Make yourself one of the test-takers who overcome this frustrating hindrance.

Special Report: Retaking the Test: What Are Your Chances at Improving Your Score?

After going through the experience of taking a major test, many test takers feel that once is enough. The test usually comes during a period of transition in the test taker's life, and taking the test is only one of a series of important events. With so many distractions and conflicting recommendations, it may be difficult for a test taker to rationally determine whether or not he should retake the test after viewing his scores.

The importance of the test usually only adds to the burden of the retake decision. However, don't be swayed by emotion. There a few simple questions that you can ask yourself to guide you as you try to determine whether a retake would improve your score:

1. What went wrong? Why wasn't your score what you expected?

Can you point to a single factor or problem that you feel caused the low score? Were you sick on test day? Was there an emotional upheaval in your life that caused a distraction? Were you late for the test or not able to use the full time allotment? If you can point to any of these specific, individual problems, then a retake should definitely be considered.

2. Is there enough time to improve?

Many problems that may show up in your score report may take a lot of time for improvement. A deficiency in a particular math skill may require weeks or months of tutoring and studying to improve. If you have enough time to improve an identified weakness, then a retake should definitely be considered.

3. How will additional scores be used? Will a score average, highest score, or most recent score be used?

Different test scores may be handled completely differently. If you've taken the test multiple times, sometimes your highest score is used, sometimes your average score is computed and used, and sometimes your most recent score is used. Make sure you understand what method will be used to evaluate your scores, and use that to help you determine whether a retake should be considered.

4. Are my practice test scores significantly higher than my actual test score?

If you have taken a lot of practice tests and are consistently scoring at a much higher level than your actual test score, then you should consider a retake. However, if you've taken five practice tests and only one of your scores was higher than your actual test score, or if your practice test scores were only slightly higher than your actual test score, then it is unlikely that you will significantly increase your score.

5. Do I need perfect scores or will I be able to live with this score? Will this score still allow me to follow my dreams?

What kind of score is acceptable to you? Is your current score "good enough?" Do you have to have a certain score in order to pursue the future of your dreams? If you won't be happy with your current score, and there's no way that you could live with it, then you should consider a retake. However, don't get your hopes up. If you are looking for significant improvement, that may or may not be possible. But if you won't be happy otherwise, it is at least worth the effort.

Remember that there are other considerations. To achieve your dream, it is likely that your grades may also be taken into account. A great test score is usually not the only thing necessary to succeed. Make sure that you aren't overemphasizing the importance of a high test score.

Furthermore, a retake does not always result in a higher score. Some test takers will score lower on a retake, rather than higher. One study shows that one-fourth of test takers will achieve a significant improvement in test score, while one-sixth of test takers will actually show a decrease. While this shows that most test takers will improve, the majority will only improve their scores a little and a retake may not be worth the test taker's effort.

Finally, if a test is taken only once and is considered in the added context of good grades on the part of a test taker, the person reviewing the grades and scores may be tempted to assume that the test taker just had a bad day while taking the test, and may discount the low test score in favor of the high grades. But if the test is retaken and the scores are approximately the same, then the validity of the low scores are only confirmed. Therefore, a retake could actually hurt a test taker by definitely bracketing a test taker's score ability to a limited range.

Special Report: The Politically Incorrect Guide to Scholarships and Merit Aid...

Ugly Fact #1 – Schools are more interested in statistics than you as a person

You've read their cute brochures, their painstaking efforts to convince you that they really respect you as an individual- but I'm going to tell you the truth. Almost every college and university sees you, at best, as a collage of numbers and statistics. Some see you just as one or two different numbers.

This CAN be a good thing- assuming you have the right numbers. In general, these are the critical factors that are most likely to land you a scholarship:

- o National Merit OR National Achievement Scholarship (the latter is actually better because it identifies you as a member of a favored minority group).
- o GPA of 3.5 or higher in high school
- o Two or three extracurricular activities with lots of "depth" in participation- surface-level memberships in many groups are ignored.
- o SAT score greater than 1300 or ACT greater than 30.

That's about it- for the most part, scholarships are awarded on the basis of test scores, as long as the candidate meets certain minimums. For example, a mid-tier state school will usually give a full scholarship to anyone with an SAT > 1300, as long as the student also has at least a high school GPA of 3.5, and some evidence of "depth" in extracurricular activities.

The "big money" scholarships to prestigious state schools are awarded almost entirely on the basis of extremely high test scores combined with National Merit status. Test scores in excess of 1400 on the SAT and 32 on the ACT are usually necessary to even qualify.

I have not mentioned merit aid to private schools for a big reason- there's not much of it:

Ugly Fact #2 – Private Schools Promise a Lot, but Rarely Deliver

Private schools are basically non-profit businesses- they have to fund their operations with student dollars, so right away you should be alert to their tactics. They will try to impress you with images of prestige, exclusivity, and tradition, initially promising lots of merit aid, and then quietly pick your pocket with their final offer after you have already emotionally committed to attending their fabled campus.

Here's why: private schools consider subsidized loans to be "financial aid." This means that they will loan you the tuition money at a reduced rate of interest and think they are helping you. You didn't actually think you could go to their fine institution for free, did you? So don't be surprised when their final aid package arrives with about 50% of the "aid" in the form of choking student loan debt.

Another tactic is their pattern of overcharging for room and board to make their tuition seem more competitive (of course, conveniently "requiring" freshman to purchase the full room an board package- often sophomores as well). A prominent private school in the South (where the cost of living is low) charges $6000 a semester per student for room and board- this buys you a half-share in a 200 square foot dorm room in a building without air conditioning!

So then, the question remains- even if you know that the most merit aid you will receive from a private school is about 50% (and is likely even lower after accounting for inflated fees and tuition), is the prestige of a private school worth the cost? The answer may surprise you:

Ugly Fact #3 – The Economics of a Private College Education

I don't mean to put down private schools- but I do think you need the facts when you make your decision. Economically, you are almost always worse off going to a private school-you can then decide if the intangible factors (prestige, exclusivity, individual attention, etc) are enough to compensate you for the economic loss.

There are basically three tiers of private schools- the "Ivy League Plus," the "Ivy Wannabes," and the "Private Pretenders."

The ILP consists of all Ivy League schools plus a few other exclusive private schools like MIT and Stanford. They give a good education, though not necessarily superior to top-tier public schools- it should be noted, however, that Ivy League schools, with their constant need to distinguish themselves in the market, are more likely to embrace academic fads- this means a good bit of your education (especially in a "soft" field like English or Sociology) may eventually be obsolete; state schools and second-tier private schools tend to teach time-tested fundamentals more likely to be relevant in the future.

The ILW's consist of various small but prestigious liberal arts schools and larger private universities- they give as good an education (or better) as an Ivy League school, and in rare cases even offer full scholarships. Prominent examples are Emory, Rice, Vanderbilt, and Duke. Other less prominent examples include Baylor, Tulane, and Amherst.

The PP's consist of a large number of overpriced private schools that prey upon the status-seeking instincts of wealthy parents with underachieving students- i.e., parents who couldn't bear the thought of sending Junior to a community college or a mainstream state school (even though Junior made C's in high school) can send their child to a private school that has all of the exterior trappings of an elite private college (these schools may even seem more prestigious than the ILW's because of their need to foster this illusion). However, this is not to say you cannot get a great education at a PP (many have very small class sizes and passionate faculty who are there because they love to teach)- it's just that, unless you are going to graduate school (where your education is validated by a standardized test), you are likely going to have a hard time convincing an employer of your exceptional status among the underachieving partying masses on campus. Even though their scholarship offer will likely be tempting, do not fall into their career death trap- in almost all cases, you are better off at a higher standard public school.

Private Schools as "Educational Insurance"

The true economic function of prestigious private schools is economic insurance for the children of the wealthy. At any private school, there is a gulf in the types of students:

1. Extreme High Achievers who are usually offered partial scholarships to attend (SAT > 1500)
2. Wealthy students who can afford the tuition with no financial assistance, but are only moderately high achieving (SAT of 1150-1250).

How does this function as insurance? Let's take a simple example like law school- there are more lawyers in this country than jobs or cases to support them- over 1/3 of lawyers are chronically underemployed. To guarantee a prestigious law job, you either have to graduate from an Ivy League-type school or graduate in the top 10% of a state law school- both achievements will offer the same salary. The prestige and reputation of the Ivy League schools (maintained by their recruited vanguard of extreme high achievers) serves as insurance for the children of the wealthy who are willing to pay up for tuition to avoid gambling their social status on grade competition in a state school. Besides, caring about grades is traditionally *déclassé*, evidence of "trying too hard." The notion of the "Gentleman's C" (i.e. a gentleman would accept no less, and tries for no more) is still alive and well.

Special Report: Prefixes and Suffixes

Prefix	Meaning	Examples
A	in, on, of, up, to	abed, afoot
A	without, lacking	atheist, agnostic
Ab	from, away, off	abdicate, abjure
Ad	to, toward	advance
Am	friend, love	amicable, amatory
Ante	before, previous	antecedent, antedate
anti	against, opposing	antipathy, antidote
auto	self	autonomy, autobiography
belli	war, warlike	bellicose
bene	well, good	benefit, benefactor
bi	two	bisect, biennial
bio	life	biology, biosphere
cata	down, away, thoroughly	catastrophe, cataclysm
chron	time	chronometer, synchronize
circum	around	circumspect, circumference
com	with, together, very	commotion, complicate
contra	against, opposing	contradict, contravene
cred	belief, trust	credible, credit
de	from	depart
dem	people	demographics, democracy
dia	through, across, apart	diameter, diagnose
dis	away, off, down, not	dissent, disappear
epi	upon	epilogue
equi	equal, equally	equivalent
ex	out	extract

Prefix	Meaning	Examples
for	away, off, from	forget, forswear
fore	before, previous	foretell, forefathers
homo	same, equal	homogenized
hyper	excessive, over	hypercritical, hypertension
hypo	under, beneath	hypodermic, hypothesis
in	in, into	intrude, invade
in	not, opposing	incapable, ineligible
inter	among, between	intercede, interrupt
intra	within	intramural, intrastate
magn	large	magnitude, magnify
mal	bad, poorly, not	malfunction
micr	small	microbe, microscope
mis	bad, poorly, not	misspell, misfire
mono	one, single	monogomy, monologue
mor	die, death	mortality, mortuary
neo	new	neolithic, neoconservative
non	not	nonentity, nonsense
ob	against, opposing	objection
omni	all, everywhere	omniscient
ortho	right, straight	orthogonal, orthodox
over	above	overbearing
pan	all, entire	panorama, pandemonium
para	beside, beyond	parallel, paradox
per	through	perceive, permit
peri	around	periscope, perimeter
phil	love, like	philosophy, philanthropic
poly	many	polymorphous, polygamous
post	after, following	postpone, postscript
pre	before, previous	prevent, preclude

Prefix	Meaning	Examples
prim	first, early	primitive, primary
pro	forward, in place of	propel, pronoun
re	back, backward, again	revoke, recur
retro	back, backward	retrospect, retrograde
semi	half, partly	semicircle, semicolon
sub	under, beneath	subjugate, substitute
super	above, extra	supersede, supernumerary
sym	with, together	sympathy, symphony
trans	across, beyond, over	transact, transport
ultra	beyond, excessively	ultramodern, ultrasonic, ultraviolet
un	not, reverse of	unhappy, unlock
uni	one	uniform, unity
vis	to see	visage, visable

Suffix	Meaning	Examples
able	able to, likely	capable, tolerable
age	process, state, rank	passage, bondage
ance	act, condition, fact	acceptance, vigilance
arch	to rule	monarch
ard	one that does excessively	drunkard, wizard
ate	having, showing	separate, desolate
ation	action, state, result	occupation, starvation
cy	state, condition	accuracy, captaincy
dom	state, rank, condition	serfdom, wisdom
en	cause to be, become	deepen, strengthen
er	one who does	teacher
esce	become, grow, continue	convalesce, acquiesce
esque	in the style of, like	picturesque, grotesque
ess	feminine	waitress, lioness
fic	making, causing	terrific, beatific
ful	full of, marked by	thankful, zestful
fy	make, cause, cause to have	glorify, fortify
hood	state, condition	manhood, statehood
ible	able, likely, fit	edible, possible, divisible
ion	action, result, state	union, fusion
ish	suggesting, like	churlish, childish
ism	act, manner, doctrine	barbarism, socialism
ist	doer, believer	monopolist, socialist
ition	action, state, result	sedition, expedition
ity	state, quality, condition	acidity, civility
ize	make, cause to be, treat with	sterilize, mechanize, criticize

Suffix	Meaning	Examples
less	lacking, without	hopeless, countless
like	like, similar	childlike, dreamlike
logue	type of speaking or writing	prologue
ly	like, of the nature of	friendly, positively
ment	means, result, action	refreshment, disappointment
ness	quality, state	greatness, tallness
or	doer, office, action	juror, elevator, honor
ous	marked by, given to	religious, riotous
ship	the art or skill of	statesmanship
some	apt to, showing	tiresome, lonesome
th	act, state, quality	warmth, width
tude	quality, state, result	magnitude, fortitude
ty	quality, state	enmity, activity
ward	in the direction of	backward, homeward

Special Report: High-Frequency Vocabulary

aberrant: Markedly different from an accepted norm.

aberration: Deviation from a right, customary, or prescribed course.

abet: To aid, promote, or encourage the commission of (an offense).

abeyance: A state of suspension or temporary inaction.

abjure: To recant, renounce, repudiate under oath.

ablution: A washing or cleansing, especially of the body.

abrogate: To abolish, repeal.

abscond: To depart suddenly and secretly, as for the purpose of escaping arrest.

abstemious: Characterized by self denial or abstinence, as in the use of drink, food.

abstruse: Dealing with matters difficult to be understood.

abut: To touch at the end or boundary line.

accede: To agree.

acquiesce: To comply; submit.

acrid: Harshly pungent or bitter.

acumen: Quickness of intellectual insight, or discernment; keenness of discrimination.

adage: An old saying.

adamant: Any substance of exceeding hardness or impenetrability.

admonition: Gentle reproof.

adumbrate: To represent beforehand in outline or by emblem.

affable: Easy to approach.

aggrandize: To cause to appear greatly.

aggravate: To make heavier, worse, or more burdensome.

agile: Able to move or act quickly, physically, or mentally.

agog: In eager desire.

alacrity: Cheerful willingness.

alcove: A covered recess connected with or at the side of a larger room.

alleviate: To make less burdensome or less hard to bear.

aloof: Not in sympathy with or desiring to associate with others.

amalgamate: To mix or blend together in a homogeneous body.

ambidextrous: Having the ability of using both hands with equal skill or ease.

ambiguous: Having a double meaning.

ameliorate: To relieve, as from pain or hardship

anathema: Anything forbidden, as by social usage.

animadversion: The utterance of criticism or censure.

animosity: Hatred.

antediluvian: Of or pertaining to the times, things, events before the great flood in the days of Noah.

antidote: Anything that will counteract or remove the effects of poison, disease, or the like.

aplomb: Confidence; coolness.

apocryphal : Of doubtful authority or authenticity.

apogee: The climax.

apostate: False.

apotheosis: Deification.

apparition: Ghost.

appease: To soothe by quieting anger or indignation.

apposite: Appropriate.

apprise: To give notice to; to inform.

approbation: Sanction.

arboreal: Of or pertaining to a tree or trees.

ardor: Intensity of passion or affection.

argot: A specialized vocabulary peculiar to a particular group.

arrant: Notoriously bad.

ascetic: Given to severe self-denial and practicing excessive abstinence and devotion.

ascribe: To assign as a quality or attribute.

asperity: Harshness or roughness of temper.

assiduous: Unceasing; persistent

assuage: To cause to be less harsh, violent, or severe, as excitement, appetite, pain, or disease.

astringent: Harsh in disposition or character.

astute: Keen in discernment.

atonement: Amends, reparation, or expiation made from wrong or injury.

audacious: Fearless.

augury: Omen

auspicious: Favorable omen

austere: Severely simple; unadorned.

autocrat: Anyone who claims or wields unrestricted or undisputed authority or influence.

auxiliary: One who or that which aids or helps, especially when regarded as subsidiary or accessory.

avarice: Passion for getting and keeping riches.

aver: To avouch, justify or prove

aversion: A mental condition of fixed opposition to or dislike of some particular thing.

avow: To declare openly.

baleful: Malignant.

banal: Commonplace.

bask: To make warm by genial heat.

beatify: To make supremely happy.

bedaub: To smear over, as with something oily or sticky.

bellicose: Warlike.

belligerent: Manifesting a warlike spirit.

benefactor: A doer of kindly and charitable acts.

benevolence: Any act of kindness or well-doing.

benign: Good and kind of heart.

berate: To scold severely.

bewilder: To confuse the perceptions or judgment of.

blandishment: Flattery intended to persuade.

blatant: Noisily or offensively loud or clamorous.

blithe: Joyous.

boisterous: Unchecked merriment or animal spirits.

bolster: To support, as something wrong.

bombast: Inflated or extravagant language, especially on unimportant subjects.

boorish: Rude.

breach: The violation of official duty, lawful right, or a legal obligation.

brittle: Fragile.

broach: To mention, for the first time.

bumptious: Full of offensive and aggressive self-conceit.

buoyant: Having the power or tendency to float or keep afloat.

burnish: To make brilliant or shining.

cabal: A number of persons secretly united for effecting by intrigue some private purpose.

cacophony: A disagreeable, harsh, or discordant sound or combination of sounds or tones.

cajole: To impose on or dupe by flattering speech.

callow: Without experience of the world.

calumny: Slander.

candid: Straightforward.

cant: To talk in a singsong, preaching tone with affected solemnity.

capacious: Roomy.

capitulate: To surrender or stipulate terms.

captious: Hypercritical.

castigate: To punish.

cataract: Opacity of the lens of the eye resulting in complete or partial blindness.

caustic: Sarcastic and severe.

censure: To criticize severely; also, an expression of disapproval.

centurion: A captain of a company of one hundred infantry in the ancient Roman army.

chagrin: Keen vexation, annoyance, or mortification, as at one's failures or errors.

chary: Careful; wary; cautious.

chicanery: The use of trickery to deceive.

circumlocution: Indirect or roundabout expression.

coddle: To treat as a baby or an invalid.

coerce: To force.

coeval: Existing during the same period of time; also, a contemporary.

cogent: Appealing strongly to the reason or conscience.

cogitate: Consider carefully and deeply; ponder.

cognizant: Taking notice.

colloquial: Pertaining or peculiar to common speech as distinguished from literary.

collusion: A secret agreement for a wrongful purpose.

comestible: Fit to be eaten.

commemorate: To serve as a remembrance of.

complaisance: Politeness.

complement: To make complete.

comport: To conduct or behave (oneself).

compunction: Remorseful feeling.

conceit: Self-flattering opinion.

conciliatory: Tending to reconcile.

concord: Harmony.

concur: To agree.

condense: To abridge.

conflagration: A great fire, as of many buildings, a forest, or the like.

confluence: The place where streams meet.

congeal: To coagulate.

conjoin: To unite.

connoisseur: A critical judge of art, especially one with thorough knowledge and sound judgment of art.

console: To comfort.

conspicuous: Clearly visible.

consternation: Panic.

constrict: To bind.

consummate: To bring to completion.

contiguous: Touching or joining at the edge or boundary.

contrite: Broken in spirit because of a sense of sin.

contumacious: Rebellious.

copious: Plenteous.

cornucopia: The horn of plenty, symbolizing peace and prosperity.

corporeal: Of a material nature; physical.

correlate: To put in some relation of connection or correspondence.

corroboration: Confirmation.

counterfeit: Made to resemble something else.

countervail: To offset.

covert: Concealed, especially for an evil purpose.

cower: To crouch down tremblingly, as through fear or shame.

crass: Coarse or thick in nature or structure, as opposed to thin or fine.

credulous: Easily deceived.

cupidity: Avarice.

cursory: Rapid and superficial.

curtail: To cut off or cut short.

cynosure: That to which general interest or attention is directed.

dearth: Scarcity, as of something customary, essential ,or desirable.

defer: To delay or put off to some other time.

deign: To deem worthy of notice or account.

deleterious: Hurtful, morally or physically.

delineate: To represent by sketch or diagram.

deluge: To overwhelm with a flood of water.

demagogue: An unprincipled politician.

denizen: Inhabitant.

denouement: That part of a play or story in which the mystery is cleared up.

deplete: To reduce or lessen, as by use, exhaustion, or waste.

deposition: Testimony legally taken on interrogatories and reduced to writing, for use as evidence in court.

deprave: To render bad, especially morally bad.

deprecate: To express disapproval or regret for, with hope for the opposite.

deride: To ridicule.

derision: Ridicule.

derivative: Coming or acquired from some origin.

descry: To discern.

desiccant: Any remedy which, when applied externally, dries up or absorbs moisture, as that of wounds.

desuetude: A state of disuse or inactivity.

desultory: Not connected with what precedes.

deter: To frighten away.

dexterity: Readiness, precision, efficiency, and ease in any physical activity or in any mechanical work.

diaphanous: Transparent.

diatribe: A bitter or malicious criticism.

didactic: Pertaining to teaching.

diffidence: Self-distrust.

diffident: Affected or possessed with self-distrust.

dilate: To enlarge in all directions.

dilatory: Tending to cause delay.

disallow: To withhold permission or sanction.

discomfit: To put to confusion.

disconcert: To disturb the composure of.

disconsolate : Hopelessly sad; also, saddening; cheerless.

discountenance: To look upon with disfavor.

discredit: To injure the reputation of.

discreet: Judicious.

disheveled: Disordered; disorderly; untidy.

dissemble: To hide by pretending something different.

disseminate: To sow or scatter abroad, as seed is sown.

dissent: Disagreement.

dissolution: A breaking up of a union of persons.

distraught: Bewildered.

divulge: To tell or make known, as something previously private or secret.

dogmatic: Making statements without argument or evidence.

dormant: Being in a state of or resembling sleep.

dubious: Doubtful.

duplicity: Double-dealing.

earthenware: Anything made of clay and baked in a kiln or dried in the sun.

ebullient: Showing enthusiasm or exhilaration of feeling.

edacious: Given to eating.

edible: Suitable to be eaten.

educe: To draw out.

effete: Exhausted, as having performed its functions.

efficacy: The power to produce an intended effect as shown in the production of it.

effrontery: Unblushing impudence.

effulgence: Splendor.

egregious: Extreme.

egress: Any place of exit.

elegy: A lyric poem lamenting the dead.

elicit: To educe or extract gradually or without violence.

elucidate: To bring out more clearly the facts concerning.

emaciate: To waste away in flesh.

embellish: To make beautiful or elegant by adding attractive or ornamental features.

embezzle: To misappropriate secretly.

emblazon: To set forth publicly or in glowing terms.

encomium: A formal or discriminating expression of praise.

encumbrance: A burdensome and troublesome load.

endemic: Peculiar to some specified country or people.

enervate: To render ineffective or inoperative.

engender: To produce.

engrave: To cut or carve in or upon some surface.

enigma: A riddle.

enmity: Hatred.

entangle: To involve in difficulties, confusion, or complications.

entreat: To ask for or request earnestly.

Epicurean: Indulging, ministering, or pertaining to daintiness of appetite.

epithet: Word used adjectivally to describe some quality or attribute of is objects, as in "Father Aeneas".

epitome: A simplified representation.

equable: Equal and uniform; also, serene.

equanimity: Evenness of mind or temper.

equanimity : Calmness; composure.

equilibrium: A state of balance.

equivocal: Ambiguous.

equivocate: To use words of double meaning.

eradicate: To destroy thoroughly.

errant: Roving or wandering, as in search of adventure or opportunity for gallant deeds.

erratic: Irregular.

erroneous: Incorrect.

erudite: Very-learned.

eschew: To keep clear of.

espy: To keep close watch.

eulogy: A spoken or written laudation of a person's life or character.

euphonious: Characterized by agreeableness of sound.

evanescent: Fleeting.

evince: To make manifest or evident.

evoke: To call or summon forth.

exacerbate: To make more sharp, severe, or virulent.

exculpate: To relieve of blame.

exhaustive: Thorough and complete in execution.

exigency: A critical period or condition.

exigency : State of requiring immediate action; also, an urgent situation; also, that which is required in a

exorbitant: Going beyond usual and proper limits.

expatiate: To speak or write at some length.

expedient: Contributing to personal advantage.

expiate: To make satisfaction or amends for.

explicate: To clear from involvement.

expostulate: To discuss.

expropriate: To deprive of possession; also, to transfer (another's property) to oneself.

extant: Still existing and known.

extempore: Without studied or special preparation.

extenuate: To diminish the gravity or importance of.

extinct: Being no longer in existence.

extinguish: To render extinct.

extirpate: To root out; to eradicate.

extol: To praise in the highest terms.

extort: To obtain by violence, threats, compulsion, or the subjection of another to some necessity.

extraneous: Having no essential relation to a subject.

exuberance: Rich supply.

facetious: Amusing.

facile: Not difficult to do.

factious: Turbulent.

fallacious: Illogical.

fatuous: Idiotic

fawn: A young deer.

feint: Any sham, pretense, or deceptive movement.

felon: A criminal or depraved person.

ferocity: Savageness.

fervid: Intense.

fervor: Ardor or intensity of feeling.

fidelity: Loyalty.

finesse: Subtle contrivance used to gain a point.

flamboyant: Characterized by extravagance and in general by want of good taste.

flippant: Having a light, pert, trifling disposition.

florid: Flushed with red.

flout: To treat with contempt.

foible: A personal weakness or failing.

foment: To nurse to life or activity; to encourage.

foppish: Characteristic of one who is unduly devoted to dress and the niceties of manners.

forbearance: Patient endurance or toleration of offenses.

forfeit: To lose possession of through failure to fulfill some obligation.

forgery: Counterfeiting.

forswear: To renounce upon oath.

fragile: Easily broken.

frantic: Frenzied.

frugal: Economical.

fugacious: Fleeting.

fulminate: To cause to explode.

fulsome: Offensive from excess of praise or commendation.

gainsay: To contradict; to deny.

gamut: The whole range or sequence.

garrulous: Given to constant trivial talking.

germane: Relevant.

gesticulate: To make gestures or motions, as in speaking, or in place of speech.

glimmer: A faint, wavering, unsteady light.

gossamer: Flimsy.

gourmand: A connoisseur in the delicacies of the table.

grandiloquent: Speaking in or characterized by a pompous or bombastic style.

gregarious: Sociable, outgoing

grievous: Creating affliction.

guile: Duplicity.

gullible: Credulous.

halcyon: Calm.

harangue: A tirade.

harbinger: One who or that which foreruns and announces the coming of any person or thing.

head: Adv. Precipitately, as in diving.

heinous: Odiously sinful.

heresy: An opinion or doctrine subversive of settled beliefs or accepted principles.

heterogeneous: Consisting of dissimilar elements or ingredients of different kinds.

hirsute: Having a hairy covering.

hoodwink: To deceive.

hospitable: Disposed to treat strangers or guests with generous kindness.

hypocrisy: Extreme insincerity.

iconoclast: An image-breaker.

idiosyncrasy: A mental quality or habit peculiar to an individual.

ignoble: Low in character or purpose.

ignominious: Shameful.

illicit: Unlawful.

imbroglio: A misunderstanding attended by ill feeling, perplexity, or strife.

imbue : To dye; to instill profoundly.

immaculate: Without spot or blemish.

imminent: Dangerous and close at hand.

immutable: Unchangeable.

impair: To cause to become less or worse.

impassive: Unmoved by or not exhibiting feeling.

impecunious: Having no money.

impede: To be an obstacle or to place obstacles in the way of.

imperative: Obligatory.

imperious: Insisting on obedience.

imperturbable: Calm.

impervious: Impenetrable.

impetuous: Impulsive.

impiety: Irreverence toward God.

implacable: Incapable of being pacified.

implicate: To show or prove to be involved in or concerned

implicit: Implied.

importunate: Urgent in character, request, or demand.

importune: To harass with persistent demands or entreaties.

impromptu: Anything done or said on the impulse of the moment.

improvident: Lacking foresight or thrift.

impugn: To assail with arguments, insinuations, or accusations.

impute: To attribute.

inadvertent: Accidental.

inane: Silly.

incessant: Unceasing.

inchoate: Incipient.

incipient: Initial.

incite: To rouse to a particular action.

incongruous: Unsuitable for the time, place, or occasion.

inculcate: To teach by frequent repetitions.

indelible: That cannot be blotted out, effaced, destroyed, or removed.

indigence: Poverty.

indigenous: Native.

indistinct: Vague.

indolence: Laziness.

indolent: Habitually inactive or idle.

indomitable: Unconquerable.

indulgent: Yielding to the desires or humor of oneself or those under one's care.

ineffable: Unutterable.

ineluctable: Impossible to avoid.

inept: Not fit or suitable.

inexorable: Unrelenting.

infuse: To instill, introduce, or inculcate, as principles or qualities.

ingenuous: Candid, frank, or open in character or quality.

inimical: Adverse.

innocuous: Harmless.

inscrutable: Impenetrably mysterious or profound.

insensible: Imperceptible.

insinuate: To imply.

insipid: Tasteless.

insouciant: Nonchalant.

insurrection: The state of being in active resistance to authority.

interdict: Authoritative act of prohibition.

interim: Time between acts or periods.

intransigent: Not capable of being swayed or diverted from a course.

intrepid: Fearless and bold.

introspection: The act of observing and analyzing one's own thoughts and feelings.

inundate: To fill with an overflowing abundance.

inure: To harden or toughen by use, exercise, or exposure.

invalid: One who is disabled by illness or injury.

invective: An utterance intended to cast censure, or reproach.

inveigh: To utter vehement censure or invective.

inveterate: Habitual.

invidious: Showing or feeling envy.

invincible: Not to be conquered, subdued, or overcome.

iota: A small or insignificant mark or part.

irascible: Prone to anger.

irate: Moved to anger.

ire: Wrath.

irksome: Wearisome.

itinerant: Wandering.

itinerate: To wander from place to place.

jocular: Inclined to joke.

jovial: Merry.

judicious: Prudent.

junta: A council or assembly that deliberates in secret upon the affairs of government.

lachrymose: Given to shedding tears.

lackadaisical: Listless.

languid: Relaxed.

lascivious: Lustful.

lassitude: Lack of vitality or energy.

latent: Dormant.

laudable: Praiseworthy.

laudatory: Pertaining to, expressing, or containing praise.

legacy: A bequest.

levee: An embankment beside a river or stream or an arm of the sea, to prevent overflow.

levity: Frivolity.

lexicon: A dictionary.

libel: Defamation.

licentious: Wanton.

lien: A legal claim or hold on property, as security for a debt or charge.

listless: Inattentive.

lithe: Supple.

loquacious: Talkative.

lugubrious: Indicating sorrow, often ridiculously.

luminary: One of the heavenly bodies as a source of light.

lustrous: Shining.

malaise: A condition of uneasiness or ill-being.

malcontent: One who is dissatisfied with the existing state of affairs.

malevolence: Ill will.

malign: To speak evil of, especially to do so falsely and severely.

malleable: Pliant.

massacre: The unnecessary and indiscriminate killing of human beings.

maudlin: Foolishly and tearfully affectionate.

mawkish: Sickening or insipid.

mellifluous: Sweetly or smoothly flowing.

mendacious: Untrue.

mendicant: A beggar.

meretricious: Alluring by false or gaudy show.

mesmerize: To hypnotize.

meticulous: Over-cautious.

mettle: Courage.

mettlesome: Having courage or spirit.

microcosm: The world or universe on a small scale.

mien: The external appearance or manner of a person.

mischievous: Fond of tricks.

miscreant: A villain.

miser: A person given to saving and hoarding unduly.

misnomer: A name wrongly or mistakenly applied.

moderation: Temperance.

modicum: A small or token amount.

mollify: To soothe.

molt: To cast off, as hair, feathers, etc.

monomania: The unreasonable pursuit of one idea.

morbid: Caused by or denoting a diseased or unsound condition of body or mind.

mordant: Biting.

moribund: On the point of dying.

morose: Gloomy.

multifarious: Having great diversity or variety.

mundane: Worldly, as opposed to spiritual or celestial.

munificent: Extraordinarily generous.

myriad: A vast indefinite number.

nadir: The lowest point.

nefarious: Wicked in the extreme.

negligent: Apt to omit what ought to be done.

neophyte: Having the character of a beginner.

noisome: Very offensive, particularly to the sense of smell.

nostrum: Any scheme or recipe of a charlatan character.

noxious: Hurtful.

nugatory: Having no power or force.

obdurate: Impassive to feelings of humanity or pity.

obfuscate: To darken; to obscure.

oblique: Slanting; said of lines.

obsequious: Showing a servile readiness to fall in with the wishes or will of another.

obstreperous: Boisterous.

obtrude: To be pushed or to push oneself into undue prominence.

obtrusive: Tending to be pushed or to push oneself into undue prominence.

obviate: To clear away or provide for, as an objection or difficulty.

odious: Hateful.

odium: A feeling of extreme repugnance, or of dislike and disgust.

officious: Intermeddling with what is not one's concern.

ominous: Portentous.

onerous: Burdensome or oppressive.

onus: A burden or responsibility.

opprobrium: The state of being scornfully reproached or accused of evil.

ossify: To convert into bone.

ostentation: A display dictated by vanity and intended to invite applause or flattery.

ostracism: Exclusion from intercourse or favor, as in society or politics.

ostracize: To exclude from public or private favor.

palate: The roof of the mouth.

palatial: Magnificent.

palliate: To cause to appear less guilty.

palpable: Perceptible by feeling or touch.

panacea: A remedy or medicine proposed for or professing to cure all diseases.

panegyric: A formal and elaborate eulogy, written or spoken, of a person or of an act.

panoply: A full set of armor.

paragon: A model of excellence.

Pariah: A member of a degraded class; a social outcast.

paroxysm: A sudden outburst of any kind of activity.

parsimonious: Unduly sparing in the use or expenditure of money.

partisan: Characterized by or exhibiting undue or unreasoning devotion to a party.

pathos: The quality in any form of representation that rouses emotion or sympathy.

paucity: Fewness.

peccadillo: A small breach of propriety or principle.

pedestrian: One who journeys on foot.

pellucid: Translucent.

penchant: A bias in favor of something.

penurious: Excessively sparing in the use of money.

penury: Indigence.

peregrination: A wandering.

peremptory: Precluding question or appeal.

perfidy: Treachery.

perfunctory: Half-hearted.

peripatetic: Walking about.

perjury: A solemn assertion of a falsity.

permeate: To pervade.

pernicious: Tending to kill or hurt.

persiflage: Banter.

perspicacity: Acuteness or discernment.

perturbation: Mental excitement or confusion.

petrify: To convert into a substance of stony hardness and character.

petulant: Displaying impatience.

phlegmatic: Not easily roused to feeling or action.

physiognomy: The external appearance merely.

pious: Religious.

pique: To excite a slight degree of anger in.

placate: To bring from a state of angry or hostile feeling to one of patience or friendliness.

platitude: A written or spoken statement that is flat, dull, or commonplace.

plea: An argument to obtain some desired action.

plenary: Entire.

plethora: Excess; superabundance.

plumb: A weight suspended by a line to test the verticality of something.

plummet: A piece of lead for making soundings, adjusting walls to the vertical.

poignant: Severely painful or acute to the spirit.

polyglot: Speaking several tongues.

ponderous: Unusually weighty or forcible.

portend: To indicate as being about to happen, especially by previous signs.

portent: Anything that indicates what is to happen.

precarious: Perilous.

preclude: To prevent.

precocious: Having the mental faculties prematurely developed.

predominate: To be chief in importance, quantity, or degree.

premature: Coming too soon.

presage: To foretell.

prescience: Knowledge of events before they take place.

presumption: That which may be logically assumed to be true until disproved.

preternatural: Extraordinary.

prevalent: Of wide extent or frequent occurrence.

prevaricate: To use ambiguous or evasive language for the purpose of deceiving or diverting attention.

prim: Stiffly proper.

pristine: Primitive.

probity: Virtue or integrity tested and confirmed.

proclivity: A natural inclination.

procrastination: Delay.

prodigal: One wasteful or extravagant, especially in the use of money or property.

prodigious: Immense.

profligacy: Shameless viciousness.

profligate: Recklessly wasteful

profuse: Produced or displayed in overabundance.

prolix: Verbose.

propinquity: Nearness.

propitious: Kindly disposed.

prosaic: Unimaginative.

proscribe: To reject, as a teaching or a practice, with condemnation or denunciation.

protuberant: Bulging.

provident: Anticipating and making ready for future wants or emergencies.

prudence: Caution.

puerile: Childish.

pugnacious: Quarrelsome.

punctilious: Strictly observant of the rules or forms prescribed by law or custom.

pungency: The quality of affecting the sense of smell.

pusillanimous: Without spirit or bravery.

pyre: A heap of combustibles arranged for burning a dead body.

qualm: A fit of nausea.

quandary: A puzzling predicament.

quibble: An utterly trivial distinction or objection.

quiescence: Being quiet, still, or at rest; inactive

quiescent: Being in a state of repose or inaction.

Quixotic: Chivalrous or romantic to a ridiculous or extravagant degree.

quotidian: Of an everyday character; ordinary.

raconteur: A person skilled in telling stories.

ramify: To divide or subdivide into branches or subdivisions.

rapacious: Seize by force, avaricious

raucous: Harsh.

reactionary: Pertaining to, of the nature of, causing, or favoring reaction.

rebuff: A peremptory or unexpected rejection of advances or approaches.

recalcitrant: Marked by stubborn resistance.

recant: To withdraw formally one's belief (in something previously believed or maintained).

reciprocity: Equal mutual rights and benefits granted and enjoyed.

recluse: One who lives in retirement or seclusion.

recondite: Incomprehensible to one of ordinary understanding.

recrudescent: Becoming raw or sore again.

recuperate: To recover.

redoubtable: Formidable.

redress: To set right, as a wrong by compensation or the punishment of the wrong-doer.

refractory: Not amenable to control.

regale: To give unusual pleasure.

regicide: The killing of a king or sovereign.

reiterate: To say or do again and again.

relapse: To suffer a return of a disease after partial recovery.

remonstrate: To present a verbal or written protest to those who have power to right or prevent a wrong.

renovate: To restore after deterioration, as a building.

repast: A meal; figuratively, any refreshment.

repel: To force or keep back in a manner, physically or mentally.

repine: To indulge in fretfulness and faultfinding.

reprobate: One abandoned to depravity and sin.

repudiate: To refuse to have anything to do with.

repulsive: Grossly offensive.

requisite: Necessary.

requite: To repay either good or evil to, as to a person.

rescind: To make void, as an act, by the enacting authority or a superior authority.

resilience: The power of springing back to a former position

resonance: Able to reinforce sound by sympathetic vibrations.

respite: Interval of rest.

restive: Resisting control.

retinue: The group of people who accompany an important person during travels.

revere: To regard with worshipful veneration.

reverent: Humble.

ribald: Indulging in or manifesting coarse indecency or obscenity.

risible: Capable of exciting laughter.

rotund: Round from fullness or plumpness.

ruffian: A lawless or recklessly brutal fellow.

ruminate: To chew over again, as food previously swallowed and regurgitated.

sagacious: Able to discern and distinguish with wise perception.

salacious: Having strong sexual desires.

salient: Standing out prominently.

salubrious: Healthful; promoting health.

salutary: Beneficial.

sanction: To approve authoritatively.

sanguine: Cheerfully confident; optimistic.

sardonic: Scornfully or bitterly sarcastic.

satiate: To satisfy fully the appetite or desire of.

satyr: A very lascivious person.

savor: To perceive by taste or smell.

scabbard: The sheath of a sword or similar bladed weapon.

scintilla: The faintest ray.

scribble: Hasty, careless writing.

sedulous: Persevering in effort or endeavor.

sequence: The order in which a number or persons, things, or events follow one another in space or time.

severance: Separation.

shrewd: Characterized by skill at understanding and profiting by circumstances.

sinecure: Any position having emoluments with few or no duties.

sinuous: Curving in and out.

skiff: Usually, a small light boat propelled by oars.

sluggard: A person habitually lazy or idle.

solace: Comfort in grief, trouble, or calamity.

solvent: Having sufficient funds to pay all debts.

somniferous: Tending to produce sleep.

somnolent: Sleepy.

sonorous: Resonant.

sophistry: Reasoning sound in appearance only, especially when designedly deceptive.

soporific: Causing sleep; also, something that causes sleep.

sordid: Filthy, morally degraded

specious: Plausible.

spurious: Not genuine.

squalid: Having a dirty, mean, poverty-stricken appearance.

stanch: To stop the flowing of; to check.

stigma: A mark of infamy or token of disgrace attaching to a person as the result of evil-doing.

stingy: Cheap, unwilling to spend money.

stolid: Expressing no power of feeling or perceiving.

submerge: To place or plunge under water.

subterfuge: Evasion.

succinct: Concise.

sumptuous: Rich and costly.

supercilious: Exhibiting haughty and careless contempt.

superfluous: Being more than is needed.

supernumerary: Superfluous.

supersede: To displace.

supine: Lying on the back.

supplicate: To beg.

suppress: To prevent from being disclosed or punished.

surcharge: An additional amount charged.

surfeit: To feed to fullness or to satiety.

susceptibility: A specific capability of feeling or emotion.

sybarite: A luxurious person.

sycophant: A servile flatterer, especially of those in authority or influence.

synopsis: A syllabus or summary.

taciturn: Disinclined to conversation.

taut: Stretched tight.

temerity: Foolhardy disregard of danger; recklessness.

terse: Pithy.

timorous: Lacking courage.

torpid: Dull; sluggish; inactive.

torrid: Excessively hot.

tortuous: Abounding in irregular bends or turns.

tractable: Easily led or controlled.

transgress: To break a law.

transient: One who or that which is only of temporary existence.

transitory: Existing for a short time only.

travail: Hard or agonizing labor.

travesty: A grotesque imitation.

trenchant: Cutting deeply and quickly.

trepidation: Nervous uncertainty of feeling.

trite: Made commonplace by frequent repetition.

truculence: Ferocity.

truculent: Having the character or the spirit of a savage.

turbid: In a state of turmoil; muddled

turgid: Swollen.

turpitude: Depravity.

tutelage: The act of training or the state of being under instruction.

tyro: One slightly skilled in or acquainted with any trade or profession.

ubiquitous: Being present everywhere.

ulterior: Not so pertinent as something else to the matter spoken of.

umbrage: A sense of injury.

unctuous: Oily.

undermine: To subvert in an underhand way.

undulate: To move like a wave or in waves.

untoward: Causing annoyance or hindrance.

upbraid: To reproach as deserving blame.

vagary: A sudden desire or action

vainglory: Excessive, pretentious, and demonstrative vanity.

valorous: Courageous.

vapid: Having lost sparkling quality and flavor.

variegated: Having marks or patches of different colors; also, varied.

vehement: Very eager or urgent.

venal: Mercenary, corrupt.

veneer: Outside show or elegance.

venial: That may be pardoned or forgiven, a forgivable sin.

veracious: Habitually disposed to speak the truth.

veracity: Truthfulness.

verbiage: Use of many words without necessity.

verbose: Wordy.

verdant: Green with vegetation.

veritable: Real; true; genuine.

vestige: A visible trace, mark, or impression, of something absent, lost, or gone.

vicissitude: A change, especially a complete change, of condition or circumstances, as of fortune.

vigilance: Alert and intent mental watchfulness in guarding against danger.

vigilant: Being on the alert to discover and ward off danger or insure safety.

virago: Loud talkative women, strong statured women

virtu: Rare, curious, or beautiful quality.

visage: The face, countenance, or look of a person.

vitiate: To contaminate.

vituperate: To overwhelm with wordy abuse.

vivify: To endue with life.

vociferous: Making a loud outcry.

volatile: Changeable.

voluble: Having great fluency in speaking.

wean: To transfer (the young) from dependence on mother's milk to another form of nourishment.

whimsical: Capricious.

winsome: Attractive.

Zeitgeist: The intellectual and moral tendencies that characterize any age or epoch.

Special Report: Additional Bonus Material

Due to our efforts to try to keep this book to a manageable length, we've created a link that will give you access to all of your additional bonus material.

Please visit http://www.mometrix.com/bonus948/sat to access the information.